False Prophets
of Peace

False Prophets of Peace

**Liberal Zionism
and the Struggle for Palestine**

TIKVA HONIG-PARNASS

Haymarket Books
Chicago, Illinois

© 2011 by Tikva Honig-Parnass
Published in 2011 by Haymarket Books
PO Box 180165
Chicago, IL 60618
773-583-7884
info@haymarketbooks.org
www.haymarketbooks.org

Trade distribution:
In the US, Consortium Book Sales and Distribution, www.cbsd.com
In Canada, Publishers Group Canada, www.pgcbooks.ca
In the UK, Turnaround Publisher Services, www.turnaround-uk.com
In Australia, Palgrave Macmillan, www.palgravemacmillan.com.au
All other countries, Publishers Group Worldwide, www.pgw.com

ISBN: 978-1-60846-130-1

Cover design by Eric Ruder.

This research project was made possible with the support of Muwatin, the Palestinian Institute
for the Study of Democracy.

Published with the generous support of Lannan Foundation and the Wallace Global Fund.

Printed in United States.

Library of Congress Cataloging-in-Publication data is available.

10 9 8 7 6 5 4 3 2 1

Contents

For Amichai Kronfeld, a man of integrity and justice;
And for my beloved grandson, Yuval: May Amichai's ethics light his way.

Acknowledgments

My special thanks to Toufic Haddad for his dedicated and careful language editing of the manuscript and for his telling, critical comments. I have also benefited a lot from inspiring discussions with my friend May Jayyusi. Both, together with the support of my daughter Sivan Parnass, enabled the completion of this study.

Introduction

This book aims to refute the prevailing myths among progressive circles in the West about the Zionist Left in Israel.[1] Western progressives believe the Zionist Left genuinely supports a just solution to the "conflict" between Israel and Palestine, as embodied in the peace initiatives brought forth by Labor governments and Zionist Left leaders. The Zionist Left has been associated with universalistic values of humanism and democracy, which guide its approach toward Palestinian citizens of Israel, and Western progressives accept the idea that the Zionist Left has truly striven to attain civil rights and equality between the Palestinian minority and Jewish majority in Israel, albeit without compromising on the Jewish identity of the state. Due to the pre-state socialist heritage of the Zionist Labor movement, Zionist Left supporters are also portrayed as Social Democrats who oppose the policies of Economic Neoliberalism.[2] They are seen as determined opponents of Israel's oppressive policies in the '67 occupied territories, the bloody wars launched in Lebanon, and Israel's role as warmonger in the service of US imperial interests in the Middle East.

This book concentrates on the discourse of the elite intellectuals and academic circles that have nourished the myths of the Zionist Left and conformed them to the Israeli Labor Party's political perspective and rhetoric. It mainly analyzes their support of an exclusivist Jewish state that acts as the central Zionist premise guiding Israel's official ideology, and their attempts to reconcile that with the definition of Israel as a democracy. It explores different dimensions of the vision for the "Jewish state" adopted by Zionist Left intellectuals, and the ways this vision fits into their ostensibly universalistic and democratic world-view. Furthermore, it seeks to clarify how this vision supports the longtime hege-mony of the Zionist Labor movement throughout the state's institutions and political culture, including the policies employed by Labor-led governments to-ward the Palestinian citizens of Israel and the failed peace plans of the past.[3]

A "Jewish and Democratic State"

The state of Israel has incorporated the philosophy of the Jewish state—"a state of the Jews for the Jews"—into its identity, official ideology, and poli-cies toward the Palestinian people within Israel and in the '67 occupied ter-ritories, and in the Diaspora. This ideology claims the Jewish people have the historic right to "return" to their homeland, from which they were ex-pelled two thousand years ago, so as to regain their national sovereignty in an exclusive Jewish state.[4] The Palestinians' recognition of Israel as the Jew-ish state, or as the recent version of the nation-state of the Jewish people, has become a condition for any peace settlement, and even for launching the peace process itself. In other words, this condition demands that Palestinians recognize and accept the Zionist colonial project and its disastrous impact on the lot of the Palestinian people—the indigenous population of the land.[5]

The notion of an exclusive Jewish state is essentially incongruous with liberal democracy, in which equal citizenship rights are granted on a territorial basis to all citizens regardless of their ethnic or national origin. But Israel, according to its self-identification and vision, is not a state for all its citizens. Rather, it is a state for the Jewish people throughout the world. This prioritizes Jews over the 1,250,000 indigenous Palestinians who by 2009 comprised around 20 per-cent of the state's population. Israeli law does not recognize an Israeli nationality. Thus, while Jewish citizens are classified as having "Jewish nationality," Israeli law methodically strips Palestinian citizens of their national identity and reduces them to mere ethnicity or religious affiliation (like Muslims, Christians, Druze, etc.).[6] As a result, Israel is not just another nation-state in which minority com-munities lack some secondary rights owned by the majority. Instead, it is a set-tler-colonial state established by the Zionist movement for advancing and expanding its colonialist project for the benefit of the Jews alone.

The inequality between the Jewish majority and the Palestinian population, a minority in its homeland after the mass ethnic cleansing of 1948—known as the Nakba (Arabic for "catastrophe")—is structural to the Jewish state. Palestinian citizens are not recognized as a national minority in their homeland, or as part of the Palestinian people and the Arab nation, deserving national rights similar to those enjoyed by the Jewish citizens. As the late progressive Hebrew University professor of sociology Baruch Kimmerling noted, "The very existence of the Arab [Palestinian] population (and not merely the Jewish state's objective to preserve a Jewish majority) is perceived as contradictory to several basic assumptions on which the state of Israel is founded as an exclusive Jewish state. . Zionist ideology has never really coped with existing non-Jewish minorities within the Jewish state, and in fact aspired not only for a Jewish nation-state but for an exclusive Jewish state." Kimmerling adds that this aspiration is the source for plans to expel Palestinians, which have loomed in Israeli discourse from the very beginning.[7]

The premises of Zionism are central to the Jewish state. They were introduced into the Declaration of the Establishment of the State of Israel (known as the Declaration of Independence),[8] signed by the temporary People's Council, which was headed by Labor Party chair David Ben-Gurion, on May 14, 1948, one day before the official end of the British Mandate for Palestine.[9] Later, elements of both Zionism and religion were funneled into Israeli laws and regulations and into the blueprints of Israel's social and political institutions.

The Declaration of Independence confirms the myths of the Divine promise to Abraham and the religious messianic content of redemption by means of the return to the "promised land." It emphasizes the Old Testament as a source of inspiration for Israel's legal system and its commitment to Zionism.

The national collective—defined in Jewish religious terms—was later institutionalized in the Law of Return, which grants every Jew (according to the Halacha[10]) the right to immigrate to Israel and reside there as a full citizen. A Jew is defined as the son or daughter of a Jewish mother or someone who has converted according to the religious procedures recognized by the orthodox religious establishment.[11] This overlapping of nation and religion runs in direct conflict with the separation of state and religion in Israel. Yet the Supreme Court has accepted this undemocratic feature based upon a basic premise of Zionism: there is no Israeli nation separate from the Jewish people. Former president of the Supreme Court Aharon Barak noted, "The Supreme Court of Israel fully represents the hegemonic ideology which prohibits the separation of State and religion."[12] Hence the Supreme Court's acceptance of the Zionist/religious essence of the Jewish state emphasized by Barak: "We are a young state in which an old people have returned to its land. The state of Israel is the fulfillment of aspirations the Jewish people have had for generations, to revive their ancient history, the beginning of deliverance and the realization of the Zionist vision. Deep is the national, religious and historical political bond between the people of Israel and the land of Israel, and between the Jewish state and the Jewish people."[13]

The Palestinian radical thinker Azmi Bishara correctly comments on Barak's perspective: "Justice Barak attempts, in effect, to codify Zionism's messianic vision through his affirmation that the Zionist bond is a religious-political one, which effectively precludes any distinction between the notions of a 'Jewish state,' a 'Zionist state,' and 'a state for Jews.'"[14] However, since its establishment Israel has claimed to be a democratic state as well as Jewish and Zionist, as highlighted in the Declaration of Independence:

> It [the state of Israel] will foster the development of the country for the benefit of all its inhabitants; it will be based on freedom, justice and peace as envisaged by the prophets of Israel; it will ensure complete equality of social and political rights to all its inhabitants irrespective of religion, race or sex; it will guarantee freedom of religion, conscience, language, education and culture; it will safeguard the Holy Places of all religions; and it will be faithful to the principles of the Charter of the United Nations.

The promise for national equality was deliberately omitted from the list of equal rights emphasized in the Declaration. Zionist liberals consistently overlook this omission and argue that the Declaration promises full equality to all Israeli citizens along with the Jewish identity of the state. Additionally, they continue to downplay Israeli laws and institutions that systematically assign Palestinians their second-class status, in contrast to the myriad prerogatives of Jewish citizens.

The Zionist Left in Israel has never challenged the prevailing belief that Israeli law implements "the democratic and egalitarian values extolled in the Declaration of Independence." Indeed, explicit legislation against Palestinian citizens, which would reveal Israel as an Apartheid state, is avoided. As the jurist David Kretzmer, a law professor at the Hebrew University, notes: "Only in extremely rare situations [like the Law of Return] does the criteria of one being a Jew or non-Jew, act as the distinguishing criterion in Israeli laws. Instead, a developed intricate language of laws allow for the systematic preference of Jews and discrimination against the Palestinian citizens."[15] Other seemingly nondiscriminatory criteria are employed to facilitate different rules or arrangements applied on national lines. For example, under the pretext of participation in military service, a wide assortment of rights have been denied to Palestinian citizens, from child allowances to privileges given under the Discharged Soldiers Law of 1984, which provides its beneficiaries (who are primarily Israeli Jews) with housing, health, and educational services. Even when the Supreme Court decides against a discriminatory governmental decision, the probability of its implementation is low, often with the acquiescence of the Supreme Court itself.[16]

It has become commonplace among many Zionist Left scholars and activists to describe the forms of discrimination in the occupied territories as analogous to South Africa's Apartheid system. In the occupied territories, different legal and administrative systems for the two populations, Jewish and non-Jewish, prevail. The parallels with South Africa are undeniable. Yet members of the Zionist Left in Israel refrain from acknowledging the Apartheid nature within the Green Line.[17] Makdisi rightly argues that almost every law of the South African Apartheid has its equivalent in Israel today.[18] A significant example of this is the Law of Return (1950), which even Kretzmer claims is explicitly discriminatory against Palestinian citizens. As mentioned above, the Law of Return grants, almost automatically, Israeli citizenship to any immigrant Jew, including any associated benefits and rights. The right of return, however, is denied to Palestinians and other non-Jewish immigrants who do not acquire their citizenship by birth, as do Jews all over the world. For non-Jewish immigrants, becoming a citizen is not a right. It is a privilege, dependent upon the almost absolute discretion of the Ministry of Interior, whose policy clearly prohibits granting citizenship to non-Jewish immigrants. The Law of Return, which determines the second-class citizenship of Palestinians, is recognized as a fundamental principle in Israel and is "possibly even its very *raison d'être* as a Jewish state."[19]

Indeed, as Makdisi points out, just as every Israeli citizen is granted a distinct national identity through the Law of Return, the notorious South African Population Registration Act of 1950 assigned every South African a racial identity, which determined if he or she had access to (or was denied) a varying range of rights. (For another parallel between Israel and South Africa, see the discussion of land access and residency rights in chapter 3.)

Still, the internal contradiction of Israel as being both Jewish and democratic ("an instinctive feeling, seldom articulated," notes Bishara[20]) has raised concern, and yet genuine attempts to disentangle each from the other inevitably ends in discord. Liberal components of democracy are doomed to undermine the notion of the Jewish state, which grants preference to its Jewish citizens. Likewise, Israel's central identity as a Jewish state conflicts with its commitment to democracy. In order to prevent any change to this definition, the Knesset (the legislative branch of the Israeli government) made it de rigueur to include the phrase "Jewish and democratic" in any Basic Law it considers passing.[21]

In 1992 the link between the Jewish and democratic elements in the definition of the state was established for the first time, anchored in the two Basic Laws aimed at safeguarding the rights of Human Dignity and Liberty, and Freedom of Occupation.[22] In the very first paragraph of each law, part of the reasoning is given: "to establish in a Basic Law the values of the State of Israel *as a Jewish and democratic state.*"

However, these two Basic Laws—considered a mini-bill of rights by Israeli legal scholars—do not include the right to equality, which is the essence of universal human rights and democracy. Palestinians in Israel are thus afforded no constitutional protection against discrimination. In fact, these laws block the legal defense for victims of human rights violations, when those violations are committed in the name of the "Jewishness of the state." Baruch Kimmerling rightly determines that the structural discrimination against the Palestinian citizens of Israel has made them the only social group in Israel that challenges the Jewish state.[23]

Hence, the consistent expectation of the Zionist Left, that the Palestinian citizens will legitimize the Zionist colonial project embodied in the Jewish state, is doomed to fail. This was exemplified in a series of dialogue meetings between Israeli and Palestinian intellectuals from January 1999 to January 2001. The meetings were hosted by the Israel Democracy Institute and aimed "to formulate an agreement that would define the relationship between the majority and minority in the state and their mutual concerns." However, the intellectuals failed to reach this goal because the Palestinian participants refused to declare their recognition of the Jewish state, a condition demanded by the Israelis.[24]

Dr. Adel Manna, director of the Center for the Study of Arab Society in Israel, the Van Leer Jerusalem Institute, acted as the Palestinian cochair of the project alongside liberal Israeli jurist and professor Mordechai Kremnitzer (of the Law Faculty at Hebrew University). Manna's firm refusal to declare the acceptance of a Jewish state reflects the Palestinian awareness that such a demand renounces their national identity and their right to equal citizenship.

I hear many Israelis say that the Arabs in Israel are not truly loyal to the state and do not identify with it. Either these people are fools or they are simply mislead. What does it mean to identify with an entity that is your contradiction? With an entity that is willing to liquidate you? With the entity which in fact is active in order to deny you elementary necessities for your existence—your security, equality and identity? This means, that they demand that I identify with a state that declares that it is Jewish and Zionist, and whose essence is to eliminate my existence here.

Manna sees this demand as antithetical to democracy: "Even in upstanding states—usually those which are states of all their citizens, non-fascist regimes— citizens are not required to be 'loyal to the state,' but to state laws, to the basic foundations which are equal to all citizens. I cannot identify with an embodiment which discriminates against me and denies me equality."[25] He later notes that "My main problem with the Jewish and Zionist state of Israel is that I am not a citizen in its full meaning, but am in the gray area between a subject and a citizen . . . I am not ready to continue living in such a situation and I don't want my children to live in it . . . I will never compromise on my citizenship status."[26]

The defiant refusal of Manna and the other Palestinian participants to recognize the Jewish state reflects a rising tide of analysis and understanding among the Palestinian citizens of Israel. Azmi Bishara, the founder of the National Democratic Assembly (NDA) in 1995, has played a prominent role in articulating this new perspective. Bishara and the NDA have challenged Israel to become "a state of all its citizens." They have also demanded that Palestinian citizens be recognized as a national group living in their homeland, not as minorities (comparable to other immigrant ethnic minorities in Western nation-states). Additionally, they believe Palestinian identity must include two dimensions—Palestinian and Arab. This double identity would imply Palestinian citizens' solidarity with their brethren in the '67 occupied territories and with the Palestinian refugees' right of return, as well as with resistance movements against Zionism and US imperialism throughout the Arab world.

The political perspective of Bishara and the NDA has been adopted in principle by the majority of the Palestinian intellectual and political leadership in Israel, as reflected in the four Position Papers, released in 2007 by leading Palestinian organizations. One of the papers, "The Future Vision of the Palestinians in Israel," was issued by the Palestinians' highest and most authoritative representative vis-à-vis the state—the Higher Follow-Up Committee for Arabs in Israel.[27] All four papers demand, first and foremost, that Israel become a state of all its citizens. The Haifa Declaration, for example, calls for canceling the Law of Return, recognizing Palestinian national identity, and implementing collective national rights for Palestinians through representatives in government. These rights include, among others, the ability to veto all matters pertaining to their interests and the right for cultural autonomy.[28]

The growing national identity among Palestinian citizens and their challenge of the Zionist/Jewish state have been sabotaged by policies and legal proposals designed to strip them of their citizenship rights or revoke their
citizenship altogether.[29] In its identification as a Jewish state, Israel has used
"security" to characterize the entire Palestinian citizenry as a threat. Each Palestinian living in Israel is considered a potential traitor. This has led to the increased involvement of the General Security Services—the Shabak—in
government policies regarding Palestinian citizens. The head of the Shabak,
Yuval Diskin, in reaction to the Position Papers, has gone so far as to announce
that the "Shin Bet security service will thwart the activity of any group or individual seeking to harm the Jewish and democratic character of the State of Israel, *even if such activity is sanctioned by the law.*"[30]

As a result of this sort of policy, Azmi Bishara was accused of "abetting the
enemy" during the 2006 Lebanon war. This allegation was merely a cover-up
for a political persecution against Bishara because of his significant role in mobilizing Palestinian citizens to challenge the Jewish state. With no chance of a
fair trial, Bishara went into exile.

The growing obsession with security in the Israeli political establishment—
a reaction to the strengthened national identity of Palestinian citizens—opened
the way for direct attack on the Palestinian leadership and activists and the depiction of them as potential traitors.

The Leading Role of the Zionist Left in Laying the Foundation for a Jewish State

The Zionist Left has maintained political and cultural dominance within
the Zionist movement since the early Yishuv, the organized Jewish settler
society in Palestine of pre-state Israel. It exercised its influence through
Mapai, Eretz Israel Workers' Party, founded in 1930. The 1933 elections of
the World Zionist Organization affirmed the political dominance of the
Israeli Labor Party, led by Mapai and chaired by David Ben-Gurion, in
both the Zionist movement and the Yishuv. It would be the Zionist Left
who led the Jewish army in the 1948 war and, after committing the ethnic
cleansing of the Palestinians, established the state of Israel. Their gover-
nance lasted until 1977 when the Labor Party lost its governmental monopoly to the right-wing Herut Party—later the Likud—headed by
Menachem Begin.[31]

Though its monopoly on government ended, the Zionist Left hegemony has remained a leading political force in Israeli state and society. Its members and supporters have maintained control over many key centers of power, including the Israeli Supreme Court, the economy, the media, and large sectors of the academy. The 1977 change of powers did not significantly transform the dominant social value system within Israel, and the Zionist Left intelligentsia has maintained their role as producer, sustainer, and disseminator of Israel's political culture.[32] While its electoral power has been diminished (see chapter 9), the fundamental principles and historical narratives that are traditionally attributed to the Zionist Left have been adopted and integrated into the political platforms of centrists and even substantial factions of the Right.[33] In effect, the hegemony of the Zionist Left was built into the core of the Jewish state from the very beginning.

Indeed, new social groups, especially Mizrahim (Jews who emigrated from Arab countries, and their descendants[34]), have risen in the political and social arenas of Israel, breaking their longtime silence. The Mizrahim, however, have not only preserved the Zionist Left's hegemonic value system—which includes the primacy of the Jewish state and its security—they have adopted even more extreme measures, particularly in regard to their support of oppressive policies toward Palestinians.[35] Their underlying motivation is to achieve a legitimate place within the Zionist-Israeli collective. (See chapter 8 for elaboration on discrimination against the Mizrahim and their protest.)

Pre-State Organized "Yishuv"

The Zionist Labor movement led the Zionist colonization project, hoping to establish an exclusive Jewish state over all of Palestine. They adopted an "organic" ethnic nationalism, similar to the romantic nationalisms of Central and Eastern Europe.[36]

The ideology of Constructive Socialism, adopted by the mainstream of the Zionist Labor movement, was a local version of National-Socialism that retained the main tenets of organic nationalism within a socialist framework. The preeminent historian of this period is Zeev Sternhell, a professor of political science at the Hebrew University, who happens to be a Social Democrat and longtime supporter of the Zionist Labor movement. According to Sternhell, "Ben-Gurion and all leaders of the Labor movement—Berl Katzenelson and A.D. Gordon,[37] in addition to other key personalities, all were not interested in Socialism but in the Zionist solution to the Jewish people."[38]

The labor movement's version of socialism was a tool for implementing colonization rather than a means of creating a new social order. It demanded absolute subservience of all class interests and individual aspirations to the Zionist project. Sternhell further details the one-dimensional character of the movement and how it lacked any genuine socialist essence: "Already at the beginning of the road, in December 1922, Ben-Gurion declared that 'The only big concern which dominates our thinking and activity is the conquest of the land, and building it through mass immigration (*aliya*). All the rest is only phraseology, deserts and 'afters' and we should not deceive ourselves.'"[39] Ben-Gurion also said, "We are the conquerors of the land confronted by an iron wall [Palestinian and Arab nationalism] which we are obliged to crash."[40]

The Histadrut (an acronym for the General Federation of the Workers in Eretz Israel) was a central organ of the colonial project. As the overarching organization of workers' trade unions, the Histadrut controlled key areas that were needed to accomplish the primary tasks of the Zionist colonial enterprise. These included economic production and marketing, defense, and control of the labor force, as well as creating jobs outside the free market so as to avoid competition with abundant and cheap Arab labor. The Histadrut thus introduced the irregular phenomenon of a "trade union" that established its own industrial, financial, construction, transport, and service enterprises.[41]

The Zionist Labor movement did not raise any principled argument against private property, nor did it challenge the capitalist system. Its demand from the emerging bourgeoisie was for private capital to fulfill its role in developing the land and absorbing immigrants. On this basis, the long-term division of labor was created between the two sides.[42]

In exchange for helping to develop the weak private industrial and commercial enterprises, and for ensuring "industrial silence" in labor relations, the bourgeoisie accepted Zionist Labor's political leadership. Ben-Gurion, the head of Mapai, chaired the Jewish Agency for Israel (also known as the "Jewish Agency" or the "Agency"), the executive arm of the World Zionist Organization (WZO). The Agency acted as the government of the Yishuv, which developed into a mostly autonomic system, recognized and supported by the British Mandate.

Through the Jewish Agency's dominant role in the Yishuv, Constructive Socialism's ideologies and policies developed the basic guidelines for the Zionist colonialist project of Palestine. Guided by a principle of Jewish exclusivism, the Agency supported a policy of separation between the Yishuv and the indigenous

Palestinian population, prohibiting Palestinians from land and labor markets and banning the goods they produced.

The Zionist Labor movement justified these policies by using slogans that camouflaged their imperatives for dispossession of Palestinians: "Kibush H'karka" (conquering the soil),[43] "Kibush H'avoda" (conquering labor), and "tozetet haaretz" (the produce of the land—implying "Jewish" produce).[44] While advancing the colonization of the land and laying the foundations of the state-in-progress, the Agency created Jewish paramilitary forces (the Hagana and the Palmach)[45] to commit the ethnic cleansing of Palestinians when the "window of opportunity opens" (*sheat kosher*).

The 1948 Nakba

Mass expulsion of the indigenous Palestinian population was considered a necessary condition for establishing a purely Jewish state on the land of Palestine. Unlike South Africa's Apartheid, which exploited the vital labor power of the Blacks,[46] Zionists rejected the Palestinians outright. Consciously and deliberately, Zionists adopted the model of pure settler colonies, following colonialist precedents set in North America, New Zealand, and Australia, where native populations were exterminated or expelled instead of used for cheap labor.[47]

Ethnic cleansing of the indigenous Palestinian population has been in consideration since the early history of the Zionist Labor movement. Ben-Gurion, in the 20th Zionist Congress, determined that the "growing Jewish strength in Palestine will increase our possibilities for conducting a large scale transfer." He avowed "this method also contains an important Zionist and humanistic idea—to transfer parts of the people to their own land."[48] Zionist Labor leaders did not view these ideas as morally deplorable at any time, and any hesitation to implement them was due to pragmatic considerations. For example, they did not want to precipitate an all-out war with the Arab countries.[49]

Even the most Left wing of the movement did not reject the idea of ethnic cleansing on moral grounds. Aharon Zisling, a member of Kibbutz Ein Harod and leader of Ahdut Ha'avoda (which in 1948 united with Hashomer Hatzair and Poali Zion Small to form the self-identified Marxist party Mapam—an acronym for the Unified Workers Party), declared in 1937: "I do not deny our moral right to propose population transfer. There is no moral flaw to a proposal aimed at concentrating the development of national life. On the contrary, in a new world order it can and should be a noble human vision."[50] This hypocritical stance—supporting socialism and claiming to uphold universal human values, while at the same time advocating ethnic cleansing—was shared by the great majority of the Zionist Left.

After the United Nations Partition Plan for Palestine was accepted on November 29, 1947, by the General Assembly, the 1948 war broke out, and the opportunity to expel the Palestinians emerged.

The UN resolution was entitled UN General Assembly Resolution 181 (II), Future Government of Palestine. It recommended the termination of the British Mandate and the partition of the territory into two states—one Jewish and one Arab—with the Jerusalem-Bethlehem area under special international protection, administered by the United Nations. The resolution also called for the withdrawal of British forces and for the Mandate to end by August 1, 1948, and for the new independent states to be established by October 1, 1948.

The Partition Plan was rejected by the representative leadership of the Arab community in Palestine (like the Palestine Arab Higher Committee) who were supported by the states of the Arab League, a regional organization of of Arab states . . .

The proposed plan however was accepted in word by the leaders of the Jewish community in Palestine, through the Jewish Agency, even though it contradicted the Zionist vision of an exclusive Jewish state in all of Palestine. As stated, the decision recommended that the area between the Mediterranean and the Jordan River be divided into two provisional states, one Jewish and one Arab. The Jewish state, according to the UN Partition Plan, had 498,000 Jews and 497,000 Palestinian Arabs—virtually equal in population—and was, in effect, a binational state.[51] However, the territories conquered by the Jewish army expanded far beyond the area allocated for a Jewish state.

The ethnic cleansing of the Palestinians created a Jewish majority in the newly established state. Between 750,000 and 900,000 Palestinians—55 to 66 percent of the total Palestinian population at the time—were expelled or forced to leave their homeland between the end of 1947 and early 1949.[52] Eighty-five percent of the indigenous Palestinian population living in pre-state Israel was displaced.[53] Furthermore, refugees were strictly prevented from returning to their villages and homes, even if they were only a short distance away.[54] More than 500 Palestinian villages were destroyed, and eleven cities were depopulated. An additional 30,000 Palestinians remained inside the borders of the new Jewish state—they either fled to nearby villages or were ordered to leave their villages for "security reasons," with the promise that their departure would be temporary. Today, known as the internal refugees, they remain displaced. In 2008 their population had grown to roughly 250,000. A secret agreement between the Zionist Left leadership and King Abdulla of Jordan, just twelve days before the UN Resolution, led to the partition of the area designated by the UN for the Palestinian state between the future Jewish state and the Hashemite kingdom, with the silent blessing of Western powers.[55]

The expanded Jewish state established itself on only a part of Mandate of Palestine, and 132,000 Palestinians survived the mass expulsion. This somewhat reduced the sense of historical achievement for the leaders of the Zionist Labor movement. Their disappointment is described by Professor Anita Shapira, a historian and enthusiastic supporter of Zionist Labor, in her biography of Yigal Alon, the admired commander of the Palmach which he commanded during the most brutal atrocities committed in the 1948 war:[56]

> Yigal had no hesitations in regard to this policy [expulsion] . . . He felt deterred by cruel deeds and robbery. But he saw in the War of Independence [the term used to refer to the War of 1948 in Israeli discourse and writing] an opportunity that would not repeat itself, for changing the demographic and settlement balance between Jews and Arabs. An opportunity which was not initiated by the Jews, and which in his opinion was not sufficiently exploited. Anything that was dependent on himself, he did as best he could—not only to conquer areas of *Eretz Israel*, but also to empty (*Leroken*) them from their Arabness. Alon even specified the territory he aspired to conquer in the 1948 war, namely, the entire area of Palestine: "I say it openly: I disagreed with the way in which the war ended . . . I was already convinced [in 1948] that we should go as far as the Jordanian desert and the Jordan [river] to create the conditions of a stable defense . : . while finding a solution to the problem of the Arab population."[57]

The 1967 occupation of the West Bank signified the completion of Alon's vision, which was shared by his colleagues in the Labor government that led the war. His plan (known as the "Alon Plan"), regarding the fate of the occupied territories, created the basis for the Oslo Accords and subsequent peace proposals that have been designed to eternalize Israel's control of Palestine with the collaboration of the Palestinian leadership.[58] (See chapter 9.)

Strengthened Zionist Left Hegemony in the Newborn State

Soon after the end of the 1948 war, the remaining Palestinians in the newly established state became completely cut off from the outside world. A military government oversaw the lives of hundreds of thousands of Palestinian citizens between 1950 and 1966.[59] Palestinians required the permission of the military governor for satisfying any basic necessity, including venturing beyond the "free" area designated to them, finding a job, visiting relatives, or seeing a medical specialist. The spatial immobility and political paralysis enforced upon the terrorized Palestinian population enabled the Labor-led coalition government along with Mapam to seize Palestinian lands, the majority of which were taken in the first years of the state.

However, to gain the legitimization of the international community for the newborn state of Israel, it was necessary to disguise the dispossession policies deployed against Palestinians.[60] Hence arose the decision to establish a formal democracy in which Palestinians, who remained within the borders of Israel, were granted citizenship and formal equality before the law. They were granted the right to vote for the Knesset and, at least theoretically, the right to organize on political lists so as to participate in general elections.

The falsely universalistic language of Israeli law, however, could not completely conceal the burgeoning Apartheid in the emerging Jewish state. Systematic institutional discrimination against Palestinian citizens was applied through the strengthened power of the Zionist Left. When the Declaration of the Establishment of the State of Israel took place on May 14, 1948, the entire leadership of the state, together with the governing institutions and organizations, were already in place. Major components of the Jewish Agency for Israel and its departments became state ministries in the first Israeli governments. The Yishuv representatives in its governing bodies, like the Jewish Agency for Israel and the Elected Assembly (Havad Haleumi), became the "Establishing Assembly," and later evolved into the first Knesset. The Hagana, the pre-state paramilitary of the Yishuv, became the Israeli Defense Forces (IDF).

The hegemony of the Zionist Labor movement was strengthened in the newborn state ruled by Mapai and Prime Minister Ben-Gurion. From the beginning, it enjoyed a dominant and even monopolist position within the political and social system. As emphasized by Baruch Kimmerling,[61] the state enlisted the bureaucratic civilian and military apparatuses for its needs and interests, as well as non-state bodies, including most political parties, the Jewish Agency for Israel, the Jewish National Fund (JNF), and the Histadrut. These pre-state national institutions now penetrated all social strata, imposed strict control over them and mobilized them to perform roles and tasks in service of the state. Thus, the first wave of industrialization that began in the late 1950s was implemented with the full consensus of Israeli society. The government controlled the state mechanisms and the majority of resources came from outside.

One of the important functions of the Zionist Left leadership was to preserve its own power and that of the Ashkenazi Jews (Jews of European origin)
and their descendants, who comprised the great majority of the pre-state settler
community. The large waves of Jewish immigrants from Arab states, which
came a few years after the establishment of the state, were exploited for cheap
labor by the Ashkenazi Zionist elite. The newcomers were construed as a potential political threat. In response, the state implemented a "melting-pot" policy
and ideology. The intention was to create a monolithic, homogeneous culture
in which the supposedly modern, Western, and progressive values of the Ashkenazi Jews were considered paramount, legitimizing their rule.

According to the dominant Orientalist ideology, Mizrahim have been perceived as descendants of undeveloped countries and as members of inferior cultures. This perception has enabled the Ashkenazi Zionist Left governments to
subordinate Mizrahim in the economy and society.

The capacity of the state to influence and control the Mizrahim was also
facilitated by the pretext of security, inscribed at the center of collective consciousness. By depicting Israeli society as existing in a constant state of siege, a
general social order and political culture of solidarity was engendered—and continues to be engendered in the present. This in turn allowed almost full co-optation of the Mizrahim and a legacy of subservience to their economic and social
discrimination.[62]

The Zionist Labor movement now applied the Constructive Socialism of
the pre-state period to the new reality of the sovereign settler state. Namely,
they replaced "socialism" with full-fledged "statism" (a state-centered approach),
which was to become Israel's dominant ideology and praxis. The state's laws,
symbols, and particularly its army were positioned at the heart of societal values,
enjoying a halo of sanctity and serving as the basis of a "civil religion," as depicted by Kimmerling.

This state-centered approach, says Kimmerling, created "*close to fascist* perceptions of the role of the state, its institutions and agencies which succeeded
to repress the development of a civil society in Israel for many years." Moreover,
"Israel's civic religion—was among the central causes of a cultural, cognitive and
civic militarism which in turn became the central agency and mechanism for
preserving and reproducing the Zionist-Ashkenazi hegemony."[63]

State-Created Class Structure
and the Role of Zionist Left Intellectuals

The prevailing political culture supported the structure of Israeli economic classes on the basis of ethnic and national divisions.[64] The Mizrahim and their Israeli-born descendants worked mostly blue-collar jobs, regardless of skill, and came to constitute the bulk of the Jewish working class. They facilitated the first wave of Israeli industrialization and played a central role in developing the strategic branches of Israeli industry in the 1960s for the Zionist Left governments.[65] The Histadrut's failure to defend the rights of these laborers forced the Mizrahim into professions with much lower salaries than jobs manned by Ashkenazim. State policies have preserved these gaps in income and standard of living between Mizrahim and Ashkenazim to the present day.[66]

Palestinian citizens, however, occupy the lowest levels of Israel's class structure. They were barred from employment in the public sector—said to consist of "strategic" industries—and from state- or Histadrut-controlled economic enterprises, all under the pretext of state security.[67] Palestinians were thus forced to seek employment in the private sector, where salaries and fringe benefits were much lower. These policies, systematically implemented by all Israeli governments, focused on repressing the Palestinian sector in Israel. Primarily concentrated in Galilee, the Triangle regions, and in the Negev, the Palestinian communities were made dependent on the Jewish economy, both in terms of jobs and purchasing basic life necessities. Due to the state's policies of dispossession, many Palestinian villages became commuter communities, and their prospects for organized social and political life were weakened.[68]

The Ashkenazi bourgeoisie and middle class were the major beneficiaries of the vast state investments in employment, education, and housing, and the encouragement of local business.[69] It is within the crucible of this class and its experience that the hegemonic culture and Israeli identity were structured and nurtured. The state and the majority of the Jewish population (in addition to internal and external researchers) view the Ashkenazi bourgeoisie as the embodiment of "Israeli culture" and "Israeli society." And by maintaining loyalty to the state and to basic Zionist premises, it continues to preserve its centrality as the leading class and culture. The Israeli intellectual elite of the Zionist Left are part and parcel of this social class. As in many other places, they fulfill the crucial function of the intelligentsia—namely, sustaining the ideology that gives a major role to state power and "manufacturing the consent" around its policies, ideology, and political culture. In Israel, Zionist Left intellectuals have enlisted in the service of the interests of the Ashkenazi political-social elite (who usually support the Labor Party) and have sustained the hegemonic ideology.[70] At the center of this ideology is the "Jewish state"—the key premise of Zionism, as imagined and implemented by the Zionist Labor movement.

This underscores the important task of this book: to study critically the prevailing discourse among Zionist Left intellectuals about the "Jewish state," and their efforts to reconcile the state with the definition of Israel as a democracy. In this context, the repeated failure of "post-Zionists" to create alternatives to the narratives of the Zionist Left is of paramount significance (see chapters 7, 8, and 9). Both Zionist Left and post-Zionist intellectuals speak of and within a liberal, humanist, conceptual, and ideological framework. This has enhanced their credibility among genuine progressives both in Israel and abroad. The Zionist Left role in granting legitimacy to Israel's version of Apartheid and "close to Fascist" political culture could not have been played by right-wing intellectuals and politicians. The latter have never claimed to base their support of the Jewish identity of the state on absolute universal human values.

One question we must ask is to what extent the Zionist Left's discourse on the "Jewishness" of the state and its perspective on democracy inevitably leads to dead-end peace plans, while the daily destruction of the Palestinian people continues unabated. Why is it that even genuine efforts to disengage from the stranglehold of the Zionist Left have failed to present a real alternative? I hope that by confronting these issues, this book will help to challenge Zionist Left ideological and political perspectives, and open the way for progressive forces among Jews and Palestinians to fight together against the Zionist/Jewish state. This is the only condition for building a democratic Israel and a free Middle East.

CHAPTER 1

The Physical and Symbolic Erasure of the Palestinian Presence from the Land, Past and Present

This chapter reviews the relentless efforts made by Israel's state agencies to erase the collective memory of the 1948 Nakba, as well as any physical, geographical, or cultural remains of Palestinian society from before the 1948 war. It focuses on the role played by Zionist Left intellectuals as the guardians of collective memory, sustaining the state's official ideology and narratives. The chapter further examines the supposition of Zionist Left intellectuals that the 1967 occupation is the root cause of the "conflict," and their associated disregard of the structural discrimination of Palestinians in the Jewish state.

Wiping Out the Pre-1948 Palestinian Presence

In the process of strengthening its hegemony, the newborn state quickly gained command over the historical legacy and narratives of the Zionist movement regarding the 1948 war and the Nakba. The state solely determined what should be erased from collective memory and what should be inscribed into the nation's consciousness. Any evidence of 1948 crimes was vehemently disputed. Deviations from the official narrative and the state's agenda were simply unacceptable. Such deviations were depicted as a challenge to "the justification of our existence in this land" and, therefore, were outside the boundaries of public discourse. Instead, Zionist themes like the rights to the land and the right to return to their homeland were made central to the official state ideology. The story of the Jews' heroic resistance to Greek and Roman occupiers in ancient times was presented as the model for the younger generation. All state agencies were involved in this comprehensive project of creating a collective homogeneous consciousness so as to ensure full commitment to the colonial settler Jewish state, led by the Zionist Left.[1]

At first the state abolished physical and geographical evidence of the pre-1948 existence of Palestinians. The housing and infrastructure of former Palestinian villages were destroyed, only after they were looted, and farmland was legally seized. The immediate purpose of this mass destruction was to preempt any threat of international sanctions. For example, if "there was nowhere to return to,"[2] Israel could not be forced to accept Palestinian refugees. Next came the physical and symbolic erasure of what was once a vigorous, pre-Nakba Palestinian civilization. All traces, memory, and records of the pastoral lifestyle of the Palestinian villages and their flourishing agriculture, and the emerging modernism that existed in Palestinian cities, which included abundant civic organizations, nationalist and women's movements, and buds of economic development—all of it was done away with.[3]

The theme of an "empty land"—the barren desert to which the Zionist settlers brought greenness and fertility—was consistently propagated by all state agencies. The narrative that Jewish settlers were "making the desert bloom" was used to mask the physical destruction of the Palestinian villages and towns. The early Zionist slogan "a land without a people for a people without a land" solicited a collective trust in the just cause of the Jewish state. "The 'emptiness' of the land," says Yitzhak Laor, "has become a central motif of the literature and ideology of the young state . . . The desolation and wilderness received a new design in the state narrative: No more swamps that had to be dried [the Zionist myth regarding pre-state times] but empty plains that need to be settled soon, in order to ensure the 'security' of the state."[4] The imagined "empty land" served well the central element in the Zionist myth: the "return" of Jews to their homeland after two thousand years in exile, a homeland that was waiting for its sons to come and redeem it from its wilderness. Radical historian Amnon Raz-Krakotzkin of Ben-Gurion University[5] has elaborated on the connection of the imagined "empty land" to the aspect of "return." The Zionist narrative relied upon a historical perception that negated the Jewish experience in Diaspora. It "emptied" the time that had stretched between the loss of sovereignty over the land and the renewal of settling it, from any significant meaning in the nation's life. In order to affirm a direct link between the Zionist project and the Biblical land and the people supposedly expelled from it, the homeland was imagined as "empty land." Thus, argues Raz-Krakotzkin, the "denial of exile" leads also to the negation of the Palestinian national memory and to the symbolic dispossession of the Palestinians from their homeland. The "empty land" was portrayed as waiting to embrace its returning sons and daughters to "make the wilderness bloom." The perception of Zionism as a colonialist project and of Israel as its implementation could thus be rejected on these grounds.

Erasing the Memory of the Nakba

There is ample evidence, from Zionist sources during the period of the 1948 war and immediately afterward, that indicates "members of the military and political elite, secondary leaders and intellectuals close to them knew very well what happened to the Palestinian Arabs in 1948, to say nothing of rank-and-file soldiers and kibbutz members, who actually expelled Palestinians, expropriated their lands and destroyed their homes." But soon after the war ended, state officials, with the help of Zionist Left intellectuals, began to consolidate an official discourse that enabled most Israeli Jews to "forget" what they once knew about the 1948 ethnic cleansing of Palestinians. [6]

Until the late 1980s, when the "New Historians" emerged onto Israel's intellectual scene (see chapters 6 and 7), the great majority of Zionist Left intellectuals were involved in the state project of forgetting or whitewashing the war crimes committed by Israel in the 1948 war. [7] They frequently downplayed the extent of the catastrophe inflicted upon the Palestinian people, and refused to acknowledge that Zionism was responsible for it. The role of the Marxist-Zionist Mapam (the Unified Workers Party) in creating the false narrative of the Nakba is emphasized by Stanford University professor of Middle East history Joel Beinin: "[Despite what they knew] after the war, it was Mapam's prescription for the conduct of Israeli forces—rather than the reality of expulsion—that became official Israeli history, and eventually, came to define the Jewish Israeli collective memory of what happened in 1948." Mapam's hypocrisy in calling for "Zionism, Socialism and Fraternity Between Nations" is demonstrated in the report of historian Yossi Amitai, a member of Hakibbutz Haartzi-Hashomer Hatzair (the extreme Zionist Left Kibbutz movement affiliated with Mapam). [8] "Most greedy [among the different streams of the Kibbutz Movement] was the Hakibbutz Haartzi-Hashomer Hatzair movement. Mapam members were not satisfied like other Kibbutzim with gaining control of abandoned lands, but demanded also lands on which their [Palestinian] owners still resided." [9]

For decades, the state of Israel, and traditional Zionist historians, argued that the Palestinian Arabs fled on orders from Arab military commanders and governments. These governments, they said, hoped to return behind the guns of victorious Arab armies. Consequently, the Zionist authorities have admitted little or no responsibility for the fate of the Palestinian refugees and their descendants.[10] The Zionist Left lacked compassion when referring to the Nakba. Even its most humanist figures often expressed justification for the 1948 ethnic cleansing in a laconic, offhand manner, claiming it was a necessary and inevitable response to the existential danger that the Yishuv was confronted with.

The perception of anti-Semitism and Arab "hatred of Jews," as a historical phenomenon, is regarded as the ultimate justification for the Zionist colonization, the Nakba, and the establishment of an exclusivist Jewish state. Moreover, these views nourished Israel's image as the eternal victim. The internationally acclaimed author Amos Oz, who is also a leading moral and ideological authority of the Zionist Left, has taken this narrative to the extreme:

> The assassination of European Jewry . . . was the ultimate, consistent conclusion to be drawn from the ancient position of the Jewish human being within the culture of the West. The Jew in Europe, in Christianity, and in the Paganism within Christianity is not a "national minority," is not "a religious group" and is not a "class problem." It has been thousands of years in which the Jew is perceived as a symbol and expression of something with a non-personable essence. Like the steeple, the Cross, Satan and the Messiah, so the Jew is a construction of the Western spirit. Even if all Jews were to have been absorbed among the European peoples, the Jew would continue being present. Somebody was compelled to play his role, to stand up as a primordial prototype in the depths of Christian souls. He ought to be brilliant and frightful, to suffer and deceive, to be liable to both genius and the most abhorrent deeds. Therefore, to be a Jew in the Diaspora means Auschwitz is intended for you. This is so because you are a symbol and not an individual person—the symbol of a vampire who is justly persecuted, or the symbol of the victim who is unjustly persecuted. But always and at any time, you are not an individual person; you are not you, who are only a fragment of a symbol.[11]

Oz assumes that the political positions of the Palestinian national movement represent the ideology of Jew hatred, which is shared by the majority of Palestinian people:

"From its very onset they [the Palestinian leadership] ignored ('closed their ears') to the disaster of Jews, hardened their hearts, named the Jew's desperate distress 'an European problem which is not of our business.' They sought the right opportunity to exterminate the Jews. This movement's wickedness reached its peak in their leaders' readiness to help Hitler with the 'solution' of the Jewish problem in Europe."[12] By contrast, notes Oz, Labor Zionism had from its inception moral supremacy over Palestinian nationalism. All it asked for was recognition that those who suffered from persecution and wanted to survive in the divided land had just cause. Zionism's arrogant claim of moral supremacy is ironic in light of Oz's disinclination to deal explicitly with the ethnic cleansing of the Palestinians in 1948:

> The justification in the eyes of the Arab residents of the land cannot rely on our centuries of longing (to return) ... What's it got to do with them? [Hence][t]he Zionist project does not have any justification but the justification of a drowning person who holds onto the only plank that he can hold on to, to save his life. There is an enormous moral difference between the drowning person [Zionism—representing the persecuted Jewish people] which is holding on to the plank and [while doing so] is pushing aside—even using force—the others who are sitting on the plank [the Palestinians], and the drowning person who takes control of the entire piece of wood and throws the others who are sitting on it [the Palestinians] into the water. This is the moral argumentation which underlies our repeated principal agreement to the partition of the land. And this is the distance [difference] between the Judaization of Jaffa and Lydda [former Palestinian cities inside Israel] and the Judaization of Nablus and Ramallah [cities in the '67 occupied territories].[13]

The Palestinian national movement, however, was indifferent to the distress of the drowning Jews and refused to create space on the plank for them, namely by agreeing to the partition of Palestine in 1947.

Political scientist Zeev Sternhell of Hebrew University makes a similar argument regarding Zionism's just cause. He also shares Oz's evasiveness about the Nakba:[14] "Not the historic right but the necessity to save those who lived was the moral basis of the conquest of the land. Hence it was the natural right of all human beings to ensure their existence by means of erecting an independent political framework that justified taking over the area, which permitted the establishment of Israel. Since as we know the land was not empty ... The Arabs' long, bitter opposition [to the creation of Israel] has not left any doubt about their awareness of the danger which confronts them."

Even after abundant historical research, which has confirmed at least the partial responsibility of the Zionist army in the 1948 catastrophe,[15] there are still many Zionist Left intellectuals who cling to the their distorted views on the Nakba. Shlomo Avineri, the renowned professor of political science at Hebrew University, famous for his enlightened worldview and for his "dovish" positions on the solution to the conflict, noted his opposition to a proposal for a law that would prohibit the official public commemoration of the Nakba on Israel's Independence Day. He calls the prohibition law proposal wicked and stupid.[16] However, he defines the Palestinians' public commemoration of the Nakba as an anti-Israeli act, which drains his opposition to the law of any genuine meaning:

> Undoubtedly, the attitude of some Israeli Arab leaders and elected officials toward what they call the Nakba is infuriating. First, because its message implies a challenge to Israel's legitimacy. Second, because they lack any self-criticism of the fact that the Arab community in pre-state Israel chose to respond to the [UN] Partition Plan with armed struggle . . . Indeed, it is hard to admit responsibility for failure in war, and one of the failures of the Palestinian leaders of the time, was their shirking of moral responsibility for the results of the war caused by their own choice.

The colonialist-style warning with which Avineri concludes his article points to the conditional nature of his support to Palestinian citizens: "The Israeli Arab leaders who continue their denial today [of the Palestinian responsibility for the Nakba] are making a grave political and moral error." Avineri's and other Zionist Left members' disregard for the pre-1948 dispossession of the indigenous population of Palestine and the crimes of the Nakba helps to enable the prevailing conception of the conflict between Israel and the Palestinians: that of two nations fighting over one piece of land.

The Zionist Left has always rejected the notion of Israel as a colonial settler state, one designed to advance and expand the Zionist colonial project with the backing of the imperialist US and the West. The Israeli Socialist Organization, known as Matzpen, was the only political group that, as early as the 1960s, adopted this stance (see chapter 6).[17] Hence, the Zionist Left understands the 1967 occupation of the West Bank and Gaza Strip to be the root cause of the conflict—and withdrawal its solution.

The 1967 Occupation as the Root Cause of the Conflict

The 1967 occupation is considered the turning point in the history of how the Zionist Left has justified the project of Zionism and the establishment of the state of Israel. In a number of articles published in *Haaretz* since 2000, Zeev Sternhell has emphasized the moral difference between pre-state Zionist aggressive policies and the 1967 occupation. While sharply condemning the 1967 occupation, Sternhell argues for the inevitability of the Zionist colonization project and its culmination in the establishment of the state of Israel. "Indeed," he admits, "already the founding fathers [of Zionism] and those who came soon after them knew that if the Jews wanted to inherit *(lareshet)* the land, they would have to conquer it by force. Until the War of Independence [the 1948 war] there was no alternative. The problem began when it became clear that even after the big victories of 1948–49 and 1967, this fundamental perception continues to dictate the national policy of Israel until the very present."[18]

Sternhell's main concern is that the 1967 occupation may in fact jeopardize the legitimacy of the Zionist project and the Jewish state, both of which offered a solution to the existential danger the Jewish people faced in the first half of the twentieth century:

> After the holocaust, which proved the justness of the cause of Zionism, and with the end of the Independence War, all the goals set by the Zionist movement were achieved. Hence, there is an essential difference between their right to Petah Tikva and Ofakim [inside Israel] and the robbery of the hills of the West Bank from their owners. Whoever challenges this essential difference will end in portraying the entire Jewish national movement, and not only the settlement of the last generation, as a colonial movement. [The Kibbutzim] Kfar Giladi, Hanita and Merhavia [erected in the pre-1948 war era] had a decisive role in our national resurrection. But Beit El, Tapuah [settlements in the West Bank] and Netzarim [a former settlement in the Gaza Strip] threatens not only the moral image of Israeli society, but its very future as well.[19]

Unlike most Zionist Left intellectuals, however, Sternhell emphasizes the superficial difference between the Zionist Left and Right, regarding their interests in retaining control over the '67 occupied territories.[20] Both the Right and Zionist Left, he argues, betray the just cause of pre-1967 Zionism:

> At the end of the 1967 War, conditions changed, but no change took place in the traditional thinking patterns and political habits . . . There was no danger for the very existence of the Israeli nation-state which would justify the negation of the national right of the *neighboring people* [emphasis added] . . . The security arguments [the need to provide security to Israel and its citizens] have never been clean of the basic will to use [any possible] opportunity to enlarge the estate [*nahla*]. The only real struggle within the [Zionist] movement took place between the school of "territorial compromise," which supported the annexation of areas not densely populated [by Palestinians], and the approach which supported permanent control of the entire West Bank, without annexing the population. These two perceptions together only made more conspicuous the weight of the occupying and violent nationalism *which was part and parcel of the heritage of the Labor movement as well.* [Emphasis added.]

The often naive position of rank-and-file activists, who like Sternhell see
the 1967 occupation as contradictory to pre-state Zionism, is demonstrated by
Dalia Golomb, the daughter of Golomb, admired founder of the Hagana.

Eliyahu Golomb played an integral part in preparing the Zionist military
forces for the victory of the 1948 war and the ethnic cleansing of the Palestinians, and was also a central leader of the Zionist Left until his death in 1945.
Dalia Golomb, now eighty-one years old, has been active in the women's organization Machsom Watch, which monitors Israeli army behavior at check-
points in the West Bank, says: "I continue the path of my father. Our paths are
not contradictory. I am asked by friends 'How are you, as the daughter of the
founder of the "Hagana" doing what you are doing?' And I answer, 'That's exactly it. My father erected the "Hagana" and not the "occupation."' The Hagana,
which became the Israel Defense Forces (IDF), was designed to defend the land
but later became the Israel Occupation Force. If my father were alive, he would
be shocked to see what I see here and now."[21]

Unlike Sternhell and activists like Golomb, Amos Oz is more equivocal in
condemning the Zionist Left's yearning for control of the '67 occupied territories, as reflected in his interview with Ari Shavit, "The Surviving Jew," published
in *Haaretz* on March 1, 2002. The interview took place a few months after the
Likud, chaired by Ariel Sharon, won the elections and the oppression of Palestinians on both sides of the Green Line escalated tremendously. In this interview
Oz attributes the persistence of the Israeli-Palestinian conflict to the uncom-
promising position of Palestinians. The ongoing conflict is portrayed as a war
for life or death for both sides. This desperate attitude toward the existential
nature of the conflict inevitably leads Oz to the conclusion that Israel must use
any means necessary in order to ensure its survival, as it did in 1948.

> As I wrote this book [on 1948], it became horribly clear to me how much we
> are standing [present tense] with our backs against the wall, in a profound way.
> But it's the same for the Palestinians. What makes it so hard is that, in this
> place, you have two peoples with their backs against the wall. To me, personally,
> I discovered that what happened to my Uncle David and Aunt Malka and to
> my cousin Daniel in Vilna [during the Holocaust] was very close to what was
> happening to us in Jerusalem [in 1948]. It was a hairsbreadth away, very close.

For Oz, Palestinian resistance to the 1967 occupation is interchangeable
with the assumed "existential war" (*kiyumi*) of 1948 in which the existence of
the Yishuv was threatened. At the same time, he objects to the occupation. The
reader is actually left with an imperative that has prevailed in traditional Israeli

political culture; namely, all atrocities must be whitewashed in the name of "security." Kill and dispossess your enemy in order to prevent your enemy from doing it to you:

> In the book [*A Tale of Love and Darkness*], I don't set out to refute this [the injustice committed in the '67 occupied territories]. Oppression is oppression and injustice is injustice and degradation is degradation. My views about the [1967 occupied] territories and the [Jewish] settlements haven't changed. But when I see the hawkish hysteria on the one side, *and the "anti-colonialist" hysteria* [emphasis added] on the other, and when I sense the tectonic shift going on below the earth that I am standing on, I go back to the beginning. And I say that every beginning has the beginning before the beginning . . . And when I was a child during the siege on Jerusalem we were sitting for eight months in caves deep underground like frightened animals and [they] made us thirsty and hungry and bombed us heavily.

Oz adds, "My Zionism begins and ends in that no person deserves to go through what my parents and their parents and their parents' parents went through. That's why, in my view, the Jewish people have a right to be a majority in one place and this right is unimpeachable." Oz elaborates on this "unimpeachable right" in his discussion of the 1948 war: "The war in 1947–48 was an all-out life-and-death war between two populations, not between armies or states. It's a war of life or death. And if it comes down to: I'm uprooted from my house and you take it from me, or you are uprooted from your house and I take it from you, then it's preferable for me to remain and for you to be uprooted. And if it's going to be that you live and I die, or I live and you die, then it's better that you die. Because, like I said, our backs are to the wall. In such a war, backs are really up against the wall."[22]

Ignoring the Palestinian Citizens

The focus on the 1967 occupation as the sole cause of the Israeli-Palestinian "conflict" denies the structural discrimination against Palestinian citizens, and their history and current oppression are excluded from the political discourse and activity of all wings of the Israeli "peace camp." The erasure of the Nakba was followed by the neutralization of its present day survivors. Only seldom has opposition to the oppressive policies of the 1967 occupation "mixed" with a rebuke of the dispossession of the Palestinian citizens. Intellectuals have publicized opinions on "internal" issues preoccupying "Israeli society," but have refrained from criticizing the atrocities committed against Palestinian citizens.

When Oz published his political articles in response to contemporary political events,[23] he repeatedly dealt with the issue of the 1967 occupation in his writings. Yet his responses fail to mention the most incendiary events, the ones that stirred up the most anger in the Palestinian community of Israel. His published collection of articles (writings from 1967–78) makes no reference to the massive land confiscation that led to militant Palestinian demonstrations on "Land Day" in 1976, during which six Palestinian citizens were killed by the police. Palestinians inside Israel continue to demonstrate every year against the ongoing confiscation of their lands and other measures of dispossession employed by the Israeli government—Zionist Left and Right alike. Oz and other Zionist Left intellectuals have never related to these commemorations, much less participated in them, as did small numbers of non- and anti-Zionist Israelis. In his 2002 collection of articles (covering writings between 1998 and 2002), Oz ignores the October 2000 Israeli police force murders of thirteen Palestinian citizens (who were demonstrating in solidarity with their brethren in the '67 occupied territories) as the second Intifada began.[24] The first article published after these traumatic events came more than two months afterward, and bore no mention of them. Oz instead chose to write about the Knesset general elections in which he supported Ehud Barak (Labor), who won. Barak engineered the Camp David Summit failure in 2000 and as prime minister was responsible for the October crimes against the Palestinian citizens committed by Labor minister of internal security.

Even Uri Avnery, one of the most dedicated opponents of the 1967 occupation and its atrocities, has joined the conspiracy of silence regarding the daily resistance of Palestinian citizens. Avnery is the founder of Gush Shalom (the Peace Bloc), which was started immediately after the signing of the Oslo Accords in 1993. Avnery has led Gush Shalom from the beginning. In 2001, on behalf of Gush Shalom, he attempted to tackle the "roots of the conflict" and suggested an outline for a peace plan in his "80 Theses for a New Peace Camp."[25]

In the document, Avnery reviews the history of the conflict since the onset of the Zionist movement. While his honest manner is unlike that of other Zionist Left intellectuals, he places the burden of responsibility evenly upon both sides, indicating that both the Zionist and Palestinian National Movements have committed equal wrongs. Palestinian resistance to the Jewish immigration and colonization of their land before the 1948 war is portrayed as the Palestinian share in the "complete oblivion of each of the two peoples to the national existence of the other." On the other hand, Avnery acknowledges the essentially dispossessive nature of Zionist colonization. Regarding the Nakba, Avnery adopts a far more honest approach than that of Oz, admitting Zionist responsibility, however partial. Avnery describes the atrocities committed by the state of Israel in the first year of its establishment: "the demolition of the 450 [*sic*] Arab villages, the confiscation of most of the lands on which Jewish immigrants were settled and even coaxed to come en masse as part of the policy to 'consolidate the Jewish state.'"

However, the mention of Palestinian citizens of Israel ends there—in the early 1950s. The systematically oppressive policies of the Israeli state toward the Palestinians are completely absent from Avnery's analysis from the 1950s to 2001.

Precisely because the thirteen Palestinian citizens were killed just a few months before the theses were published, and because the campaign against the Palestinian citizens' civil, political, economic, and social rights escalated thereafter, one cannot accept this omission as a case of mere negligence. Rather, it demonstrates Avnery's disregard for Palestinian citizens' struggle for national collective rights and identity. Within the Israeli political context, silence is no less political than a declared position.

Since 2001, Uri Avnery has continued his struggle against the atrocities committed in the '67 occupied territories with even more determination and fortitude. Nevertheless, in his more recent writings, Avnery has tended to romanticize pre-state Zionism. In this way, he negates the Palestinians from the political and cultural discourse of these early years. This negation works against Palestinians in the contemporary state of Israel, too. By defending the history and aims of pre-1967 Israel to opponents of the 1967 occupation, Avnery contributes to the hegemonic narrative of an "empty land," both past and present.

This tendency is reflected in Avnery's August 2009 response[26] to a letter sent by Res. Lieutenant Colonel Dov Yermiya. Yermiya sent his letter to a limited number of friends a few months after the "Operation Cast Lead" massacre in the Gaza Strip (which began on December 27, 2008, and ended when Israel completed its withdrawal on January 21, 2009). Yermiya, a supporter of the former Marxist party Mapam, has been a respected figure among the Zionist Left and the peace camp in general. In the past, he has often raised his voice against the atrocities committed in the '67 occupied territories and in Israel's assaults on Lebanon and Gaza. In his letter Yermiya declared his break with Zionism:

> Therefore I, a 95-year-old Sabra [native-born Israeli Jew][27] who has plowed its fields, planted trees, built a house and fathered sons, grandsons and great-grandsons, and also shed his blood in the battle for the founding of the State of

Israel, declare herewith that I renounce my belief in the Zionism which has
failed, that I shall not be loyal to the Jewish fascist state and its mad visions, that
I shall not sing anymore its nationalist anthem, that I shall stand at attention
only on the days of mourning for those fallen on both sides in the wars, and that
I look with a broken heart at an Israel that is committing suicide and at the
three generations of offspring that I have bred and raised in it.

Yermiya, however, does not challenge the vision of the first founders of Zionism, the leaders of the colonization project, and most of the "pioneers" who
settled the land. "They were people of conscience and morality, who held to the
axiom that human beings are decent." It is the means by which their vision was
implemented "over [which] there is the waving of the black flag of the frightening contempt for the life and blood of the Palestinians. Israel will never be
forgiven for the terrible toll of blood spilt, and especially the blood of children,
in hair-raising quantities.

In his efforts to win Yermiya back into the fold, Avnery chooses the Dalia
Folk Dances Festival as the embodiment of the beautiful state that he and Yermiya dreamed of in their youth. This festival took place twice before the establishment of the state (in 1944 and 1947) and a number of times in the first two
decades after 1948. It came to symbolize, especially in the time of the Yishuv,
the Zionist Labor movement and its values of settling the land, as realized by
the pioneers of Kibbutzim and Moshavim. Avnery describes the Festival as the
embodiment of the admired Zionist culture:

> When I think of our youth, yours and mine, one scene is never far from my mind:
> the 1947 Dalia folk dances festival. Tens of thousands of young men and women
> were sitting on the slope of a hill in the natural amphitheater near Kibbutz Dalia
> on Mount Carmel. Ostensibly it was a festival of folk dancing, but in reality it
> was much more—a great celebration of the New Hebrew culture which we were
> then creating in the country, in which folk dancing played an important role. The
> dancing groups came mainly from the kibbutzim and the [Zionist Left] youth
> movements, and the dances were original Hebrew creations, interwoven with
> Russian, Polish, Yemenite and Hassidic ones. A group *of Arabs danced the Debka
> in ecstasy*, dancing and dancing and dancing on. [Emphasis added.]

Kibbutz Dalia was set up by Hashomer Hatzair, the Marxist faction of the
Kibbutzim movement. It was founded in 1939 as part of the "Wall and Tower"
(*Choma ve Migdal*) project—a series of fifty-three fortified settlements, most of
which were Kibbutzim and Moshavim, erected during the Arab Rebellion of
1936–39. They were designed to expand the borders of Jewish colonization, and
thus increase the area that would potentially be recognized in the future as the

Jewish state. Dalia was surrounded by a number of Palestinian villages like Daliyat al-Rawha' and Umm az Zinat, whose inhabitants were eventually expelled in 1948.

Avnery continues to describe the young audience who longed for the UN decision for an independent state: "In the middle of the event, the loudspeakers announced that members of the UN Commission of Inquiry, which had been sent by the international organization to decide upon the future of the country, were joining us. When we saw them entering the amphitheater, the tens of thousands spontaneously rose to their feet and started to sing the 'Hatikva,' the national anthem, with a holy fervor that reverberated from the surrounding mountains."

So what happened to the wonderful pre-state colonial society, according to Avnery? What happened to the "Hebrew society, the Hebrew culture, the Hebrew morality that we were so proud of then? [What happened] to the dreams of this beautiful youth, who half a year after the Dalia festival fought like me and you in our war of Independence—their Nakba"?

> Did we dream of this corrupt society, a society without compassion, where a handful of the very rich live off the fat of the land, with a large band of politicians and media people and other lackeys groveling in the dust at their feet? Did we dream of a state that is an isolated and shunned ghetto in the region, lording over an oppressed Palestinian ghetto-within-a-ghetto? There were days when we could stand up anywhere in the world and proudly declare "I am an Israeli." [Since the Gaza war] no one can do that now. The name of Israel has become mud . . .

However, all in all, Avnery's dreams regarding the Jewish state do seem to have come true. "Yes, we did create a state. As the old song goes: 'On the battlefield, a town is now standing'[28] [and we have] brought millions of people to this country. From a Hebrew community of 650,000, we have grown into a population of 7.5 million. A fourth and fifth generation speaks Hebrew as their mother tongue. Our economy is large and solid, even in these times of crisis. In several fields we are in the first rank of human endeavor."

Of course, Avnery completely fails to mention the Palestinian citizens of Israel. He thus joins the Zionist Left in their project of symbolically erasing them from the present, thus confirming Israel as a state for Jews alone.

The omission of the Palestinian citizens is not limited to those at the front of the struggle against the 1967 occupation (like Uri Avnery). Zionist Left progressives in other political arenas do the same. A case in point is the small group of self-proclaimed Social Democrats and socialists who challenge the economic Neoliberal policies supported by Zionist Left political parties—Labor and

Meretz. For example, in May 2009, a number of Labor members of Knesset (MK's) strongly opposed the Likud government's annual budget, claiming that it reflected a wildly capitalist policy. They did not, however, protest with the same intensity when the Labor Party joined this right-wing government, which includes as its foreign minister the arch-racist Avigdor Lieberman, who calls for expulsion of Palestinians.

Daniel Gutwein, professor at the Department of History of the Jewish People at Haifa University, is one of the few Zionist Left intellectuals to critically analyze Israel's neoliberal ideology and policies.[29] Two months after the end of Israel's bloody assault against Gaza, while the Labor Party was negotiating entrance into the Likud government coalition, Gutwein published an article in *Haaretz* that demonstrated the prevailing tendency of Social Democrats to exclude the political "questions of peace and the [1967 occupied] territories" from their mission of building a just "Israeli society."[30] Unsurprisingly, Palestinian citizens are not even mentioned.

In his aspiration to abolish the current neoliberal economy, Gutwein calls for splitting from the Labor Party and the creation of a party of Social Democrats. The adoption of the Labor Party's "two-states flag" by the "centrist" Kadima Party makes clear the need for a Social Democratic party.[31] Namely, to "replace Labor's courting of the well-to-do with addressing the down-trodden and dispossessed classes, working for organizing a power which struggles to halt the deterioration of Israeli society towards the right."[32]

Not only does Gutwein accept the proven empty slogan of "two states solution" adopted by the Kadima Party, he has nothing to say about the political approach of the new progressive party toward Palestinian citizens in the desired welfare state. Apparently their oppression is not considered relevant to just economic values.

As Noam Chomsky correctly notes: "Historical amnesia is a dangerous phenomenon, not only because it undermines moral and intellectual integrity, but also because it lays the groundwork for crimes that still lie ahead."[33] This is exactly how the erasure of the 1948 Nakba's history has allowed the Zionist Left intellectuals and activists to ignore the Palestinian citizens' distress and to support the prevailing systematic persecution of the Palestinian citizens. The differentiation made by the Zionist Left between the 1967 occupation and the Zionist creation of the Jewish state not only excuses the absence of a moral condemnation against the oppression of the Palestinian citizens, but it is also viewed as compatible with the struggle for "peace." This position disregards the Pales-

tinian citizens' daily fight for equal rights. It boils down to depicting their militant expressions as violence committed by "extremists."

A rather severe but telling example of this approach, which prevails among
the peace camp and the Zionist Left, is the case of the defamed ex-police officer
Alik Ron. Ron was well known for his racist attitudes and behavior against Palestinians when he served as the police commander of the North District before
and during the aforementioned mass demonstrations of October 2000. The Orr
Commission, established to inquire about these events, stated that "[Alik Ron]
was responsible for the live fire of snipers . . . that this firing was unjustified, and
resulted in injuries to at least seven people and the death of one of them." The
commission recommended that Alik Ron "not fulfill in the future any command
or administrative position which is connected to Internal Security."[34]

All this, however, did not prevent Israeli Zionist liberals from accepting Alik
Ron into the core group of supporters of the "Geneva Initiative." Headed by former Meretz chair Yossi Beilin and Yasser Abed Rabbo, a member of the Palestinian Authority, the initiative claimed to provide a "just solution to the
Israeli-Palestinian conflict." The initiative was enthusiastically accepted by Zionist Left intellectuals.[35] Moreover, Ron was a member of the delegation of Israeli
public figures who were invited to the signing ceremony of the Geneva Accords
in the Jordanian Dead Sea Movenpick Hotel on October 12, 2003.[36] His presence
did not trigger disgust or horror from the two Israeli "champions of peace" who
attended the event (authors David Grossman and Amos Oz), nor for that matter
from the members of the Palestinian delegation. Indeed, what does the cold-
blooded murder of "extremist" Palestinians in Israel have to do with the noble
aspirations of a "just" peace with the Palestinians in the occupied territories?

The unbearable ease with which Zionist Left, intellectuals, and activists ignore the daily oppression and discrimination of Palestinians in Israel, in contrast
to their professed commitment to humanism and peace, constitutes a message
of complicity to the wider Israeli Jewish public. This message of complicity is
far more significant than any stated support for a peaceful solution of the disputed '67 occupied territories.

The Zionist Left intellectuals can justify escalating repression of the Palestinian citizens' national identity and demands as part of their commitment to a
Jewish democratic state. This conception of a Jewish democratic state includes
several key elements. The first of these—the principle of a "Jewish majority" in
the state of Israel—we turn to in the following chapter.

CHAPTER 2

"Jewish Majority" Spells Racism

Traditionally, a Jewish majority has been associated with the very notion of a Jewish state. Hence, it is generally accepted by all streams of Zionist thought. The aspiration for an exclusively Jewish state inspired the ethnic cleansing of Palestinians in 1948 and heavily influenced the legal infrastructure of the newborn state of Israel. Retaining a Jewish majority has remained sacred and guides all Israeli governments' legislation and policies.

Haifa University sociologist Sammy Smooha, known for his democratic and humanistic worldviews, describes what this means:

> What is a Jewish state for me? It is of two foundations: The first is a Jewish majority. But not a coincidental majority. In many countries, there is a certain ethnic or national majority. The Jewish majority in the state of Israel [however] is a planned majority, an ideological majority; a majority which was planned throughout history, a part of the [Zionist] national aspirations, part of an intentional policy which entailed the expulsion of Arabs in 1948 and many other additional decisions.

For Smooha, the second foundation of the Jewish state, which in fact is connected to the first, relates to the attachment of the state of Israel with Jewish people throughout the world. "The Jews here see themselves as part of that people . . . Their interest that the Jewish People continue to exist makes Israelis see in them allies. These are the two foundations. On the remaining issues Jews can compromise. But not on these two foundations."[1]

At face value, the "planned" Jewish majority may seem related to "internal" Israeli and Jewish issues: the shared identity of Jews in Israel with their co-religion-
ists abroad. But Attorney Hassan Jabarin, the founder and director of Adalah,
the Legal Center for Arab Minority Rights in Israel, strips the concept of its
false innocence. "A Jewish majority with regards to whom?" notes Jabarin when
discussing the entrenched agreement among Supreme Court judges that the
superiority of Israeli Jews should be preserved. "It is clear that this means a Jewish majority with regards to Arabs. This logic, in fact, grants the Jewish state
the legitimacy to commit acts which violate the rights of the Arab citizens in
order to retain this supremacy."[2]

This chapter deals with the issues raised by Jabarin: How has the state of
Israel confronted the "demographic threat" of losing a Jewish majority? What
laws and policies have been inspired by the logic of preserving a Jewish majority
and denying citizenship rights to Palestinians in Israel? How does the discourse
of Zionist Left intellectuals attempt to reconcile this discriminatory ideology
with their claimed adherence to democratic values? Finally, how do all these issues encourage the reprisal of ethnic cleansing "transfer," in common political
parlance, as a legitimate topic of discussion?

Laws Aimed to Retain Jewish Majority

First and foremost is the 1950 Law of Return, discussed in the introduction.
This law aims to safeguard the Jewish majority that was achieved through the
mass expulsions of 1947–49 and the prevention of refugees from returning to
their homes and property and reuniting with their families.[3]

Rarely does one find acknowledgement of how this law discriminates. Even
Smooha, when saying that the Law of Return means "the exclusion of the Palestinian citizens," does not point to the basic living necessities conferred to Jews
and denied to Palestinians.

Responding to Smooha, Attorney Osama Halabi notes:

> You [Smooha] want both a Jewish state and a linkage to the Jewish people. The
> question is what is the nature of this linkage? Retaining the linkage with the
> Jewish People as practiced today, means that the Law of Return is not only
> about arriving in an aircraft and being given a nice welcome and direct trans-
> portation to a house. It is also a comprehensive parcel of benefits which you
> have avoided mentioning in your suggestions on how to limit discrimination—
> perhaps accidental, perhaps not. A Jew who is willing to immigrate to Israel is
> not only provided with an automatic citizenship, but also with a priority in ac-

quiring land. Until this very day, not one Arab locality has been built, and for a good reason: The land reserve is saved for members of the Jewish people alone.[4]

A variety of laws, regulations, and policies that aim to preserve and increase the present majority of Jews in Israel have been adopted in the past few years. For example, the 2003 New Citizenship and Entry into Israel Law prohibits granting residency or Israeli citizenship status to Palestinians from the '67 occupied territories who are married to Israeli citizens.[5] It was originally enacted for one year, but has been reissued every year since. In March 2007 the Knesset expanded the scope of this law to include banning spouses who are residents or citizens of Iran, Iraq, Syria, or Lebanon, defined in the law as "enemy states."[6]

Adalah and the Association for Civil Rights in Israel (ACRI), among others, have submitted a number of appeals to the Supreme Court in the last five years, emphasizing the discriminatory essence of the amendment to citizenship law and demanding its repeal. But these have been rejected, mainly on grounds of security and of the danger posed by Palestinian and Arab spouses. Says Jabarin:

> Supporters of the Amendment to the Citizenship Law want to justify it for demographic reasons. They are not satisfied with giving preference to one group because of its ethnic affiliation but want to deny basic freedoms to the other group, because of its ethnic affiliation. Therefore, the amendment to the law reflects a transition from a situation of invalid discrimination to a situation of racist oppression . . . If this goal [to maintain a Jewish majority] allows the government to take such a drastic step, and to undermine basic constitutional rights such as the right to a family life, then why shouldn't the [Jewish] Upper Nazareth municipality, for example, prevent Arab citizens in the future from purchasing apartments in its jurisdiction, claiming that this is essential in order to retain the Jewish character of Upper Nazareth, or alternatively, impose a higher property tax on Arab residents, in order to deter them from building a house in its jurisdiction? That is the slippery slope of the demographic argument, behind which lies racism.[7]

Indeed, as emphasized by Azmi Bishara, the principle of "a Jewish majority" that underlies Israel's policies is racist. The policies of "separation" between Jews and Palestinians have been portrayed as a necessary condition for preserving the "Jewish identity" of the state.[8] But in fact they aim to achieve a Jewish majority on both sides of the Green Line.

Policies of "Demographic Separation"
The "separation" principle that guided Israeli policies in both the '67 occupied territories and Israel has constantly pushed Palestinians into diminishing

areas, ensuring a Jewish majority in an ever-growing territory. The Zionist Left's "pragmatic" slogan of "maximum territory, minimum Palestinians," has been adopted by most Israelis, and helped to direct the settlement projects on both sides of the Green Line.

However, the "separation" between Jewish and Palestinian communities has never been complete and was not intended to be so. Separation projects have been organized to escalate the submission of "separated" Palestinians. In other words, they have strengthened the state's control of Palestinian access to resources, and weakened the Palestinians' ability to resist oppression.[9] Inside Israel, this policy has targeted Palestinian-concentrated areas, such as the Galilee and the northeastern Negev. Creating a Jewish majority in these regions has become a top priority of the Jewish state.

The major aim of "Judaisation" of these regions has been to prevent the emergence of a social/political/economic nucleus among the Palestinians.[10] These policies have been supported by the Supreme Court, which sees them as implementing the Zionist aim of "absorbing new immigrants (*Olim*)" or "dispersing the population" (*Pizur hauchlosia*).

In order to make sure they wouldn't be obliged to accept Palestinians into their communities, a number of Jewish settlements in the Galilee, largely in the Misgav Regional Council, named Mitzpim (lookouts), initiated a change in their regulations regarding the acceptance of new members. The Mitzpim and the yishuvim kehilatyim (communal settlement) in the Galilee and in Wadi Ara were erected in the 1980s, scattered between Palestinian localities as part of the state's efforts to "Judaise" the regions. Together they form a legal body that collectively decides on the qualifications of applicants for membership in their communities, a decision that would grant the applicant a plot of state land on which he/she could build a home. In the 1980s, 170 Mitzpim and communal settlements were built mostly for middle-class Ashkenazis, who were provided with the high "quality of life" of a suburban neighborhood under the pretext that their localities were essential for the "security" of the state.[11]

These lookouts and communal settlements were positioned on state lands that had previously been transferred to the Jewish National Fund (JNF) as a way to keep them in Jewish-Israeli hands. Many of the middle-class Ashkenazi settlers were self-declared liberals or members of the Zionist Left who supported territorial concessions in the '67 occupied territories as well as a "two-state solution."

A decision by the Supreme Court in 2007 raised the panic level of Jewish settlers in the Galilee. The ruling upheld the right of Ahmed and Fahima

Zubeidat to buy a house in the lookout of Rakefet, part of the Misgav bloc of lookouts in the Galilee. To stop this perceived threat to their exclusivist communities, the Jewish settlers of Misgav reached a resolution on May 2009, determining that only those who declared their commitment to Zionism and the Jewish state would be qualified to join their Mitzpim.

The ensuing battle, launched by Israeli settlement bodies against the original owners of these lands in the Galilee, had horrible consequences. While Palestinians now comprise 72 percent of the population of the Galilee, they control only 16 percent of the land. This situation is reflected in the town of Sekhnin, which supplies services to a large rural area in the lower eastern part of the Galilee. The town's 25,000 residents live on roughly 9,000 dunams of land, due to expropriations of land to the neighboring settlement of Misgav. By contrast, the 15,000 Jewish citizens of Misgav enjoy the use of 180,000 dunams.[12]

The zero-sum game regarding state lands does not allow for even the smallest concession. All the land must be controlled, which will cause the economic suffocation of Palestinian localities. At the beginning of December 2005, the Borders' Committee of the Ministry of Interior rejected the Sekhnin municipality's request for an addition of 8,400 dunams. Instead only 1,700 dunams were transferred to the municipality. Worse yet, the allocated land was in a geographically problematic area. Israeli sociologist Dani Rabinowitz emphasizes this lethal blow to the Sekhnin community: "The decision of the committee to add to it [Sekhnin] a limited and hilled area to the east, intentionally ignores its potential natural growth towards the north and west . . . Following the recent decisions of the committee, the quantity of municipal land per capita in the nearby Jewish regional council of Misgav will now be 36 times more than the quantity per capita in Sekhnin."[13]

Ron Shani, the chair of the Misgav Regional Council, defended the aforementioned resolution to condition acceptance of new members to the Mitzpim on the applicants' declared commitment to Zionism and the Jewish state:[14]

"A community which Zionist values and Israel [Jewish people's] heritage are in the heart of its being and walks of life, seeks to accept people for whom these values are close to their heart . . . There is nothing racist about it because Zionism itself is not a racist movement despite its addressing the Jewish people [alone] as we do not see any racism in the right of our Arab neighbors to absorb into their communities only locals [sic]."

Soon enough, however, the falseness of Shani's peaceful "separate but equal" argument is revealed by his acknowledgement that the very Zionist rationale of

Judaising the Galilee is a declared war on the Palestinians' presence in the region. "The lookouts in the Galilee are a strategic aim of the state . . . Their disappearance [as only Jewish] would constitute a direct and concrete threat to the continued sovereignty of Israel in this part of the land."

The same logic has led to the fragmentation of the '67 occupied territories, care of a joint US-Israeli strategy. As emphasized by Noam Chomsky:

> The total separation of the Gaza Strip from the West Bank is one of the greatest achievements of Israeli politics, whose overarching objective is to prevent a solution based on international decisions and understandings and instead dictate an arrangement based on Israel's military superiority . . . Since January 1991, Israel has bureaucratically and logistically merely perfected the split and the separation: not only between Palestinians in the occupied territories and their brothers in Israel, but also between the Palestinian residents of Jerusalem and those in the rest of the territories and between Gazans and West Bankers/Jerusalemites.[15]

The "unilateral" disengagement from the Gaza Strip in September 2006, supported by both Labor and Meretz, and the blanket siege enforced since then has aimed and succeeded to "virtually reduce it [the Gaza Strip] to a state of abject destitution, and its once productive population transformed into one of aid-dependent paupers."[16] In exchange for this farce, Israel was given a free hand in the West Bank, namely to build settlements, and to fragment any remaining areas such that a sovereign entity of Palestinians could not be established.[17]

Thus, the "Separation Wall" in the West Bank, initiated by a number of Labor leaders and supported by the majority of the Zionist Left, was not trying to determine the political borders between two sovereign entities, Israeli and Palestinian, as some on the Zionist Left want to believe. Rather, the logic and inspiration of the wall, and the accompanying checkpoint system, was to create a collaborationist Palestinian Authority whose primary function is to ensure that Palestinians in the West Bank and Gaza are detained and enclosed. The wall was built precisely for this reason, to prevent Palestinians from developing a viable mass resistance. However slow, these policies are part of the comprehensive systematic strategy of ethnic cleansing carried out in the '67 occupied territories, as emphasized by the radical left linguist Ran HaCohen from Tel Aviv University. "Ethnic cleansing is the motivation behind every new acre taken by Jewish settlements, behind 'security zones' and 'by-pass roads,' behind fences and military outposts. It is behind every siege and closure, aimed at reducing Palestinian movement to their immediate surroundings, confining them to their enclave, to their town or village, to their house."[18]

This is why Meron Benvenisti, researcher, political analyst, and genuine democrat, dreams of the day "when believers in this illusion will realize that 'separation' is a means to oppress and dominate," which, in turn, "will mobilize to dismantle the apartheid apparatus."[19]

The Majority Discourse among Zionist Left Intellectuals

Israel's demographic phobia—the fear that the Palestinians' higher birth rate will translate into a Palestinian majority—is widespread. The irony is that Israel's control over the '67 occupied territories has already brought about this change, and it has increased the level of fear. The '67 occupied territories have in fact become part and parcel of the Israeli regime, rather than an entity "external" to Israel "proper." According to the data provided by the Central Bureau of Statistics, 11.43 million people live under Israeli domination. Of these, 5.6 million are Jewish, while 5.83 million are not Jewish. That's a total of 49 percent Jews and 51 percent non-Jews currently living in the Israeli empire.[20]

This demographic situation has brought Israel back to square one. Namely, to the 1947 UN decision that partitioned Palestine, in which the future Jewish state was designated to include almost equal numbers of Jews and Palestinians. However, Israel's official legal-political language is more affiliated with the 1967 occupation, indicating that its control over these areas is "temporary." Zionist Left intellectuals are more than eager to adopt such misleading terms. They avoid having to admit that the denial of basic rights from Palestinians in the '67 occupied territories is part of the regime in which they live. (See chapter 5 for discourse on the consolidation of one Israeli regime throughout Historic Palestine.)[21]

The "demographic" discussion has spread into liberal circles. Some have gone so far as to suggest limiting the birth rates of Palestinian citizens and Ultra Orthodox Jews (the majority of whom are non-Zionist).[22] Ruth Gavison, a law professor at Hebrew University and the former president of ACRI, represents many among Israeli intellectuals who left the Liberal/Left camp. They have now explicitly adopted the logical conclusions of the (Jewish) state-centered ideology they had nourished. Namely, a total disregard for Palestinian human rights, which the right wing has always openly expressed.

In 2005 Gavison came out with strong views on the Jewish majority, which in her belief reflected a wide consensus. "Israel has the right to control Palestinian natural growth," she said. "Control of birth rates is not racism."[23]

The "demographic ghost" dominates the discourse in Zionist Left circles. The ultimate Zionist aims of maintaining an exclusively Jewish state and retaining a Jewish majority are inseparable to the Zionist Left. Moreover, safeguarding the present Jewish majority has become a condition of one's commitment to the state. This is explicitly admitted by Yossi Beilin, the former chair of the Meretz Party and one of the initiators of the Oslo Agreements and of the Geneva Initiative (see chapter 9), in his response to Avraham Burg, former leader of the Labor Party and former chair of the World Zionist Organization. Burg published sharp criticisms of Israel in 2007, comparing it to Germany on the eve of Nazism's ascendance. He suggested changing the Law of Return, and doing away with the definition of Israel as a Jewish state. "If this state is not the state of the Jews," Beilin rebukes Burg, "and there is not within it a Jewish majority, it [the state] does not interest me."[24] The leftist author Sami Michael, the current president of ACRI, goes a step further, saying he would rather leave the entire region if he belonged to a minority in the state.[25]

The Right in Israel has no difficulty justifying the existence of a non-democratic regime in which Palestinians are second-class citizens, because they have never pretended to uphold universalist-socialist values like the Left. The latter are compelled to defend the democratic values in the definition of the state of Israel, and while the Jewish majority principle contradicts the idea of a "Jewish Democratic State," the Left uses it to confer legitimacy to "democracy," as described in the next section.

The "Majority" Principle as a Cornerstone of Democracy

The argument for Jewish majority is based on a simplified idea of democracy: sanctification of the decisions and interests of the majority, which are then foisted upon the "people." The supreme value attributed to the majority—which just happens to be Jewish—allows Zionist intellectuals to take a hypocritical stance, preserving their image as democrats. They can thus support various aspects of Israel's Apartheid regime without needing separate legal systems for Jews and Palestinians. The majority rule becomes a tool to justify Jewish dominance. It is an expression of the most genuine democratic process, "the very accumulation of the personal decisions of the members of the majority" (namely the Jews).[26]

Through this process, which is disguised as a participatory, direct democracy, all state policies and laws—including those that aim to preserve the Jewish majority and its dominance—are whitewashed. Indeed, it is a form of circular thinking in its most illogical expression: a democratic value (the rule of "the majority") that legitimizes undemocratic policies to sustain this exact process.

Asa Kasher, a professor of philosophy at Tel Aviv University and the author of the "Code of Ethics" of the Israeli army, has, like Gavison, deserted the liberal/left camp while claiming to represent humanist values. He attempts to reconcile his belief in both a Jewish state and democratic values through the principle of a Jewish majority.

> Kasher: I want a democratic state, in the most moral meaning of the expression, and I want a decisive Jewish majority, which enjoys national, political and social freedom, among other things, by being the ruler in all unorganized aspects of the social life of the state, [and through] the very accumulation of the personal decisions of the members of the majority.
>
> The interviewer: Everything is conditioned on being the majority here [in Israel]?
>
> Kasher: Everything is conditioned on being a decisive majority, not just a majority.[27]

The insistent denial of the state's role in initiating and implementing policies that aim to preserve the dominant Jewish majority reaches its absurd climax in the writings of a professor of philosophy in the Hebrew University, Menachem Brinker, an expert on Sartre and existentialism and one of the founders of Peace Now.[28] Brinker fails to see the conflict between his commitment to the Jewish state and his liberal values. By elaborating on Kasher's misleading portrayal of the majority concept, as if it were an expression of the most genuine, popular democratic processes, Brinker deludes himself further. He rejects the common understanding that the state of Israel has been the embodiment of Zionist goals, one of which is to preserve the Jewish majority. As emphasized in the introduction, these premises are part of the hegemonic Zionist ideology, officially declared so by the state,[29] and adopted in Supreme Court decisions. Ignoring this fact permits Brinker, like Kasher, to rely on the miracle of "participatory democracy" in which collective/state decisions are but the expression of the decisions made by the individuals that comprise the Jewish majority. The free will of the "majority" is thus presented as having an existence disconnected from the Zionist project, which he argues, has ended its role. "In my opinion there is here some instrumental distortion regarding the relation between the state and Zionism, because people who say 'a Jewish state' or a 'Zionist state' think that the state of Israel was established to serve Zionist goals. And Zionism is not an infinite idea. On the contrary: Zionism was erected in order that there will be a state where the majority of its citizens are Jews. And once the state was established with a majority of Jewish citizens, it [Zionism] has more or less finished its job as Zionism."[30]

Brinker depicts the state of Israel as being neutral to the aims of Zionism, befitting his image of a liberal democracy. That is, a state without common themes and plans that it enforces upon its citizens, as in a totalitarian regime. Despite the fact that Israel continues to implement Zionist goals, such as the "absorption of the Diaspora," it does so only because it is a democratic state, and not because it is a means for implementing something pre-defined: "Not because it is the aim of the state of Israel but because it is the will of 83 percent of its citizens which is expressed in general elections . . . What grants the state its Jewishness is its democracy and not vice versa. It [the state] is a means to implement what all its citizens want, as is expressed in the general elections every four years."[31]

Again, a remarkable twist in logic: Brinker avoids the essence of a liberal democratic state, in which neutrality to the identity and interests of its major ethnic group allows for universal citizenship. He avoids it by using the argument that one of these groups is the "majority" and can deny equal citizenship to the minority—the very perspective that is contradictory to liberal democracy!

This distorted concept of liberal democracy is the basis for Brinker's defense of his obligation to accept the "Jewish and Zionist identity of the state." He himself is prepared to give up the Jewishness of the state and live with its democratic definition alone. Nor does he care if Jews outside Israel are assimilated into the nations where they live. However, it is precisely his democratic values, he notes, and not his commitment to Zionism, that compel him to accept the will of the Jewish majority. In other words, it is they (the 83 percent)[32] who are interested in the "ingathering of the Exiles" (*kibutz galuyot*) and in the "absorption of immigrants" (*klitat aliya*)—goals that have been defined by all Israeli governments, the Zionist Labor movement, and the Israeli Supreme Court as the ultimate mission of the state.

However, it does not take long before Brinker's commitment to Zionism materializes. Despite sanctifying the democratic values of majority rule, Brinker is unable to remain "neutral" to the preservation of the Jewish majority and its dominance. The Jewish majority is so important to him that he cannot just leave it to the "accumulation of individual spontaneous decisions." On the other hand, his loyalty to the approach of the Zionist Left, and to his self-professed democratic values, precludes his support for further legislation that would explicitly and directly maintain the present demographic supremacy of Jews.

Thus, after announcing he does not hold "that there should be any other basis for the Jewish nature of the state except the fact that its majority of citizens are Jews," the interviewer insists on asking him "From what you say I understand that you have no interest in preserving it [the Jewish majority] by using special means [except the will of the Jewish majority]?" Brinker responds:

> Surely not by means of legislation, but by means of the fact that we are in charge of preserving it [the Jewish majority]. All Jews in the state of Israel, all Zionists [and even] post-Zionists who still see in Zionism an important stage [agree with me]. We are in charge of the fact, the reality, that the majority of the citizens will be Jews, speak Hebrew, are connected to the Hebrew culture, and to the history of the Jewish people. All these elements, are the ones needed to ensure the Jewishness of the state, not by [applying] legislative means or by means of an *a priori* definition.[33]

The hypocrisy embedded in "the rule of the majority" is disclosed in the arguments used by the Zionist Left to support the Law of Return, which in its design maintains this majority. Brinker and others cling to a humanist argument that Jewish people who are persecuted in Diaspora need asylum. In other words, the state of Israel must perpetuate the discrimination and dispossession of its Palestinian citizens because of the presumed discrimination faced by Jews all over the world. Moreover, one is supposed to believe Brinker's distress is brought on by his professed need to support such an undemocratic law. "But I am longing for the day in which it will be possible to cancel it."[34]

Others reason the Law of Return is fair because it falls within the boundaries and powers of a sovereign state, quietly excusing its discriminatory nature. According to this logic, the state of Israel, like any other sovereign state that has a monopoly on power, can decide who has the right to enter the state and under what status they can enter. Israel defines those who enter as tourists, foreign residents, or citizens based upon criteria that seeks to preserve the "cultural homogeneity" of the Jewish majority.

Again and again we are faced with the misleading comparison of the Jewish state of Israel with other "nation states." This comparison ignores the fact that the immigration laws of those nation states do not condition the right to immigrate and qualify for citizenship on the religious-ethnic criterion, as does the Israeli Law of Return.

Indeed the irrational arguments used by the Zionist Left, in order to appear committed to justice, often reach high levels of absurdity. A case in point is Avishai Margalit and Moshe Halbertal's[35] proposal to achieve equality, which the Law of Return denies Palestinian citizens. Margalit and Halbertal are professors of philosophy at Hebrew University and Bir Sheva University, respectively, and are known for their liberal-democratic worldviews and as supporters of the Israeli "peace camp." Their identity as representatives of Israel's enlightened intelligentsia makes their idea especially dreadful.

"It [the Law of Return] in fact ensures the permanent existence of a Jewish majority in the state of Israel while the Arabs remain a minority within it."[36] It grants clear preference to the Jewish majority and its culture, determining the character of Jewish public space, without granting special rights to the Jewish majority. The "unequal situation" it creates "needs to be balanced" through granting the Palestinian minority special rights alongside state laws that apply to Jews alone, "so they too can preserve their culture." In order to regain justice, these two liberal intellectuals come out with a racist solution in which the Zionist principle of "separation" takes its most cynical form.

Their suggestion to "gain balance" boils down to a tolerance for two "reservation areas" where the indigenous Palestinian population (who managed to survive the 1948 Nakba) will be granted the "right" to maintain its majority (the Galilee and the Triangle). Through their benevolent gesture of opposition to the government's "Judaisation" policies in these areas, they end up strengthening the prevailing acceptance of Palestinian second-class citizenship. Here, the "separation" principle is used in the service of a legal dimension of Apartheid, which the Zionist Left has always been careful to avoid. Namely, a "separation" between geographical areas in which different laws will be implemented. "It is justified to balance the situation and grant the Arab public in Israel the right to maintain an Arab majority in its regions of concentration, in order to enable Israeli Arabs a public space of their own, alongside the public space of the Jewish majority."[37] "Separate but Equal" at its best.

Arabs' Primordial Nature as Justification for "Jewish Majority"

Some Zionist Left writers who are not committed to academic "neutral" and "objective" analysis express their Orientalist tendencies openly in an attempt to defend the principle of the "Jewish majority." This is done by means of transferring the "political" appearance of the "majority discourse" into the irrational arena of the supposed primordial collective characteristics of Islam and the Arabs. Moreover, the distorted picture these writers create is infused with apocalyptic dimensions that blur the line between the loss of the Jewish definition of the state and its Jewish majority, and the elimination of the state's actual "existence." Once the Jewish majority is lost, they insinuate, the extermination of the Jewish population is made possible.

Some of the most renowned among them, icons of human values and justice in the eyes of international progressives, have added moral authority to the atmosphere of hysteria around the "demographic problem" in Israel. Author Sami Michael is well known for wanting just peace in the framework of a two-state solution. In an interview with David Grossman he elaborates on the Palestinians' refusal to accept the Jewish state, which he defines in majority/minority terms:

> But there is one thing that the Israeli Arab has not and will not come to terms with [namely] that he is a minority. "True" he would say, "I'm a minority here on this small island, but look behind you and you'll see a whole ocean of Arabs." Because in international terms, the Arab world is great—economically, numerically, in the number of countries, the number of votes at the UN . . . And the Israeli Arabs still have a living memory of the way things were fifty years ago: [They say] "the fact we turned into a minority is only a temporary malfunction. We look to the future. We, with our birth rate, will again be a majority here. And you, the Jews, are in a crisis, both economic and moral. You are failing. The day will come, and with one good battle, everything would change." That's still in the back of their minds. "So why," the same Arab asks, "should I wear the suit you've sewn for me, the suit of a minority? I'll just wait."[38]

Arab cultural stubbornness not only prevents them from giving up all of Palestine, but it also won't allow them to internalize their defeat in Spain seven hundred years ago. Grossman notes, "I asked him [Michael] if it is possible that among the Arabs in the Middle East would emerge an internalized acceptance of the existing of the state of Israel in the region? Michael answered: 'If today some Arab tells you he came to terms with the fact that in Madrid and Spain, there is a Christian, European state, don't believe him . . . To this day, every Arab feels the pain of the loss of Andalusia, and when was that—seven hundred years ago? So this is my answer [to your question]."[39]

Arab culture, which is responsible for their incapacity to truly accept the Jewish state, is not the only stumbling block in the way of peace. Their higher birth rates can topple the Jewish majority and thus the very existence of Jews in Israel are in danger. "What are we going to do here?" Sami Michael sighs. "I really bang my head over it. My ideal would be to reach some kind of joint state, but I don't think that either we or they are ripe for that. And we'd be a minority very quickly—their natural increase has always been larger than ours. Ten years from now, fifty years from now, they'll be the majority and they'll make the decisions."

Michael concludes: "And I, if I've got to be a minority, I'd rather not live in this region. I'm willing to be a minority in the U.S., in Australia. But not in this region, so intolerant of minorities. Look at the Kurds in Iraq, the Christians in Lebanon . . . I wouldn't want to be like them. Not that I'm a big fan of Zionist ideology. I never was. But I'm Zionist enough in that I don't want to be a minority in Israel. I'm not willing."[40]

Twelve years later (but only two years after this interview was republished[41]), Sami Michael began serving as the chair of the ACRI, a post whose qualifications should be, at minimum, a worldview free of bias against cultural traditions, an ethos without racist biological premises. However, he has not changed his reliance upon the "national character" of the Arabs to explain the inability to solve the "conflict": "The Arab culture bears a grudge; blood feud is an honor command. It is forbidden to let time blur the memory, to bring to forgiveness and renunciation. A Bedouin who revenged the blood of his father after 40 years was scolded: 'What is the hurry?' . . . A number of Arab intellectuals condemn the Palestinians who negotiate with Israel aimed at bringing about peace between the two peoples and throw at them the terrible accusation: 'They are apt to reconcile with the loss of Andalusia.'"

Indeed, since his interview with Grossman, Michael has become more cautious and politically correct. He has not changed his belief that the larger Arab culture dictates the Palestinian refusal to accept Israel's offers of peace. However, he now pays lip service to a Jewish culture that also inscribes "deep in our heart" the wrongs committed against the Jewish people. "Till this day we hate the ancient Egyptians, the Babylonians, Greeks, Romans, the Inquisition in Spain and the pogromists in Hebron early in the last century." But when the implication of these Jewish cultural traits are raised in regard to the Israeli preparedness to make concessions for peace, Michael's accusations focus primarily upon the fanaticism of Jewish settlers and right-wing extremists, and steer clear of any critique of the Zionist center, let alone left politicians or intellectuals. He implies that peace plans initiated by progressive Israelis are in accordance with a different, "real" Jewish cultural tradition, which "poses life above anything else [. . .] The Jewish people are still alive because it has disdained empty slogans and chosen life . . . The Judaism that guarded my people, the tradition which is rooted deep in my soul, both tell me to give up (make concessions) for the sake of life." One wonders what parts of Arab culture peace-loving Palestinians can turn to for making similar noble concessions "of any piece of land." According to Michael's article, the reader cannot find any.[42]

These words echo the Israeli Left's cry that "there is no partner for peace"— a slogan that allowed them to retreat to the warm bosom of the Zionist consensus after Labor Party prime minister Barak's pre-planned collapse of the Camp David talks in October 2000, and after the breakout of the second Intifada, which put an end to the Oslo "peace process." (See chapter 8 for the backlash of Zionist Left and post-Zionists.) Only Michael prefers to stay in the realm of "culture," and leaves the reader to draw the conclusion of what political strategy is required to confront the Jewish state's existential danger.[43]

Left intellectuals' discourse on the existential importance of retaining a Jewish majority raises a question that most of them refrain from answering: What is to be done in order to preserve the Jewish majority? How can Israel prevent the higher natural growth rate of Palestinians, which may change the demographic balance inside Israel and which has already tipped the balance when one considers the entire Israeli empire? Zionist Left intellectuals are well aware of the way Zionists dealt with this issue in 1948. Their failure to warn their readers against ethnic cleansing makes them complicit to the growing discourse of "transfer" in Israeli society.

Return of the Discourse of "Transfer"

The collective closing of ranks behind a Jewish state with a Jewish majority has laid the groundwork for a demographically obsessed, full-fledged fascistic culture. This has made mass ethnic cleansing and its variants a legitimate topic within Israeli public discourse. Openly planning to expel Palestinian citizens was seen in the past by mainstream Israel as racist and part of the agenda of the loathed far Right. However, in recent years, the idea of "transfer" has been publicly endorsed by various "Doves" and other figures associated with the Zionist Left. Senior *Haaretz* political commentator Aluf Benn confirms the concept's pervasiveness among many Zionist Left public figures: "This is what happened to the 'security-obsessed Left,' which during the [second] Intifada has become a 'demographic Left.'"[44]

The case of Benny Morris illustrates the logical conclusion drawn from the concept of a Jewish majority and the need for separation embedded in Zionist Left thinking—namely, mass expulsion of Palestinians. One of the first "New Historians," Benny Morris, whose book, *The Birth of the Palestinian Refugee Problem, 1947–1949*, contributed to unearthing the truth about the Nakba (see chapter 7 for elaboration on the New Historians), returned in 2002 to the bosom of Zionist mainstream historiography.[45] The principle of a "Jewish majority" is inherent in Morris's argument for supporting the ethnic cleansing of Palestinians in 1948. He expresses regret that Ben-Gurion understood that there could be no Jewish state "with a large and hostile Arab minority" in it, and did not complete the job then. Morris emphasizes that the unfinished job can and should be completed in the future, but this time, "cleaning" refers to the entire territory of Palestine.[46]

Following Morris's call for expulsion, the *Haaretz* interviewer Ari Shavit asks him: "Including the expulsion of Israeli Arabs?" to which Morris answers: "The Israeli Arabs are a time bomb. Their slide into complete Palestinization has made them an emissary of the enemy that is among us. They are a potential fifth column. In both demographic and security terms they are liable to undermine the state. So that if Israel again finds itself in a situation of existential threat, as in 1948, it may be forced to do it."

The very fact that this interview was published in the liberal daily *Haaretz*, according to Adi Ophir, professor of philosophy at Tel Aviv University, reflects the growing trend of supporting the transfer and elimination of Palestinians far beyond the traditional base of the extreme Right. "The most frightening thing is that this logic is creeping into *Haaretz* and peeks out from the front page of its respected Friday Supplement. The interviewer and editors thought it proper to interview Morris. They appreciate the fact that he has dropped the vocabulary of political correctness and says what many are thinking but do not dare to say. If there is a sick society here, the publication of this interview is at one and the same time a symptom of the illness and that which nourishes it."[47]

The notion of transfer has been included in the agenda of the annual Herzliyah Conference on the Balance of Israel's National Security, arguably the country's most prestigious conference. Over three hundred personalities attend, representing the Israeli academic, economic, and security professions—"the center of the center." Many of them support various Israeli-US peace initiatives and are sympathetic to the Zionist Left.

The conference is so well respected in international academic and political circles that it attracts marquee names from around the world. At the 2001 conference, the conclusion of the forum, which was submitted to the president of Israel, included the following transfer solution, reported by the late radical linguistic Tanya Reinhardt:[48]

> It will be necessary to find some place for resettlement outside the state of Israel (perhaps to the East of the Jordan River) for the Palestinian population of the ['67 occupied] territories. Israeli Palestinians would be deprived of their citizen-

ship by "transferring them to areas of Palestinian sovereignty." As to policies regarding Israeli society, "The state resources should be invested in 'fostering equality,' that is, in the strong population [in Israel] and not in the 'non-Zionist population,' which includes 'Arabs, ultra-orthodox Jews and foreign workers' whose natural increase is a source of concern."

At the 2004 Herzliyah Conference the idea of "a land swap"—a more delicate version of transfer—was suggested by Uzi Arad, then chair of the Herzliyah Conference and director of the Institute for Policy and Strategy (as well as former director of the Israeli Mossad).

Arad proposed "a fair deal" to the Palestinian citizens—an exchange of lands, suggested under the name "the great land swap." The plan consisted of Israel handing over large Palestinian population areas contiguous with the West Bank (such as the Little Triangle in the center of the country), and in return receiving the large settlement blocs in the West Bank and the Jordan Valley, up to the Southern Hebron Hills and West Bank mountain ridges.[49]

The hypocrisy of this quest for "a fair exchange" is expressed in Arad's own words: "The beauty of a swap is that you trade in kind . . . It's not I give you money, and you give me land, or you give me peace and I give you land. It's I give you land, and you give me land."[50]

However, while blurring the underlying principle of transfer, Arad reveals the unchanged Zionist power politics behind it: disregard for the civil rights of Palestinians, be they citizens of Israel, or those living under the 1967 occupation, all in the name of preserving the Jewish majority in Israel and all the areas under its control. With frightful ease, Arad would abolish the citizenship status of Palestinians in Israel, and justifies this version of transfer through the principle of separation, needed for sustaining a Jewish state that is sanctioned by all streams of the Zionist Left. His interviewer from the *Jerusalem Post* reports: "Arad says that his logic in promoting the idea is simple: 'I want a Jewish state as Jewish as it can be, with a substantial majority of Jews. The Palestinians of Umm el-Fahm and the rest consider themselves Palestinians, they have mixed loyalties to Israel, about one-third are Islamic radicals, many of them have trade relations with the West Bank and they are contiguous to it. So rather than them being—in their own eyes—second-class citizens here let them be patriotic, first-class citizens in their own entity."

The depiction of the Palestinian citizens as a "fifth column" is used to justify their transfer. Their non-acceptance of the "Jewish state" is distorted, and made to look like a dangerous betrayal.

Interviewer: But what if they don't want it, what if the residents of Tira and Taiba would rather stay second-class citizens here?

Arad: They don't want to be second-class citizens here. They want to be subversive from within. They do not accept Israel as a Jewish state. If you ask them, "Do you accept being Israelis?" they say yes. But when you ask if they accept Israel as a Jewish state, they say "Hmm."

The "fair deal" offered to the Palestinian citizens in the future peace settlement actually makes them pay twice: they are transferred from their homeland through the revocation of their citizenship and denied the right as citizens to fight or to change the nature of the Jewish-Zionist state in order to obtain equal rights. At the same time they are asked to consent to the fragmentation of this future Palestinian state through the remaining blocs of settlements, which Arad and his colleagues well know precludes any chance for genuine viability and sovereignty. Even the self-professed Zionist Left has given up declaring their support for dismantling settlement blocs.[51] The "fair deal" of swapping land offers Palestinians compensation for the annexation of these settlement blocs. But this would fragment the future Palestinian state into a number of "Bandustans" encircled by Jewish settlements.

Still, the core of Zionist Left intellectuals cannot explicitly accept a transfer solution to the problem of the Jewish majority. They continue to conceptualize a Jewish-Zionist state in which equality between Jews and Palestinians in pre-1967 borders can be and, in fact, is, largely sustained. The following chapter will address their attempts to prove their conviction that the state of Israel can be both Jewish and democratic.

CHAPTER 3

Equal Rights

Zionist Left discourse on equal rights for Palestinians takes place within the boundaries of the hegemonic Zionist ideology and state policies. The Zionist Left collectively strives to perpetuate an exclusive Jewish state with a substantive Jewish majority, and in effect negates the indigenous Palestinian population. As emphasized in previous chapters, recognizing Palestinian citizens as a national minority with national rights would undermine the ideological justification of Jewish domination. Structured discrimination against Palestinian citizens is inevitable. Writes Haifa University sociologist Sammy Smooha, "The meaning of a Jewish state is that Jews have a certain advantage, [or] preference, over Arabs. It cannot be otherwise. And about this we are arguing."[1]

But what exactly does this "certain advantage" mean in terms of rights? What rights are denied to Palestinians because of the state's Jewish identity? Is there any space left within Zionist boundaries for equal rights for Palestinians, and what is the nature of these rights? Can these rights be safeguarded when Jewish identity and supremacy are virtually boundless? Can these rights satisfy, at least partially, Palestinian demands? Or is the gap so wide that common ground is no longer possible?

In June 2009 former Supreme Court president Aharon Barak said, "Jews have the exclusive right to immigrate to Israel, but the moment they arrive, their rights must be equal to those of Arabs."[2] In light of the wide symbolic and tangible implications of the Law of Return, and its promise of rights and services to Jews alone, how has the Supreme Court itself safeguarded the principle of equality? This chapter attempts to answer these questions.

Civil Equality vs. National Equality

The Jewish identity of the state of Israel is considered an unchangeable fact, a fait accompli, which Palestinians must accept. Zionist Left intellectuals do not challenge the fact that the Jewish state has been created and sustained by Israel's might. Professor David Kretzmer, a genuine democratically inclined jurist at Hebrew University, notes, "In this stage when Jews have the power, it is impossible to expect, and even to ask them to renounce this power [of a Jewish state] as long as they are not offered an alternative settlement which ensures them a collective security. Nowhere in the entire world is there a way to create collective defense and security for a threatened group but through a powerful state."[3]

Most Zionist Left intellectuals share the conviction that Palestinians in Israel should be denied the rights that embody and sustain the national identity and existence of Jews. The intellectuals agree that Palestinians should instead be granted "civic equality"—namely, equal access to state resources and services. These include social and economic rights, such as access to funds from local Palestinian municipalities or public institutions, and equal funding for religious, educational, and welfare services. Says Kretzmer, "the fundamental principle should be that citizenship is equal. Hence allocation of resources should be equal irrespective of the religious and national ascription of the citizens."

"The Jewish identity of the state is unchangeable. Hence the question of the Arab minority should be dealt with by means of dismantling the issue into its element and supplying an answer to the troubles of the Arab population embodied in each of these elements." The Jewish identity of the state should not prevent equality in citizen rights.[4]

Kretzmer believes that, despite its "ethnic identity," the state of Israel has generally managed to secure civil rights for its Palestinian citizens. "In most cases, the tensions between majority and minority within each area of life, do not necessarily derive from the very definition of Israel as a Jewish state. Historically, yes; practically, no."[5] In other words, like most of his Zionist Left colleagues, Kretzmer believes that the seemingly contradictory elements in the definition of Israel—as both Jewish and democratic—can be reconciled, and are not adverse to the rights of Palestinian citizens.

The Palestinians, however, refuse to recognize the Jewish state and their limited rights as a fait accompli. They affirm their rights as citizens to struggle for change. For Palestinians, altering the Zionist essence of the state is a necessary condition for full equality.[6] What the Palestinians demand and what the Zionist Left wants for Palestinians are two entirely different things. Unlike immigrant ethnic minorities, who are willing to be integrated into the state, its institutions, and its ideologies, and who will accept the hegemony of the majority group, the Palestinians demand more than just civil rights. They are the indigenous people of the land, and they have no aspiration to integrate into the Zionist/Jewish state. The state was erected on their land, and, by definition, it denies them their national identity and national rights.[7]

As discussed in the introduction, Azmi Bishara and the National Democratic Assembly's (NDA) influence helped crystallize the widespread challenge among Palestinian intellectual and political elites against the Jewish state, which was expressed in the four Position Papers of 2007. The NDA was the first to translate this challenge into a discourse focused on rights. It concentrated on strengthening the national consciousness and self-organization of Palestinian citizens, encouraging them to fight for recognition as a national minority in their homeland. As Bishara notes, "Focusing the demand on citizenship or civil rights alone within the limits of a Jewish state is inherently unrealizable, as it would inevitably entail forsaking Palestinian national identity without obtaining true equality. Instead of assimilation there would only be further marginalization."[8]

The rationale for founding the NDA was to the huge wave of "Israelization" that followed the support of the Oslo Accords. The growing awareness in the mid-1980s among Palestinians of their civil rights paved the way for an integration drive within Israeli society, which demanded equality within the framework of the Jewish state. This wave included Hadash, the Communist Party–headed front for which Palestinians in Israel had traditionally voted. "In that period" says Bishara, "in which the NDA was alone in opposing Oslo, one could witness hundreds of cars of Arabs from Nazareth lifting the Israeli flag in their 'Independence Day' which is our Nakba. Palestinians massively streamed into Zionist political parties, encouraged by the stupid and misleading slogan of Hadash that 'We are part of the Israeli Left.'"[9] Since the mid-1990s, however, as national awareness gained impetus, due in great part to the work of Bishara and the NDA, the "Israelization" process has gradually been halted. Nevertheless, "this danger still looms," warns Bishara.

As early as 2002, senior *Haaretz* commentator Uzi Benziman clearly understood the radical meaning of Bishara's discourse, which combined the Palestinian struggle for full equality with a challenge against the Jewish state and its
Zionist essence.

> Bishara is an eloquent and impressive person. From a Zionist perspective he is
> also a dangerous man. He is the most consistent and zealous [leader] in the
> Arab sector who represents the perception that denies the Zionist logic inherent
> in the establishment of the state of Israel . . . Bishara aspires to turn Israel into "a
> state of all its citizens"—namely, to get rid of all the Jewish and Zionist ele-
> ments from the definition of the state. He aspires to replace them by another
> world of values—civic and non-nationalistic [implemented in a de-Zionized
> state]. Bishara is the vanguard of the stream which Dr. Dani Rabinowitz and
> Dr. Khawla Abu Baker name in their new book *The Stand Tall Generation*. This
> is an ever-widening stream, which demands collective equality of rights—and
> not only personal [rights]—for the Arab citizens of the state.[10]

Indeed, Bishara's and the NDA's influence, as expressed in the four Position
Papers, has been supported by many Palestinians. A 2007 annual survey on "the
attitudes of Arab and Jewish citizens toward each other and toward the state,"
conducted by Sammy Smooha, confirms the wide gap between the Palestinian
and Jewish public. The survey tried to assess the conflicting attitudes toward
the collective, national demands presented in the Position Papers.[11]

> "The state of Israel must stop being a Jewish state and become the state of all its
> citizens"—Palestinians: 90.5 percent; Jews: 8.6 percent.
>   "The Arab language must be in use like Hebrew"—Palestinians: 91.3 per-
> cent; Jews: 33.8 percent.
>   "The state must grant the Arab citizens an adequate expression in its sym-
> bols, flag and national anthem"—Palestinians: 89.3 percent; Jews: 16.6 percent.
>   "The state must recognize its responsibility for the Nakba which happened to
> the Palestinians in the 1948 war"—Palestinians: 90.9 percent; Jews: 11.3 percent.
>   "The state is obliged to receive the agreement of the leadership of the Arab
> citizens for any law or decision related to them"—Palestinians: 93.6 percent;
> Jews: 27.9 percent.
>   "The state should recognize the Arab citizens as Palestinians, and ensure
> their right to maintain their connections with the Palestinian people and the
> Arab nation"—Palestinians: 91.7 percent; Jews: 26.5 percent.

The Jewish respondents to the survey follow, in principle, the positions of
Zionist Left intellectuals. They refuse to recognize the national rights of the
Palestinian citizens and will not relinquish their supremacy within the Jewish
state. The question remains—regarding the civil rights the Zionist Left claims

to support—to what extent do High Court rulings, state policies, and Jewish public discourse confirm Bishara's warning that equality of civil rights cannot be realized in the Zionist/Jewish state?

Futility of the Distinction between "National" and "Civil" Rights

Zionist Left intellectuals differentiate between "national" and "civil" rights. They claim that Palestinian citizens can enjoy full, equal, civil rights, but must be denied national rights. Time and again, reality has proven the futility of perceiving national and citizenship rights as distinct. There are hardly any discernible boundaries to the vague "preference" and privileges of Jews in the Zionist/Jewish state. The state's Jewish identity is infused into almost every aspect of individual and social life in Israel, making the separation between "civil" and "national" rights impossible: Attorney Hassan Jabarin, the founder of Adalah (the Legal Center for Arab Minority Rights in Israel), studied Supreme Court rulings on appeals for cases of Palestinian rights violations.[12] He found that, regarding appeals related to the Jewish identity of the state, judges always agreed on "the level of [Zionist] values or ideology," such as the obligation to preserve a Jewish majority. If they differed in relation to these matters, it was "on the pragmatic level only." "Judges agree that the principle of prohibition of inequality between citizens should not be accepted as an absolute principle."

In demonstrating how the Supreme Court's commitment to Zionist principles violates basic democratic citizenship rights, Jabarin refers to a case in which the Supreme Court seemingly defended the democratic rights of Palestinian citizens: the 2003 decision to reject the state's attempt to disqualify Bishara and the NDA from participating in the Knesset elections. The appeal was based on Clause 7(a) to the "Basic Law: The Knesset," added in 1985. This clause requires that all those who run in elections must recognize Israel as the state of the Jewish people. In this way, the political establishment's intention was to block democratic challenges to the nature of the Jewish state. In the 2003 ruling the majority of the Supreme Court judges did not criticize the law itself. Instead they argued that the appeal lacked a "factual base which could confirm the disqualification." The minority of the judges, however, tried to disqualify Bishara and the NDA despite this lack of "factual base," only for "the very contradiction between Zionism and their call for the state of all its citizens."

On the other hand, in rulings that dealt with issues of "civil equality," there was almost no division of opinions among Supreme Court judges, regardless of the Court's decision. "The assumption is that since these cases deal mainly with equality of budgets allocated to Jewish and Palestinian localities, the question of national identity is neutralized. Hence one would expect that in these matters the principle of equality would apply and the Court would accept Palestinian appeals whose 'civil' rights were violated. But this has not been the case. The Supreme Court's support was not guaranteed." The Court's tendency in civil rights issues is inconsistent. "In fact it is consistent in its inconsistency," says Jabarin. There are cases in which judges have admitted the existence of discrimination and nevertheless rejected the appeal. As an example, Jabarin mentions Adalah's first appeal, demanding equality between Jews and Arabs in budgets granted for religious services. The High Supreme Court determined that, indeed, there was clear discrimination in this area since Arabs received less than 2 percent from the entire budget [Arabs comprised 20 percent of the entire population], but "the appeal is too general since it was not based on [a] factual base." Jabarin asks, "How is it possible to admit that discrimination indeed existed but at the same time to determine that the appeal lacks a factual base? Isn't the very existence of discrimination a factual matter?!"

Jabarin concludes that the distinction between rulings on "national identity" and "civil equality" is artificial because the principle of equality is not divisible. "We have seen that when there is no recognition of equality between national identities, there has not been full equality on the civic level as well. The recognition of national identities is the recognition of equal collective rights on all levels. The lack of this kind of recognition which is based on [democratic universal] values, inevitably leads to a pragmatic approach to the equality issue in other levels, and this approach will be consistent in its inconsistency."

The lack of equality before the Law is a decisive extension of the Jewish state's Apartheid nature. However, the discrimination of Palestinian citizens in rulings of the Supreme Court is not based on specified laws. The laws that indirectly determine Apartheid inequalities, like the Law of Return (discussed in the introduction and in chapter 2), are undoubtedly in the background of Supreme Court rulings and are conferred semi-legally.

Like the Law of Return, the system of regulations that provide Jews with exclusive access to lands in Israel has a direct equivalent in South African Apartheid law. The Group Areas Act of 1950 assigned different areas in South Africa for the residential use of different racial groups.[13]

Blocking Access to Lands—an Explicitly Legal Apartheid

The official, exclusively Jewish access to 93 percent of the land in Israel, classified as "state lands," is of uppermost importance in sustaining Israel's version of Apartheid. Denying Palestinians the very permission to purchase land precludes a whole range of additional rights and benefits, which Jewish settlers are afforded, in housing, education, health, and job opportunities. As a result, Palestinians have been stuffed into overcrowded towns, blocking prospects for adequate living conditions and collective economic and social development.

The fait accompli attitude of the Jewish state and the prerogatives conferred upon its Jewish citizens prevent any reversal of dispossession policies against Palestinians. Leaders of the peace camp, and Zionist Left intellectuals who have called for dismantling Jewish settlements in the '67 occupied territories, have never asked the same of the Mitzpim or yishuvim kehilatyim built on confiscated Palestinian land in the Galilee or Wadi Ara, nor even to freeze their expansion. The very existence of "state lands," most of which was Palestinian land, is uncritically accepted by the Zionist Left intellectuals as a "fact." Nor have they ever challenged the cunning institutionalized means by which the lands have been retained.[14]

The set of laws and institutions in the newborn state were established to ensure that confiscated Palestinian lands became "state lands," defined as property of the "Jewish nation."[15] Accordingly, the vast majority of Jewish "landowners" in the state of Israel are "tenants" who do not actually own the land on which they live, but lease it from the state, either directly through the Israel Land Administration (ILA) or through "national institutions," such as the Jewish Agency for Israel and the JNF (the Jewish National Fund), which transfer lands to Jewish localities for exclusively Jewish use.[16]

These institutions, which continue to play their pre-state colonizing roles on behalf of the World Zionist Organization, openly declare that they aim to "develop the country" for the benefit of Jews alone. Working alongside the Jewish Agency for Israel, the JNF "has served as the main fig leaf covering up the continued Zionist mission of preserving the ownership and use of lands for Jews alone, and in fact is the organization most responsible for the Jewish apartheid project."[17]

Zionist Left intellectuals have indeed betrayed their fundamental democratic role. "What should democrats in this case demand?" asks Azmi Bishara. "They should demand equality—one citizenship for all, and they should demand the land to be the land of its citizens, because democrats should refuse to accept concepts like the 'land of the nation,' when a considerable part of this nation according to its definition, does not live in this land but in the United States, and other countries. This is the ideological basis for the laws in this country that enabled confiscation of the land owned by Arabs. This was the process of the nationalizing the Arab land."[18]

The implementation of different strategies of "Judaising the land" continues unabated in the present day. As mentioned in chapter 2, around 170 settlements were scattered between Palestinian localities in the Galilee and Wadi Ara. Established on lands expropriated from the private and public holdings of neighboring Palestinian towns and villages, this policy expanded the already disproportionately large amounts of land reserved for the use of Jewish townships and citizens.[19] The Palestinian minority has been prevented from establishing even one new town since the foundation of Israel.[20] The 132,000 Palestinians who remained within the borders of Israel after the 1948 ethnic cleansing inhabited only 3 percent of the land, and were only allowed to build upon 2 percent. Today, 1,300,000 Palestinians live on the same 3 percent of the land. Because of various administrative procedures, they cannot build on their meager space.[21] This was the background for the Qa'dan case, also known as the Katzir ruling,[22] in which a Palestinian family applied for membership to a Jewish communal settlement. The case lays bare all dimensions of the Zionist Left's position on equal rights, as represented by the Supreme Court. It also highlights the gap between the Zionist Left and Palestinians on the issue of civil rights, conditioned on "integration" within a Zionist community.

The Katzir Ruling—Different Agendas of the Zionist Left and Palestinians

Katzir is a communal settlement in Wadi Ara that was established in 1982 on "state lands." The Israel Land Administration (ILA) allocated these lands to the Jewish Agency for Israel, and ultimately to the Communal Association of Katzir, for the purpose of settlement. Katzir was part of the aforementioned ongoing efforts to "Judaise" areas where a majority of Palestinians live, and to prevent development of large, contiguous Palestinian areas. Like other Jewish settlements, it was largely established on confiscated Palestinian lands, a substantive part of which originally belonged to an Arab family from the village of Arara.[23] Bitter legal struggles and violent confrontations had taken place between regional Palestinian residents and the Israeli police force—struggles that escalated in September 1998, but failed to prevent the confiscation of most of the land.

The Supreme Court was asked to resolve a dispute between the applicants: Iman and Adel Qa'dan, represented by the ACRI; and the defendants: the Katzir community representatives, the ILA, and the Jewish Agency for Israel. The Qa'-dan couple had requested permission in 1995 to lease a plot of land to build their house in the Jewish communal settlement of Katzir, but the association turned them down. The decision was based on its internal regulations, which determine, albeit indirectly, that only Jews can be accepted as members of the association. (The agreed code was "a person who among other things has completed his army service or was discharged from the army.") It took four years for the Supreme Court to finally begin discussing the Kaadan case. In order to avoid confrontation with this "most difficult" issue, the Supreme Court tried diligently, but in vain, to convince the state authorities to solve the problem without bringing it to the courts. Only after these attempts failed did the Qa'dan case return to court for a judicial ruling.

The Supreme Court was well aware of the significance of their decision in this case, which, besides the question of "civil rights," dealt with a central Zionist mission undertaken by the state of Israel—Judaising the Galilee. Aharon Barak, then president of the Supreme Court, said in one of the preliminary discussions that "the problem which arises here is the most difficult one I had come across as a judge," and that "the difficulty in reaching a decision stems from [knowing] that it has far-reaching results which are hard to predict in advance and that the subject is not sufficiently ripe for judicial decision."[24] The 1999 Court's decision stated that Katzir had no justification to exclude Arabs and that the Qa'dan couple should be accepted by the Katzir community. It emphasizes that, although Israel is a Jewish state, the discrimination of "non-Jews" who live in Israel is unjustified. Furthermore, the state cannot avoid its obligation to treat non-Jews fairly and still allocate lands to the Jewish Agency for Israel and the JNF, or to any similar organization with bylaws that discriminate against Palestinians.

The Supreme Court decision, however, failed to properly address the contradiction between equality and the Zionist principle of "redeeming the land for the Jewish nation." The judges were very careful not to reject discrimination on nationalist grounds as a universal principle. In fact, they limited their ruling specifically to the Katzir case.[25] The court tried to refrain from setting a judicial precedent, and it did not prohibit or even discourage discrimination against Palestinian citizens in areas defined by "Zionist aims." On the contrary, it pointedly left the door open for the continued exclusion of Palestinians from Jewish localities. "There are different types of settlements, like Kibbutzim, cooperative settlements or lookouts, which may raise different problems . . . Also there is need to take into consideration the possibility of special circumstances other than the type of locality, such as state security, which may be important. We have not heard any claims regarding the significance of such circumstances [for accepting Palestinians]. Therefore we shall not express our opinion on their significance."[26]

To introduce their decision in the Qa'dan case, the Supreme Court judges outlined the ideological framework within which their subsequent ruling—and for that matter any discourse on equal rights—should take place. The court clarified its deep identification with Zionism and its goals, and with state institutions whose role is to implement those goals. The judges were also not shy about expressing their admiration for the Jewish Agency for Israel, which openly declared in court that its project was intended to develop the country for the benefit of Jews alone ("to settle Jews throughout the country, particularly in regions where the Jewish population is sparse"). The court praised the agency's Zionist efforts to help settle the country, and maintained that it had yet to complete its role in "the realization of the Zionist vision," which was granted by the state, "to disperse the [Jewish] population and thus strengthen the security of the state." The judges emphasized that the arguments of the applicant (ACRI) clearly indicated the Qa'dans accepted the ideological values of the Zionist/Jewish state of Israel; they did not raise historical demands; they did not challenge the legitimacy or function of the Jewish Agency for Israel's work; and they expressed loyalty to the "Jewish People." "The applicants do not focus their arguments on the legitimacy of the policy which prevailed regarding this matter in the pre-state period and during the years since its foundation. They also don't object to the decisive role that the Jewish Agency played in settling Jews all over the land during this century."

The hot-button issue of assimilation provoked a wide range of reactions to the Qa'dan (Katzir) ruling. Zionist Left circles saw it as a historic decision, a giant step toward the equal rights of Palestinian citizens and the annulment of prevailing discriminatory land policies. The Palestinian public, on the other hand, was largely indifferent toward the decision, and some central public figures came out with sharp criticism of the Zionist Left who celebrated it.[27] Attorney Jabarin repudiated ACRI's appeal and the Supreme Court's decision for having dealt with civil rights inadequately, decrying the idea that Palestinians were like immigrants who only aspired to assimilate into the culture and ideology of their host country.

Jabarin argues that the Qa'dan's request to be included in Katzir—a settlement that is part of the Zionist-Jewish project, and helps to negate the Arab presence in Wadi Ara—legitimizes the empowerment of the Jewish presence in this region. The Qa'dan request indicates their willingness to live in a place with Jewish-Zionist values, where their children will be educated at the local school. There the children will celebrate Zionist holidays, like "Independence Day," which celebrates the 1948 establishment of the state of Israel, the expulsion of the Palestinian people, and the destruction of Palestinian society.

In an article published in *Haaretz* soon after the Supreme Court ruling,[28] Attorney Jamil Dakwar explores the differences between the Palestinian fight for equality and the struggle in the United States for Black civil rights, using the historic 1954 US Supreme Court ruling *Brown v. Board of Education* as a point of comparison (the landmark ruling determined that having separate school systems for blacks and whites was unconstitutional). For Dakwar, the Brown case does not apply to the case of Katzir, as some in the Zionist Left believe. Indeed, both the Katzir and Brown cases deal with the issue of integration of a minority in a community of the majority.

> But unlike the Afro-American public, for whom integration was at the top of their agenda in the 1950s, the Palestinians in Israel have never demanded their integration into Jewish localities. They demanded solutions to the severe distress of Palestinians who live in mixed cities and towns,[29] but Tel Aviv, Hadera and Netanya [pre-1948 Jewish towns], Karmiel and Maalot [post-1948 localities in the far north, built with the aim of "Judaising" the area] have not been an attraction for Arabs, despite the fact that there was no ideological or legal obstacle to live there. All the more so in the case of an ideological locality like Katzir, which has been erected by the Jewish Agency on confiscated Arab lands explicitly for Jews alone.[30]

According to Dakwar, the Supreme Court ruling does not qualify as a historical event because of two unfulfilled conditions. The first is realized "when the court accepts the minority position on an issue which is at the very center of the political-historical struggle of that minority, and which did not succeed to create change—except with the help of the court." Dakwar protests because the Palestinian agenda consists of totally different topics than that of the Katzir ruling. These topics include the actual return of residents of the dispossessed villages (for a discussion of internal refugees, see the introduction), recognition of unrecognized villages,[31] recognition of the Palestinian citizens as a national minority, expanding the jurisdiction areas of Arab localities, equalizing the budgets of local authorities and municipal councils, halting the confiscation of land, and canceling the thousands of house demolition decrees issued to Palestinian citizens.

The Katzir ruling does not deal with any of these urgent issues on the Palestinian community's agenda. Notes Dakwar, "This is how the infinite gap between the Arabs' demands to get back their confiscated lands because they are a homeland group, and the demand of an Arab individual like Qa'dan, to purchase a house on confiscated Arab land, was created, through the acceptance of this individual claim, which was presented as 'victory.'"[32]

Hence, as Jabarin states, "It is not by chance that the 'victory' achieved by the Supreme Court decision did not stop the commemoration of Land Day through mass demonstrations, which took place two weeks later . . . signifying the continued collective struggle against confiscation of lands and other oppressive policies."[33]

The second condition of the ruling, that "it creates an immediate social and political change beyond the specific case whose problem it solved," was also unfulfilled. In the case of the Brown ruling, just one day after the court decision, Black families felt an actual change. They were asked to send their children to any school they chose. In the case of Katzir, however, not only was the wording of the ruling lacking in universal applicability, but the Qa'dan family itself was not accepted into the communal settlement of Katzir until 2009—nine years after the Supreme Court decision. Repeated legal appeals by the Katzir community and the Jewish Agency for Israel, as well as procedural demands, delayed the ruling's implementation. The Supreme Court's ambivalent position also contributed to this delay.

In the meantime, as *Haaretz* reported on January 5, 2003, Jews from Argentina were encouraged by a delegation from Katzir to immigrate to Israel and settle there. Furthermore, Katzir is part of a regional municipality that includes the "mixed" community of Harish. The plan to bring Jews from Argentina to Katzir was part of a comprehensive project aimed "to curb the settling of Arabs in the municipality communities by encouraging groups from France to settle in Harish as well . . . This project is part of the struggle between Jews and Arabs over the lands—which Katzir and Harish have become its symbols," noted the Harish mayor.

Interestingly, a new land reform law, approved in August 2009, would bring to an end the loopholes in laws and regulations that permitted challenges against the exclusively Jewish access to land. The new law allows for land exchanges between the state and the Jewish National Fund, as well as for allocations of land in accordance with "admissions committee" mechanisms. It grants decisive weight to JNF representatives in a new Land Authority Council, which would replace the Israel Land Administration (ILA). The land privatization aspects of the new law are extremely prejudicial, affecting properties confiscated by the state from Palestinian citizens of Israel, Palestinian refugee property classified as "absentee" property, and properties in the occupied Golan Heights and in East Jerusalem. In fact, it confirms the expiration of any right available to the owners of these properties, defined as "absentees" under the Absentee Property Law.[34]

The Jewish State's Use of "Security" as a Justification for Inequality

The idea of directly conditioning Palestinian citizenship rights on whether they accept the Jewish state and its Zionist principles has long loomed in Zionist Left discourse. For example, at a meeting hosted by the Israel Democracy Institute (mentioned in the introduction), some of the Jewish intellectuals presented their views on the citizenship rights of Palestinians. These intellectuals declared rights for Palestinians must be contingent upon the renunciation of Palestinian national identity and collective memory, and an acceptance of the Jewish-Zionist definition of the state of Israel. Other Jewish participants declined to critique this arrogant attitude. For what it's worth, they did not support the enraged reactions of Palestinian participants either.

In defending this undemocratic stance, the Jewish intellectuals made the argument that Palestinians are "a security threat" to the state. Says Smooha, "Palestinians are depicted by the majority of the Jews as a real security threat to the state and to them [the Jews], which explains their opposition to granting equal rights to the Palestinian citizens." The reason Jews feel threatened is because, "From the point of view of the Jews, the Palestinians delegitimize not only Israel as a Jewish state. They negate its very existence. The Jew does not differentiate between the state's right to exist and its right to exist as a Jewish state. This is a differentiation made by the Arab. The Israeli Arabs don't accept the state of Israel as a Jewish state."[35]

Again we face the Zionist Left's confusion between a "security" threat—in its usual physical meaning—and a challenge against the Jewish state. This in turn is depicted as delegitimation of the state itself, which implies physical elimination of its Jewish population. David Kretzmer joins Smooha's defense of Jewish fear, and he explicitly conjoins Israel's "collective security" with its Jewish identity. When asked what he means by "collective security," he refers to the Jewishness of the state, namely "the capability to exist as a community, which if it chooses to live as a group that owns unique religious and historic characteristics, it can do so."[36] The conceptual jump, from mixing the "Jewish state" with "security" to seeing all Palestinian citizens as potential traitors, is not far. As Smooha says, "I speak as a sociologist: they are 20 percent of the population; they are part of the Arab world, part of the Palestinian People; they are accessible to the Palestinian people, accessible to the enemy side and discriminated against. Therefore they cannot be loyal. They cannot identify with the state; they live in areas which were not supposed to be part of the state of Israel at all. The reasons are many."[37]

Given that Palestinians can never confer legitimacy upon a Jewish state, and since they shall remain a "threat" for a long time, it is their responsibility to find some solution to the problem of their inequality, says Smooha. They should contribute their share in a deal between themselves and the state of Israel. Namely, in order to achieve more rights, they would need to soften their delegitimation of the state and renounce their national identity: "The more the Arabs in the state of Israel retain a separate identity and a separate culture, the more it will be difficult for them to achieve social mobility."[38] Palestinians are hence expected to give up their national history as the indigenous people of the land, and to integrate into Zionist society. The deal they are offered inheres no principles or values. Each of its clauses is articulated as a separate give-and-take issue: "If you choose, for instance, to commemorate the Nakba instead of the Day of Independence of the state, you increase the threat [against Israel]. Maybe you have a justification to commemorate the Nakba, but you should know that in doing so you increase the threat . . . If on Independence Day you send your children to school, it means that you challenge the Jewish character of the state and this increases the delegitimation [of the state] and the feeling of threat."[39]

Giving up their national identity, however, is not enough. For winning citizenship rights, says Smooha, Palestinian citizens are required to commit to their obligations as law-abiding citizens—a commitment they are assumed to neglect:

> Besides being a threat in the eyes of the Jews and beside the Arab's delegitimation of the state, one has to note also the inequality in obligations. When you want to realize citizenship rights, you have to deal with responsibilities and not only with rights. Again and again [you] speak about implementation of [your] rights, but from the Jewish perspective, obligations are not less important than rights. And a service in the state and for it [the state]—including avoiding building without legal permission and paying property tax—this is what would be on the agenda [of the Jews' argumentation against equal rights].[40]

Moreover, Palestinians are expected to be humble and submissive, so as not to irritate "the majority of Jews." Additionally, they are "to avoid certain declarations by Arab leaders or certain harmful declarations" in general.

Dr. Khaled Abu Usba, manager of the Massar Institute for Research, Planning, and Educational Counseling, responded to this arrogant idea of conditioning one's citizenship rights on fulfilling "obligations:"[41]

> I think that even the dialogue which is taking place here is not equal due to the simple reason that the [Jewish] majority is in possession of resources. Hence the idiomatic phrase a "transaction"—a transaction of give and take—fits here well. I [Abu Usba] have accepted the defeat with quotation marks or without them. And you come and say to me: "what would you give me in exchange for giving you part of your rights?" You, Sammy Smooha and Ruth Gavizon, even tell *me* in advance: even if you do your military service, you will not receive all the rights . . . This discussion about military or civil service or serving the state, is not simplistic or naïve. It is neither about education for morals and values. The Arabs who participate here in this discussion are members and activists and even heads of NGOs which supply civil services . . . That is to say, there is no need to educate me for civil service. This moral asset is already in my possession. Since the issue does not have to do with educating for values, it is not naïve nor a kind of "we are all one family, come and give. Why don't you give?" Precisely because of this reason, Smooha insists on naming the service, as service to the state, with a possibility for a military service, and not simply civil service. The assumption is that part [of the Palestinians] will serve in the army and [another] part, in civil fields. Sammy Smooha has already noted in the last meeting: The military service should symbolize the legitimation of the Arabs in Israel to the state of Israel. "Hence the military service of the Arabs in Israel is not a military need of the state of Israel."

As mentioned in the introduction, the determined rejection of the Jewish state by Dr. Adel Manna and colleagues is part of the ever-strengthening national identity of Palestinians in Israel. This includes a shift among parts of the Palestinian community toward a more open rejection of the limited "civil rights" offered to them by the Zionist Left intellectuals. In the Position Papers of 2007, Palestinian national identity received an additional dimension, namely the reviving of history, the memory of the Nakba, and the Palestinian reconnection to the Arab nation. The demand for Israel to recognize them as a national minority, a people who deserve national rights, is at the center of these documents.

By 2009, however, the process of disconnecting from the futile dialogue of rights has accelerated. As in the past, Azmi Bishara has spoken on national rights and tried to encourage Palestinian citizens to move forward, doing so from his place in exile. The demand for the recognition of Palestinian national rights as citizens of Israel is dealt with in the context of redefining citizenship and its accompanying rights. First and foremost is the demand to recognize the Palestinian people as the original owner of the land. Their rights must be restored. These include the return of refugees to their homes, the return of confiscated lands, and the elimination of both de-Arabization and the Apartheid regime of the Zionist colonial state.[42]

> For many years I've been advocating a Palestinian interpretation of citizenship in Israel that Israel continues to reject, with consequences to myself that readers may well be aware of. According to this interpretation, the Palestinian citizen effectively tells the ruling authorities, "My loyalty does not go beyond the bounds of being a law abiding citizen who pays his taxes and the like. As for my keeping in touch with Palestinian history and with the Arab world in matters that should be inter-Arab, such things should not have to pass via your [The Israeli ruling authority's] requirement or your approval." Such talk was previously unheard of in Israel and it came as quite a shock to the ears of interlocutors used to liberal-sounding references to "our Arab citizens who serve as a bridge of peace and proof of the power of Israeli democracy." Rejecting such condescension, the new type of Palestinian says, "My Palestinianness existed before your state was created on top of the ruins of my people. Citizenship is a compromise I have accepted in order to be able to go on living here in my land. It is not a favor that you bestow on me with strings attached."

Bishara openly departs from any commitment toward "coexistence" or "patriotism" implied by the demand to recognize the Jewish state. "It is not the Palestinians' duty to assimilate to the Zionist character of the state," says Bishara. "The attempt to transform them into patriotic Israelis is an attempt to falsify history, to distort their cultural persona and fragment their moral cohesion. A Palestinian Arab who regards himself as an Israeli patriot is naught. He is someone who has accepted to be something less than a citizen and less than a Palestinian and who simultaneously identifies with those who have occupied Palestinian lands and repressed and expelled his people."

Far away from the developments taking place in the Palestinian community and its growing alienation from the Apartheid regime of the state of Israel, Zionist Left intellectuals continue their self-centered discourse on "the Jewish and democratic state." They ponder the meaning of the Jewishness of the state while ignoring its Apartheid essence, desperately twisting the meaning of liberal democracy for it to reconcile with the Jewish identity of the state.

CHAPTER 4

A Theocratic Jewish State

Previous chapters dealt with the Apartheid nature of the state of Israel, the structural discrimination of Palestinian citizens, the determined campaign against Palestinian national identity and rights, and the readiness of Zionist Left intellectuals to forgo universal human values in order to retain a Jewish majority. All this advances the goal of sustaining the Jewish identity of the state of Israel.

However, the concept of the state's Jewish identity remains vague. Indeed Zionism has always claimed, whether explicitly or in more subtle forms, to be based on the Divine promise between God and the Jewish people, as stated in the Bible and Jewish Halacha law.[1] These religious sources have served as the basis for legislation and for interpretation of laws by the Israeli Supreme Court. However, the question remains: What is the impact of religion upon the hegemonic ideology, culture, society, and political regime? Why and how do self-declared secular Zionists from the Left come to terms with the religious components in the Zionist ideology and the state? This chapter is dedicated to the religious dimension of the settler Jewish state—the reasons for its central status in the ideology and institutional structure of the state, and the secular Zionist Left's approach to the centrality of religion in Israel.

Jewish Religion—the Ultimate Justification
for Zionism and the State

The intense connection between Zionism and the Jewish religion began with Zionism's conception, even though the founders were secular people, outside of the religious Jewish communities and their rabbinical leaderships.

Jewish religion was the only criterion for delineating the boundaries of the "imagined" Jewish nation[2] assumed to have existed throughout the centuries. The first Zionist leaders soon realized that their attempts to "secularize" the concept of the nation, and to consolidate a national collective as something separate from the religious collective, had failed. "All attempts to reconstruct the annals of Jews as a 'national' history of an exiled territorial nation whose origin is one, is saturated with internal insolvable contradictions," says critical historian Shlomo Sand of Tel Aviv University. Yoav Peled, a progressive political scientist also of Tel Aviv University, adds another reason for the religious definition of the national collective which was adopted by first Zionist leaders: "Of all the political movements spawned by the crisis of Eastern European Jewry in the second half of the 19th century, Zionism alone claimed to speak on behalf of a world wide Jewish nation. The only cultural attribute holding this Jewish nation together, however, was the common religion to which the vast majority of Jews still held. Claiming to speak in the name of world Jewry, both internally and externally, Zionism needed at least the tacit approval of those universally recognized as the representatives of the Jewish communities: Orthodox rabbis."[3] Many of the rabbis actually opposed the emerging Zionist movement as a threat to Orthodox Judaism and the Jewish communities' religious way of life.

The national collective, defined in religious terms, later became institutionalized in the Law of Return, which identifies a Jew as the son or daughter of a Jewish mother, in accordance with Jewish Halacha.[4]

Jewish religion came to play an important role in designing Zionist ideology itself. Zionist leaders realized the inherent political and ideological advantages of using Jewish religion and tradition to sustain the Zionist colonial project. They set out to incorporate Jewish religion and tradition into the emerging hegemonic collective identity and culture of the colonial settlers society, the Yishuv—spearhead of the world Zionist movement.[5]

The myth of the Divine promise served as the "ultimate legitimacy" for choosing Palestine for Zionist colonization, despite the presence of the indigenous

Palestinian population.[6] Jewish religion and tradition supplied Zionism with a capacity to mask the colonialist project behind the innocent "return to Zion."

The Jewish religion's centrality, for delineating the boundaries of the "Jewish nation" and supplying legitimacy to the Zionist colonial movement and state, is summarized by Baruch Kimmerling:

> [The] essence of this society and state's right and reason to exist is embedded in symbols, ideas and religious scriptures—even if there has been an attempt to give them a secular re-interpretation and context . . . [This society] was made captive from the beginning by its choice of a target-territory for immigration and a place for its nation-building, for then neither the nation nor its culture could be built successfully apart from the religious context, even when its prophets, priests, builders and fighters saw themselves as completely secular.[7]

In establishing religion as central to the identity of the Jewish state, the decisive step was the pre-state "Status Quo Agreement" forged between the orthodox non-Zionist "Agudat Israel" movement and the leadership of the Jewish Agency (headed by Ben-Gurion, the chair of Mapai).[8] This agreement helped to lay the foundation of the inseparability between religion and state in Israel, which the legal later codified. Accordingly, certain state legislative and judicial powers were transferred to the realm of the religious establishment, which made its judgments according to Halachic law. For example, all major aspects of marriage and divorce are dealt with according to Halachic interpretation, based upon the Orthodox stream of Judaism. Jewish religious elements have also been incorporated into other areas of legislation as well.[9] Additionally there is statewide and local legislation that consists of public norms, which are also based upon the Halacha.[10]

In this way, the everyday life of the state, its symbols and holidays, the curriculum of schools, and in fact the entire collective identity were made subservient to a mixture of Zionism and religion, to the extent that "Zionism itself became a kind of version of the Jewish religion which includes within it civil foundations as well."[11]

Almost all members of Israeli society—on the right and left, religious and secular—claim this overlap between Jewish religion and nation. In a social order that made hegemonic Zionism a central characteristic, the conformity of secular Zionists to the rule of religion was inevitable. "There are in Israel individuals and groups and even secular sub-cultures. Their daily behavior and self-identity is secular . . . But when the majority of the public in Israel relates to their collective national identity, this identity is defined by terminology, values, symbols and collective memory, most of which are anchored in the Jewish religion."[12]

Thus Zionist Left intellectuals have accepted the authority of the rabbinate and Halachic laws in a number of central areas. They have refrained from launching a consistent campaign for separation of state from religion, even in the case of civil marriage, which doesn't exist in Israel.

The unique nature of the "secularism" adopted by Zionist Left liberals is exemplified in the way philosopher Menachem Brinker deals with the right to civil marriage. He discusses this issue in the same misleading way he dealt with the right to equality. That is, he uses the democratic decisions of the majority in the Knesset as a pretext for avoiding confrontation with the issue of civil marriage. In an interview, Brinker says:[13] "The Knesset legislated a law that marriage and divorce are under the authority of religious institutions. I would have liked for the Knesset to have legalized these matters differently and to recognize civil marriage. But as long as this is the law, so this is the law."

However, when asked directly about his stance on separation between state and religion, his passivity as a "law abiding" citizen is insufficient. Refusing to explicitly reject this cornerstone of liberalism, he pretends that separation of state and religion already exists in Israel "except in marriage, divorce, and burial and except that the state pays for the religious schools"—as though these are minor matters. He thus misleadingly limits the social, cultural, and personal space which Jewish religion dominates, and disregards the violation of basic liberties in family and educational affairs. Hence, Brinker would not call for changing the current status of religion in the areas he limits. "Thus I don't support the separation of religion from state if this is its [the state's] model. I would also not fight against the present law of marriage and divorce which ensures that they take place under religious law, even not through the means of writing new legislation . . . The ability to marry in civil marriages in the state of Israel should be preserved only for those who can not marry according to the Jewish Halacha"—that is, marriages between Jews and non-Jews.

The Zionist Left does not lead even the sporadic and weak anti-religious struggles against "religious coercion" that occasionally emerge, such as objections to closing shopping malls on Saturdays, or closing roads or even highways that pass close to Orthodox neighborhoods. To quote Brinker—who is at least honest enough to break the silence of his "liberal" colleagues and openly declare his objections to these campaigns, however disguised they are in the rhetoric of humanistic values—on the need to fight the closing of malls on Saturdays: "There is no place for such a campaign which was launched by secular circles. I would have liked the malls to close down during the weekdays as well. All these malls are cultural rubbish. I would like them to be closed seven days of the week . . .

In my opinion, even the secular campaign to open at least one restaurant that serves pork, does not seem to me to be a campaign for civil rights. It does not seem like an important struggle to me."[14]

Despite their acceptance of the institutional and legal centrality of religion in the state and its culture, the Zionist Left still see themselves as trying to reconcile the national collective religious identity with their support of secularity and universal enlightenment.

A New-Old Hebrew/Zionist Culture in the "State of the Jews"

The reluctance to identify the Jewishness of the state with the Jewish Halacha (which includes observance of religious commandments) can be seen in the rhetorical preference of "the state of the Jews" over the "Jewish state."[15] This preferred definition is used by secular Israelis to free themselves from the diasporic Halacha that the concept of "Jewish state" inheres. Writes author A. B. Yehoshua:

> What does it mean, a Jewish state called "Israel"? It is not entirely clear. My assumption, which I think can be proven, is that the word "Israel" means the total, absolute Jewish identity. A Jew is only a partial Israeli, an Israeli is a complete Jew . . . In the past, there was only the name Israel, and for a thousand years the name "Jew" did not exist. The first time this name was adopted was when we went into exile. Before that, it was the "people of Israel," "the sons of Israel," "Eretz Israel" [the land of Israel], and everything connected to it . . . When we say Israelis we mean total Jews. Jews who all parts of their life are Jewish, and are therefore named "Israelis."[16]

Yehoshua returned to express this semantic position in 2009:[17]

> If Moses, the kings and prophets of the biblical times could be asked "Please, identify, who are you?" They would answer "we are Israeli or the sons of Israel." If they would be asked again: "and what about the 'Jewish character'?" They would say, "we don't understand what you mean."
>
> The decision to name the state "Israel" and not "Yehuda" or "Yehudia"—was a natural logic. Why then we insist on defining our state as "a Jewish state"? The moment you inflate the use of the concept "Jewish and democratic," you either consciously or unconsciously connect the religious element to the concept of state.

In response, Shlomo Avineri confirmed the Zionist claim of the connection between religion and nation, which he assumed Yehoshua ignored:[18]

> He [Yehoshua] errs when he says that Jewish religion is an optional element in the definition of a Jew, as [for example] Catholicism or Christianity is an optional element in the definition of an Italian. The paradox is that despite the

fact that the concept "Jew" is wider than its religious meaning, the majority of
Jews (and the majority of Israeli Jews) agree that a Jew who converts to another
religion, also stops being a Jew in terms of its nationalist meaning. Herzl, a par
excellence secular Jew recognized it when he determined that "We are a nation,
according to religion 'in the meaning that indeed religion is not the content of
Jewish identity but it determines its boundaries.'"

In trying to come to terms with the religious essence of Zionism, the Zionist
Left has interpreted Jewish religion in such a way as to make it compatible with
their alleged commitment to Western humanism. The assumption is that the
renewed, resurrected, national culture ("Hebrew culture"), like any other national
culture, absorbs the history and collective memory of the nation, but creates a
new identity that is not connected or affiliated with Jewish religious Ortho-
doxy.[19] The new "Hebrew culture" signifies the most humanist of values, namely
"the centrality of the value of the individual human being, who was created in
the image of God and who is the whole world and whose life is sacred."[20]

The selection of the aspired for humanistic elements in Judaism is assumed
to be in the Old Testament, and not in Halachic literature created during the
years in "exile." The belief that these elements (found only in the Bible) can integrate with "secular" universalistic and democratic values squares with the fundamental Zionist perspective of "Negation of Exile" *(shlilat hagola)*. Chapter 1
addresses how this ideology was presented through the Zionist notion of "an
empty land," to which the Jewish people "returned" in order to renew their political and cultural life after two thousand years of exile.[21] However, "Negation
of Exile" also points to the nature of the Jewish identity of the state of Israel and
its culture. It is thought to sustain the "normalization" of Jewish existence, and
the fulfillment and "solution" to Jewish history. Accordingly, "centuries in exile"
are perceived as an interim period that lacks any significance in "the life of the
nation." The centuries are marked by an incomplete and faulty existence, in
which "the spirit of the nation" could not find its full expression. The Zionist
assumption is that the "return" will lead to the renewal of a national culture, and
will ensure the resurrection of the cultural creativity that was lost in exile. The
"totality of the Jew," as emphasized by Yehoshua, can be achieved only by participating in the Zionist colonization of "Eretz Israel," in which the old-new
Hebrew culture has emerged.[22]

Against this background, the images of the "sabra," the anti–"ghetto-like,"
"new Jew," were crystallized.[23] These images are presented as the authentic Jewish national culture, of which only the Zionist project (emphasizing "sovereignty
in this land") can ensure its full development. This in turn is conditioned upon

the erasure of "Diasporic consciousness" and the characteristics attributed to the stereotypical image of "ghetto-like" Jews: weak, submissive, passive, cowardly, and even physically deformed.[24] The contradictory image of the "sabra," the embodiment of the new Jew, has been portrayed as physically beautiful, masculine, determined, brave, proud, and healthy, known to have a "beautiful forelock and appearance"—(*yefe hablorit ve hatoar*).[25] Underlying this mythological Eretz Israeli cultural hero is the sanctification of force and militarism so prominent in Zionist culture today.[26]

The concept of the "Negation of Exile" delineates the boundaries of the "legitimate" Zionist collective. It excludes the non-Zionist Orthodox Jews, who are perceived as ghetto-like *(galuti)* and contradictory of Western enlightenment and humanism. On the other hand, religious Zionists who support the settlers' movement are recognized as part and parcel of the collective, together with "secular" Zionists.

Amos Oz shares the ideology of the renewed Hebrew culture and directs his rage against the "ultra-orthodox" non-Zionist who represents the presumably "exilic,""backward" way of life developed within Eastern European culture:[27]

> I say this particularly to people who uphold some sort of contradiction that it is supposedly impossible to reconcile between Israel's culture and humanism, between Israel's culture and democracy. There is no such contradiction. Indeed, there is a contradiction between, humanism, democracy, pluralism, and sanctity of the individual, and the few who have assumed for themselves the monopoly over Judaism, because it has been given to them . . . They, the ultra-orthodox Jews, come and demand of us to be original and not imitate the Gentiles. They come and say that putting wreaths on a grave, or singing the national anthem, or firing rifles during a military funeral, or flying the flag is a custom of the Gentiles. And who says this to us? People who go around in this [modern] world, dressed in clothes of Polish landlords from the 17th century, the clothes which were then those of Polish nobility [the origin of the Orthodox clothes from the 19th century] and who sing beautiful Hassidim songs in Ukrainian melodies—which I love but they are still Ukrainian melodies—dance ecstatic Ukraine dances . . . but from us, they demand originality.

Oz thus dispenses with "them," the Ultra-Orthodox Jews, because of the Gentiles' influence on their Hassidic garb, music, the Yiddish language, and various other religious rituals, such as the mezuzah (a piece of specified parchment inscribed with Hebrew verses from the Torah). On the other hand, says Oz, "we," the secular, represent the authentic Hebrew culture.[28]

Zionist Secularism Identified with "Peace"

The humanistic "Hebrew culture" adopted by the "secular" Zionist Left includes their declared commitment to "peace." As mentioned in chapter 1, the 1967 occupation is considered the turning point that led to the distortion of the "peaceful" side of Zionism. However, the blame for this distortion is put on the strengthened powers of religious and right-wing streams of Zionism.

The late Amos Elon, self-claimed non-Zionist and supporter of an independent Palestinian state, was a historian and political analyst. He also served for years as a correspondent on European and American affairs for the newspaper *Haaretz,* and was a frequent contributor to the *New York Review of Books* and the *New York Times Magazine.* His "enlightened" secularism in the context of analyzing Zionism is exposed in an interview he gave to *Haaretz* in 2004. "I definitely agree with the idea that there was a need to establish a state-of-the-Jews in Israel for those Jews who want to live here . . . [Now] I think that Zionism has exhausted itself, precisely because it accomplished its aims. If Zionism of today isn't a success story, it's the fault of the Zionists. It's because of the religionization and Likudization of Zionism and because what was supposed to be a state-of-the-Jews has become a Jewish state."[29]

Elon depicts "Gush Dan" (Tel Aviv and the towns around it) as the stronghold of the secular enlightened middle class, who have supported Zionist Left peace initiatives, unlike the semi-fascist "religious":

Q. Do you find Israel to be barbaric, unenlightened, nationalistic?

A. In Israel there's the "Gush Dan" state and the political state. The "Gush Dan" state is a state of live-and-let-live. Of tolerance. Of the desire for peace and for good life. But the political state, well, you know what it looks like.

Q. What does it look like?

A. It's partly quasi-fascist and partly religious with narrow horizons.

Q. Quasi-fascist?

A. Quasi-fascist in the sense that abstract principles of religion are dictating our fate without any democratic process. There are religious people here who believe they've put their finger on the very essence of being. They know everything. They're in direct contact with God.

Q. You have some profound anti-religious sentiment.

A. I'm not being original when I say that religion that enters politics is dangerous. Such religious people would be better off behind bars and not in politics.[30]

Among Zionist Left intellectuals, the support for the 1993 Oslo Accords (signed by Labor Party prime minister Yitzhak Rabin and the late PLO (Palestine Liberation Organization) chair Yasser Arafat) became the criterion for "Is-raeli" identity in the years thereafter. The Zionist Left intellectuals misleadingly depict this support as indicating recognition of Palestinian national rights and commitment to universal values. However, as Noam Chomsky reminds us, "the Oslo Agreement gave a green light to continued settlement building and their development, thus rendering the agreement virtually useless. [It has thus] estab-lished the Palestinian Authority not as a 'partner' but as a police force to keep Palestinians under control while Clinton-Rabin-Peres continued with their pro-grams of integrating crucial parts of the territories within Israel—quite openly."[31]

Like Elon, the majority of the Zionist Left blames religion for the rise of the extreme Right in Israel, which in turn has objected consistently to the Zionist Left's peace initiatives—first and foremost, the Oslo Accords. "This is an ideo-logical construction," says historian Raz-Krakotzkin, "designed to eternalize their [Zionist Left intellectuals'] enlightened self-image identified with secularism."[32]

However, it is not the centrality of religion in state and society that has con-cerned the Zionist Left intellectuals. Instead, they are focused on how different factions of religious Judaism are committed to the hegemonic Zionist ideology. Challenging the supreme authority of Zionist ideology, namely Israel, is the real reason why opponents of the Oslo framework became identified with the rejection of humanism and enlightenment. The Left's arrogant stance toward Palestinian national rights and humanism was demonstrated in the fact that support for Oslo (which does not recognize Palestinian national rights) was paradoxically used as a criterion to delegitimize the non-Zionist Orthodox (most of whom do not serve in the army), but not the National Religious parties, which represent the settlers and strongly objected to the Oslo Agreements.

The Zionist Left discourse following the November 4, 1995, assassination of Israeli prime minister Yitzhak Rabin is a case in point.[33]

The assassination was carried out by a religious Jew, who argued that he acted in response to a rabbi's commandment. This was used to justify the en-suing outburst of "anti-religious" sentiment from the Zionist Left. They largely ignored the fact that the assassin came from national-religious Zionist circles that headed the settler movement. More than anyone else, these circles were responsible for inciting the assassination. Moreover, the rhetoric used by the assassin was a political Zionist rhetoric, not a religious one. He objected to Is-rael making territorial concessions to any Palestinian sovereign—a position held by many non-religious Jews. His positions were not born of extreme reli-giousness, but rather from extreme Zionism. Nevertheless his religious identity was presented as the central motive for the assassination. "It was more convenient to attack the assassination on the religious level, of a man wearing a skullcap, than on the nationalist level. Because if the reason [for the assassination] is religious, the derived conclusion is that you need to develop a 'secular' identity. You can then divide the world into good Jews and bad Jews. And this indeed was the central tendency [in Zionist Left discourse at the time]." Accordingly, "religion" was scapegoated for all manifestations of fanaticism in Israel. "But," continues Raz-Krakotzkin, "if the reason is nationalistic, even if indeed most of those who held it were religious, then you would have to develop against it an anti-nationalistic position. In this context, it is first and foremost a position which grants high value to the realization of the national rights of the Palestinians [and which the Zionist Left objects to]. This position precisely may constitute a basis for a joint activity of religious people and those who do not practice religious commandments."[34]

The Zionist Left claimed the assassination of Rabin embodied the split in Israeli society between the "Jewish" side and the "Israeli" side. This position was well represented by political scientist Shlomo Ben Ami, a Social Democrat labor leader and ideologue who was elected to the Knesset in 1996. He served as minister of internal security in Ehud Barak's government (1999–2001), and later as foreign minister.[35]

At a 1998 roundtable discussion of Rabin's assassination and legacy, Ben Ami depicts the assassination as the rebellion of the "Jew" against the "Israeli."[36] "The assassination of Rabin was the embodiment of the split in Israeli society. It was an additional step in a civil war which takes place here . . . The split is between the Jewish side in the state of Israel and the Israeli side . . . Those who voted for the Likud in the 1996 elections which took place soon after the assassination were the more Jewish part in the society—a public for whom the Jewish influences, the connection with Judaism, were more close to their hearts."

What motivated the assassin was not the issue of restoring part of the '67 occupied territories, says Ben Ami, but hatred of Arabs, which is not part of hegemonic Zionist Left culture. "Those, who in the footsteps of the assassination of Rabin won the elections, were those groups that in 1948 either were not in the land or, if they were, did not influence its image and the directions of its development . . . These groups want to erect a different state—not the state which the beautiful forelock and appearance youth [the sabra] wanted and not that which his heroes wanted."

Responding to Ben Ami's misleading interpretation of Rabin's assassination, that "the Jew stood up against the Israeli and killed him," MK Jamal Zahalka (of the NDA), who participated in the roundtable discussion,[37] noted:

> This is but an attempt to locate evil outside the boundaries of "Israeliness." In my opinion Yigal Amir [Rabin's assassin] is one hundred percent "Israeli." In it one must search for the problem not in his Judaism. His Israeliness discloses the ugly face of Israeliness. Moreover, this nationalistic-religious Messianic is an Israeli product *par excellence,* which indeed has roots in certain aspects of Jewish history prior to the establishment of Israel, but has mainly grown out of Israeliness and its values. The Israeliness is Messianism, and it emphasizes admiration of power.

Historian David Ochana of Ben-Gurion University confirms the affinity toward messianism that has been embedded in the Zionist movement from its inception. Moreover, he admits "the secular messianism of the Labor movement played no small part in the birth of *Gush Emunim.*" Gush Emunim is the "Bloc of the Faithful," the settler movement, which Ochana defines as "the great enemy of Israeli society." Additionally, he says, "Fascism is embedded inherently in the messianic Zionism of Ben-Gurion."[38]

The common roots of left- and right-wing Zionists help to explain both the empathy felt by Zionist Left intellectuals toward the settlements and their support for Labor governments active in expanding them.

Affinity with Religious Settlement Movement

Though the Zionist Left has declared its objections to the settlement movement, there is no denying the deep affinity that many of them have for settlement members.

This fundamental "brotherhood" was expressed by Amos Oz while meeting with the settlers of Ofra, a settlement between Ramallah and Nablus, deep within the West Bank. It is considered the "Jewel of the Crown" of the "ideological" settlement movement, as opposed to the "quality of life" settlements, whose members mainly join for the high level of housing and social services subsidized by the Israeli government. Oz's report on the meeting at Ofra is included in his book *Journey in Israel, Autumn 1982,* which discusses meetings with representatives of different sectors of "Israeli society" on both sides of the Green Line.[39]

The friendly meeting took place in the autumn of 1982 in the midst of the Israeli bloody assault on Lebanon. The assault began on June 6, 1982, and continued with the massacre in the Palestinian refugee camps of Sabra and Shatila on September 16–18. The popular movement against the horrors committed by Israel grew exponentially. It reached its peak on September 25, with a mass demonstration in Tel Aviv of 400,000 participants. Many other mass demonstrations took place during the months Oz's voyage occurred, led by the radical wing of the peace camp, the Committee Against the War in Lebanon. In all of the demonstrations, the connection between the war in Lebanon and Sharon's plan to annex the West Bank by expanding the settlements was emphasized time and again.[40]

However, the raging storm sweeping over a large part of the peace camp had no effect upon the calm, pleasant, and friendly atmosphere that characterized the meeting between the Zionist Left icon and the fascist settlers of Ofra. The war on Lebanon was an attempt to destroy the PLO leadership in residence; the intention was to fully subjugate the Palestinians in the '67 occupied territories. In failing to mention the war in Lebanon, Oz also ignores the role his hosts played in implementing this scheme.

This is what Oz said in the 1982 meeting at Ofra:

"All of us would readily agree that Zionism means that it is good for the Jewish people to return to Eretz Israel and that it is bad for it to be dispersed among the nations. From this point on however there is a division of opinions [amongst us]."[41]

According to Oz, this dispute is over humanism and liberalism: "As to the question of the sanctity of tradition, ritual or cultural creativity, the settlers are totally oriented toward the past, instead of adopting Western European humanism, mainly in its liberal and socialist interpretation."[42]

Asked to explain what he means by Western humanism, Oz replies: "It means a supreme and absolute sanctity of the life and liberty of any human being. It means a universal justice . . . not only in the Jewish-tribe circle."[43] From someone who highlights the essential conflict between his humanist, universal values and the aspirations of the settlers—who want to occupy the land by whatever means—one might expect an ardent declaration of war. But Oz does nothing of the sort. Instead, he indicates that universal values are subordinate to Zionism. Additionally, his arguments and lengthy discussions are noticeably absent of moral argumentation and of recognition of Palestinian national rights. After paying lip service to "Western humanism," his argument boils down to *realpolitik* considerations. He relates mainly to the joint concern, shared by both Right and Left, about the "continued existence of the state of Israel and Zionist-Jewish culture." However, while the settlers are convinced that giving up

"*Judea and Samaria*" (the Biblical names for the area which comprises the West Bank) constitutes an existential danger to Israel, Oz adds that the annexation of the settlements "would bring about disaster on the Jewish people [*Am Israel*—referring to Jews all over the world]."

Oz frequently emphasizes legitimate differences of opinion "within the family." Moreover, he acknowledges the settlers' place within the "pluralism of Zionism" is a blessing, because "this tension is creative and fertilizing."[44] During the meeting, the appalling theft of Palestinian lands, water resources, and livelihoods goes completely unmentioned. Instead, Oz provides an egocentric articulation of his own reaction to what he terms the "legitimate positions" of the settlers, his feelings of fraternity with them as Zionists, and a shocking indifference to Palestinian dispossession.

> All streams of Zionism, including those which are strange to me and scare me, *all of them attract me like the stories of a story teller* [emphasis added]. Of course, I am not an amused observer sitting in an elevated point of observation entertainingly watching these tribal conflagrations. But even when certain positions make me lose control, the sense of excitement I experience watching this sight is unending. Namely, that people of different intentions and different worldviews basically agree with each other that the Jews should return home, though they may not agree, and in fact bitterly fight [among each other], over the plan of the home and its content. I [usually] willingly accept the mosaic of beliefs and opinions.[45]

Oz's book has been continually reissued since the first edition, published in 1982, without reservations from him. In the introduction to the 1993 edition, he ignores the tremendous expansion of the settlements in the '67 occupied territories, including Ofra, using evasive language: "What has changed since then? I don't have a generalized answer. I also can not tell what has changed among my partners to the dialogue [that took place] eleven years ago because I have continued talking with only few of them." Oz emphasizes, "The writer still adheres to the viewpoints which he expressed in the debate on life and death in Ofra . . . and he still has the same hopes expressed in the last two pages of this book—hopes which maybe are seen now closer [than then]."[46]

Because Oz is viewed as a moral authority, his book has become a significant source of political education for the Israeli public and "remains to this day [2009] among the most conspicuous components in the comprehensive canon of one of the greatest Hebrew writers in modern times."[47] The book's ninth edition (July 2009) was celebrated in the Israeli daily *Yediot Ahronot*, which printed a long article that included an interview with the author. Again Oz says nothing new about the horrific events in Lebanon that coincided with his meetings in Ofra, though he does refer to that period as "the bad autumn of 1982." In the article Oz also declines the opportunity to speak out against the current settlement movement; the number of settler colonies has tripled since the book's initial publication. Nor does he call for the support of US president Barack Obama's demand to freeze settlement construction. (Not to mention a call to support an international inquiry committee on the massacre in Gaza that took place just a few months before this article was written (in December 2008–January 2009). As in the past, Oz refrains from criticizing his expressed "brotherhood" with the most ideological fanatics of Ofra, who have continued to steal Palestinian lands for further settler expansions.[48]

Indeed, the essential division between the Israeli peace camp and the Right (both secular and religious) revolves around "the plan of the home," and not whose right it is to live there. In other words, it is a disagreement over the scope of territorial concessions as a condition to the "solution of the conflict," and over the nature of Israel's continued control over the '67 occupied territories. And on the issue of the Palestinians' national rights, both sides are in accord.

Closing Ranks with the Secular and Religious Right—the Kinneret Covenant

The Labor government headed by Ehud Barak (1999–2001) brought about the final collapse of the Oslo framework in 2000. This was followed by the brutal repression of the second Intifada. The military reconquered the '67 occupied territories and squelched mass demonstrations of Palestinians in Israel,[49] while Zionist Left intellectuals framed the Palestinians' uprising as terrorism. They blamed Arafat for refusing to accept the "generous proposal" of the Labor government.[50] Prime Minister Sharon, who ascended to power as chair of Likud in February 2001, enthusiastically pursued Labor's strategy, which was supported by the Zionist Left, including Meretz.[51]

The belief that Palestinian resistance in the '67 occupied territories would require even more cruel policies, and that Palestinians in Israel would give up neither their challenge of the Jewish state nor solidarity with their brethren, inspired Zionists to reunite around a joint left-right tribal fire. As the self-righteous, hegemonic Zionist ideology, conditioned on the subdued acceptance of Palestinians, began to falter, Israelis hurried to close ranks. They gathered around the shared Zionist premises of the Jewish state and its need for "security," both of which easily trump the absoluteness of human rights and democratic procedures.

These developments resolidified the relationship between many left Zionists and national religious streams, which had been somewhat weakened during the false liberalization of the Oslo peace years. The rediscovered fraternity between the Zionist Left and Right (both secular and religious) during the first three years of the second Intifada was made evident in university events, research institutes, and individual projects and discussion groups, all of which confirmed their shared adherence to the "Jewish state." Discussions amongst academics and other liberal circles—regarding the "demographic issue" (see chapter 2) and how to preserve the Jewish majority inside Israel—began to multiply like the sprouting of mushrooms after the rain.

One such series of discussions resulted in the Kinneret Covenant, which was developed while the Likud-Labor government was waging war against the Palestinian people from February to July 2001. The Kinneret Covenant (*Amanat kineret*) was published on January 11, 2002, a few months after Labor resigned from Sharon's government. Its final text was followed up with an aggressive and expensive media campaign. The document was sent out to hundreds of thousands of homes in Israel, and was published as large advertisements in the printed media.

The Kinneret Covenant was produced by a group of sixty Israelis from a wide spectrum of Israeli Jewish society, confirming shared Zionist ideology embedded in the definition of Israel as "a Jewish and democratic state."[52] Its signatories included prominent figures—both religious and secular, left wing and extreme right, those identified with the settlement movement, academics, and former high commanders in the army, as well as current members of the political and security establishment. Its stated goals were "finding a renewed common identity for Israelis; closing schisms in society; narrowing social gaps; and repairing society's failures. Among the left-wing signatories and supporters were public figures who had long been known as the most vocal advocates of peace in Israel, and who, up until the failed Camp David Summit of July 2000, were known for their support of the Oslo framework. This grouping included political scientist Shlomo Avineri, and Yuli Tamir, one of the founders of Peace Now[53] and former Minister of Immigration and Absorption under Barak's Labor government.[54]

Representing the right wing were fanatical figures like Brig.-Gen. (Res.) Efraim "Effi" Eitam (from the National-Religious Party Mafdal), who called

for greatly expanding the settlements and for reoccupying and annexing the
West Bank, and geographer Arnon Sofer of Haifa University, the foremost Israeli academic warning about "the demographic danger of Arabs in Israel."[55]

In an interview with *Haaretz*,[56] Eitam presents the Kinneret Covenant as,
"above all, an attempt to build trust . . . This is a document of partnership, not a
document of compromise. We were able to [jointly] define everything without
which there is no people and no state." In reviewing the Left and Right's ideological battle for Israeli public opinion, Eitam notes, "Each side tried with all
means at its disposal to impose its agenda on the other, and did not succeed. The
Left with its lunatic rush to Oslo; the Right, with the settlements." But the meeting between both camps strengthened the affinity between the participants, who
"discovered in their deliberations preparing the document something we all knew
in our hearts: *that we are all brothers* [emphasis added]."

The iconic Zionist Left member Yuli Tamir confirms the atmosphere of respect and understanding that prevailed in the meetings, and says of the future,
"Everyone will translate his personal commitment into operative moves. We'll
say to the political system: Listen, there is a parallel reality [indicated by the
Kinneret Covenant] in which people communicate with each other in a completely different way without cynicism, and with a lot of mutual respect and
empathy, and with a readiness to listen to each other. Our contribution will be
the example, the model."[57]

The Left and Right were able to find common ground by making particular
concessions. The extreme Right was willing to abandon its bellicose language
and accepted both the Zionist Left's "universalistic" vocabulary and its alleged
commitment to democracy. On the other side, important issues in the Zionist
Left intellectual discourse, such as the "objection" to the 1967 occupation and
Jewish settlements, were simply omitted from the covenant. Other positions
were presented in a blurred or generalized language that rendered the ideas
fairly meaningless.

The first article of the covenant declares, "the State of Israel is the national
home of the Jewish people," thus loudly confirming a core tenet of Zionist
ideology.

> Israel is "the national home of the Jewish people" . . . Throughout its history, the
> Jewish people maintained a profound and unbroken connection to its land. The
> longing for the land of Israel and for Jerusalem stood at the center of its spiri-
> tual, cultural, and national life . . . The Jewish people's adherence to its heritage,
> its *Torah*, its language, and its land, is a human and historic occurrence with few

parallels in the history of nations. It was this loyalty that gave rise to the Zionist movement, brought about the ingathering of our people once more into its land, and led to the founding of the State of Israel and the establishment of Jerusalem as its capital . . . We believe that it is out of supreme and existential necessity, and with complete moral justification, that the Jewish people should have a national home of its own, the State of Israel.

There is no acknowledgement here, or anywhere else in the covenant, of the Palestinians as the indigenous population of the land, thus perpetuating the myth that Jews are the only nationality on the land.

The second article identifies Israel as a democracy. "In accordance with its Basic Laws and fundamental values, the State of Israel believes in the dignity of man and his freedom, and is committed to the defense of human rights and civil rights. All men are created in God's image." As explored in the introduction, while these basic laws strive to safeguard human rights, they fail to do so because these rights are conditioned on recognition of the Jewish state.

Representatives of the Right, who have never cared about the violation of citizenship rights of Palestinians, accepted the Zionist Left's pathetic need to cover up and justify the "shortcomings" of Israel's democracy. They did this by adopting the "will of the majority" argument. The article states, "The State of Israel is a democracy, accepting the decisions of the majority, and honoring the rights of the minority." However, in line with the Zionist Left's contradictory stance (see chapter 2), a Jewish majority is both a reality and a mission: "In order to guarantee the continuity of a Jewish-democratic Israel, it is imperative that a substantial Jewish majority continues to be maintained within the state. This majority will be maintained only by moral means."

The Jewish character of Israel (article 3):

Is expressed in a profound commitment to Jewish history and Jewish culture: in the state's connection to the Jews of the Diaspora, the Law of Return, and its efforts to encourage *Aliya* [Jewish immigration] and absorption [of Jewish immigrants]; in the Hebrew language, the principal language of the state, and the unique language of a unique Israeli creativity; in the festivals and official days of rest of the state, its symbols, and its anthem; in Hebrew culture with its Jewish roots, and in the state institutions devoted to its advancement; and in the Jewish educational system, whose purpose is to inculcate, along with general and scientific knowledge and the values of humanity, and along with loyalty to the state and love of the land of Israel and its vistas, the students' attachment to the Jewish people, the Jewish heritage, and the book of books [the Bible].

This definition of the Jewish state fixes on identity and culture, and excludes

Palestinians from full citizenship. That the Jews are given preference (in terms of legislation and state resources) is omitted from the covenant, allowing the Left to cling insistently to its fallacious belief that there is no contradiction between the Jewish state and democracy.

The prevailing image of Israel, as a state seeking peace while sustaining and developing its security capabilities, is preserved by the covenant's sixth article "From the day of its birth, Israel has been subject to conflict and bloodshed . . . [But] Israel did not lose its belief in peace, nor its hope of attaining peace." And, of course, "With that, Israel reserves the right to defend itself. It is imperative that this right be safeguarded, and that Israel maintain the ability to defend itself on a permanent basis." Recognition of the Jewish state is presented as a condition for reaching a peace settlement with the "neighbors." By 2009, this has become an official demand by the Likud-Labor government, knowing full well that it creates yet another obstacle to any peace agreement. In line with the traditionally blurred language of the Zionist Left, the requirement is presented as an existential condition. The phrasing makes equivalent the physical elimination of the state with the dissolution of Jewish identity of Israel. "Israel has no wish to rule over another people, but it insists that no people and no state try to bring about its destruction as a Jewish state. Israel sees the principle of self-determination and its expression within the framework of national states, as well as a readiness for compromise on the part of both sides, as the basis for the resolution of the conflict."

When the words "occupation" and "settlements" are not mentioned throughout the entire document, we know Israel does not truly aspire for peace. Ignoring the implications of the settlements for "the principle of self-determination of the Palestinians and its expression in a nation-state" signifies the Left's betrayal of its own beliefs.

Palestinian citizenship in the Jewish state is addressed separately in article 5. It recognizes "the need to implement the principle of civil equality in those areas in which non-Jewish citizens are discriminated and neglected." Moreover, "Israel will ensure the right of the Arab minority to maintain its linguistic, cultural, and national identity." But again, neglecting to mention the 1948 Nakba, the historic heritage of the Palestinians, and their connection to their brothers in the '67 occupied territories (and in exile) mark this recognition as conspicuously empty. Also, the idea that the "Jewish character of the State of Israel will not serve as an excuse for discrimination between one citizen and another" is contradicted by the stated need to ensure a Jewish majority for the continued existence of the Jewish democratic state. The inequality of Palestinians is structural. The laws and policies aimed at realizing the Jewish identity of the state go to the core of Israel's brand of Apartheid.

It is not by accident that the article on the religious character of the state (article 9) is presented separately from the article emphasizing the "Jewishness" of the state. In this context, the "Jewish state" represents the Zionist Left's declared commitment to the Bible and "Jewish heritage," but not to the Halacha. Separation of the two articles misleadingly differentiates between a "Jewish" state and "religious" state, and implies, incorrectly, that the Zionist Left and Israel are secular entities.

The way is thus opened for a reconciliation between religion and secularism, via a rather wide common denominator: agreeing in principle to mitigated descriptions of the state's religiousness and presenting the dispute between religion and state as a negotiation over details, not as a philosophical, ideological battle over the essence of the state and regime.

"We, secular, traditional, and religious Jews, each recognize the contribution of the others to the physical and spiritual existence of the Jewish people. On the other hand the 'seculars' believe that the Jewish tradition has an important place in the public sphere and in the public aspects of the life of the state, but that the state must not impose religious norms on the private life of the individual. Disagreements over matters of religion and state should be resolved through discussion, without insult and incitement, by legal and democratic means, and out of a respect for one's neighbor."

The common denominator of the secular and religious, and of the Left and Right, as Zionists, and as Jews, supersedes all contradictions. "We belong to the same people. We have a joint past and a joint lot. Despite the differences in opinions and viewpoints, all of us are committed to the continuity of Jewish life, to the continuity of the existence of the Jewish people and to the assurance of the future of the state of Israel."

The summary of the covenant assigns a common task for the Left and Right to complete together—the as yet-to-be-accomplished Zionist Project. "In establishing the State of Israel, the forefathers of the state performed an extraordinary historic deed. This deed has not ended; it is at its height. The return to Zion and the effort to found Jewish-democratic sovereignty in the land of Israel stand, in the 21st century, before great challenges." How else to conclude but to say the state of Israel is indeed a tool to further the Zionist project?

The feeling of brotherhood with the extreme Right has been affirmed through the Labor Party's participation in right-wing governments. In 2006 the government launched a second onslaught against Lebanon, and in 2009 they were responsible for the massacre in Gaza. Both interventions had the support of left intellectuals. The elaboration of their shared perspective on the meaning of the Jewish state, and the legitimacy provided by Zionist Left intellectuals to Israel's Apartheid, does not leave much hope for genuine criticism of Israel's "democracy."

CHAPTER 5

The Assertion of the Democratic Nature of the State

This chapter addresses the way the Zionist Left intellectuals discuss the issue of democracy—the second element of the "Jewish democratic" state formula. The question is: how do they deal with Israel's democracy when their shared perspective on the meaning of the Jewish state includes a legitimization of Israel's Apartheid?

Very few Zionist Left intellectuals see Israel as a colonial settler state. They do not attribute its "internal" regime, laws, and political culture to this central characteristic of state and society (not to mention Israel's Apartheid nature). The majority refuses to see the Zionist movement as an ongoing colonial project.

Matzpen, the anti-Zionist socialist organization, was one of few exceptions. (See chapter 6 for a history of Matzpen and its political positions.) As early as the 1960s, it portrayed Zionism and Israel as a colonial enterprise supported by Western imperialism, partnering to advance Western imperialist interests in the Middle East.[1] Says Moshé Machover, a founder of Matzpen: "Present-day Israel is not only a product of the Zionist colonization but also an instrument for its further extension and expansion."[2] Colonization continued in 1948 to 1967 in the territory then ruled by Israel within the Green Line. Lands belonging to Palestinian Arabs—including those who remained within the Green Line— were expropriated and given over to Zionist colonization. And soon after the 1967 war, colonization continued in the newly occupied territories, regardless of the party in charge: Labor, Likud, and grand coalitions.

In the mid-1990s, Azmi Bishara and the NDA also identified Zionism as a colonialist project. They also saw the Palestinian lot as connected to that of the entire Arab nation, oppressed by Western imperialism. The NDA won a large sector of the intellectual and political elite of Palestinians in Israel, as expressed in the position documents discussed in the introduction. Azmi Bishara has elaborated on the colonial nature of Israel: "Zionist colonialism inhabits the space between two extinct models—those provided by South Africa and by French practice in Algeria. It is not a blend of the two, but rather a distillation of the worst in each." However, Israel's policy toward Palestinians on both sides of the Green Line has a single motive: "its endeavor to sustain the Jewish hegemony all over Palestine."[3]

'67 Occupied Territories Excluded from the Discourse on Israel's Regime

The Zionist Left refuses to acknowledge Israel's prolonged rule over the '67 occupied territories as a structural characteristic of the Israeli political regime. The occupation is considered irrelevant to the debate on the definition of Israel as democracy.

The Zionist Left has never seriously confronted the question raised by Idith Zertal: "Can a democratic state hold a population of millions in a territory which was occupied in war, while their liberties are limited and they are disposed from fundamental democratic rights and from minimal human life conditions—without its very own democracy, their very perception of democracy—being incurably damaged?"[4]

In response, progressive scholars have rejected the Zionist Left's position that excludes the 1967 occupation from the debate on the Israeli regime. They contend that this debate cannot be limited to "Israel proper" because such a geopolitical entity does not exist anymore. Since 1967, Israel has ruled over the entire area between the Mediterranean and the Jordan River as though it were one unified political unit. And in fact the collaborationist Palestinian Authority helps to sustain Israeli control and to disguise Israel's nature.

Ariella Azoulay and Adi Ophir assert that Israel was transformed into one big state that includes the West Bank and in which one-third of its subjects are denied political status that would confer even minimal human rights. This transformation has been institutionalized in a new regime, subcontracted through the Palestinian Authority. Every indication is that it is there to stay.[5]

Despite this, Azoulay and Ophir argue that in fact they are speaking about "two regimes within one": an occupation regime in the '67 occupied territories and an ethnic-democratic regime in Israel proper.[6] This stance, which prevails among the Zionist Left, was criticized by Oren Yftachel of Ben-Gurion University in the Negev:[7]

> How can the crippled, wounded and excluded citizenship of the Palestinian in Israel constitute a basis for defining the state as democracy? Moreover, the superficial approach to the Israeli state is conspicuous precisely when you compare it with the thorough description of the control system in the [1967 occupied] territories. There, Azoulay and Ophir bothered to punctiliously examine "How is it working." They however lightly skip this punctiliousness, when they come [to deal with] the state of Israel and simply omit an analysis of the Israeli regime: How does it work in [Palestinian] NGOs and schools which are under the control of the Shabak? How does it work in the "unrecognized" villages where "citizens" live without water? How does it work in the continued space oppression? How does it work in the gaining control over the Arab neighborhoods of Jaffa, Acre, Ramle and Lydda? How does it work in the Jewish designing the curriculum in Arabic? Here the presumption of democracy is prior to [the facts about] their [Palestinians'] exclusion.

Already in the early 1980s, progressive researcher Meron Benvenisti argued that the occupied territories were actually annexed. Contrary to the Zionist Left's position, he says, this annexation was an irreversible fact. He describes post-1967 Israel as "a democracy of a master nation *(Herrenvolk Democracy)*."[8] Benvenisti criticizes the Zionist Left for its perception of the '67 occupied territories as a separate unit, and for claiming that the methods used to colonize the territories are different from those still used within the Green Line. Thus, for example, the Zionist Left perceives methods of confiscating "state lands" in the '67 occupied territories as a "novelty," when, in reality, they are entirely identical to those that have been employed in Israel since 1948.

Moreover, Benvenisti points out, emphasizing the 1967 occupation as "a colonial project," undertaken by an ostensibly peaceful pre-1967 Israel, enables some among the Zionist Left to avoid seeing the occupation as one link among many in the chain of the Israeli-Palestinian conflict. In the unified Israeli regime over entire Palestine, all Palestinians lack civil rights. Indeed, the Palestinians in Israel are citizens of the state. But according to state laws, their citizenship status does not ensure them political, economic, or personal equality.[9]

Sociologist Sammy Smooha rejects Benvenisti's definition of Israel as a Herrenvolk Democracy, as well as his claim that the occupation is permanent.[10] Regarding the lack of any human rights for the residents of the '67 occupied territories, Smooha uses the absurd argument that "they have never demanded to be Israeli citizens with equal rights." Smooha thus avoids rendering a moral judgment on the brutal violation of human rights in the '67 occupied territories. He also wrongly equates universal human rights with the equal citizens' rights "they have not demanded." By implication, resistance to the occupation is viewed as a rejection of Israeli "citizenship."[11]

The ease with which the Zionist Left dismisses any challenge to the Apartheid nature of the state of Israel is demonstrated in Smooha's analysis of the Oslo Accords near the end of 2000. To him, the Oslo Accords demonstrate that the Palestinian situation in the '67 occupied territories is only temporary. In rejecting Benvenisti's model of a "masters' democracy," Smooha joins with the rest of the Zionist Left, who see in the autonomic West Bank towns, established in 1994 under the Oslo Agreement, an indication that the "solution of the Palestinian issue is very close." Excluding the 1967 occupation from the discussion of Israel's democracy implies that Palestinians on different sides of the Green Line have a separate status from one another. Only the question of "Israeli Arabs," when not ignored, is seen as relevant to this discussion. In most cases, however, Zionist Left intellectuals do not believe that the conditional second-class citizenship of Palestinians inside Israel harms the essentially democratic features of Israel's regime. The precarious rights of Palestinians in Israel to organize politically and socially, and to participate in general elections, is for them the sum total of their rights under the "democracy."

Democracy in Israel "Proper"

Soon after its establishment, Israel set out to implement the main features of a Western liberal democracy on a formal level. These features consisted of multiple political parties, a representative parliament, free and universal elections, and an independent judicial system.[12] But what Israel failed to do—deliberately—was to apply the central concept of citizenship, the cornerstone of democracy. In democratic theory, "citizenship does not depend on ethnic, religious, or cultural origin. The affiliation of the individual to the state is direct and unmediated through any other identity or belonging."[13] Israel, however, functions in the opposite way.

Democracy in All Senses

Being the state of the entire Jewish people creates two different levels of citizenship for Jews and Palestinians, notes Azmi Bishara. "The right of a Jew to become an Israeli citizen is absolute because it is essential to their definition of being Jewish." Obviously this right is denied to Palestinians.

> Unlike the 'essential' citizenship given to Jews as affiliated with the Jewish people, Palestinian citizenship is "incidental," given to those who happened to remain in Israel after the 1948 Nakba. The existence of two kinds of citizenship based on ethnic-religious affiliation contradicts the principle of a universal, equal citizenship, the most basic element of a genuine liberal democracy. Israel's linking of ethnicity and citizenship highlights the lack of other characteristics of liberal democracy. This [lack] even makes the accidental citizenship granted to Palestinians something much less than it appears.[14]

As discussed in the introduction, the state of Israel did not, and does not, aspire to establish a nation of citizens. Nor does it recognize an Israeli nationality, let alone a separate Palestinian nationality. Arabs are categorized as a group of religions—Christians, Druze, Muslims, etc. Moreover, the hegemonic ideology that emphasizes and recognizes Jewish nationality alone (supported by the Zionist Left) denies Palestinians the ability to claim their own nationality as Palestinians and Arabs.

> They [Palestinian citizens] are still detained in a pre-national phase of development. And if you claim to be an Arab, you are a nationalist. If you want to take it a step further, and say we are not only pre-nationals, religions and tribes, there is a higher degree of organization of society called nation, nationality, and we are Palestinian Arabs, then you become, especially in the eyes of left-Zionists, a nationalist. Because to be a left-Zionist is not nationalism, to be a Zionist is no problem. But to be a Palestinian Arab is the problem. You can't be a democrat and a Palestinian Arab nationalist. This logic is adopted by the U.S. ideology in Iraq.[15]

This results in the systematic denial of Palestinian rights to freedom of expression and organization, and to equal participation in the Israeli political process. Since 2000, the state has increased its efforts to empty Palestinian citizenship of any substantial content, including stripping Palestinians of some fundamental citizenship rights. While this tendency has existed since Israel's inception, over the last decade it has found new impetus in the drive for "security." The worship of the state and its "security" supports a regime structure that gives the security establishment independence from the three governmental branches. The executive branch and especially the army have almost total authority in determining the definition of groups and activities that "endanger" the state of Israel, to the extent that "Israel is not a country with an army, but rather an army that has a state."[16] Despite the undemocratic nature of the state, which has been revealed in part by even mainstream scholars, members of the Zionist Left continue to miscategorize Israel's regime as essentially a democracy.

Second-Class Palestinian Citizenship Is Irrelevant

When discussing what type of democracy Israel represents, some of the most renowned scholars in the social sciences ignore the citizenship status of Palestinians and their marginalization in the Jewish state. Almost all of these scholars find Israel's regime comparable to other Western democratic nation-states, while avoiding its essence as a settler-colonial state. But ignoring this central fact makes any comparison between Israel and Western democratic nations dishonest.

The views of Zionist Left professors Moshe Lissak and Shlomo Avineri are emblematic of this disregard for Palestinian citizenship within Israel's political system. In an interview with *Haaretz* three days after the sweeping victory of Sharon and the extreme Right in the 2001 Knesset elections, Lissak expressed his concern for the deterioration of Israeli democracy due to the changes in power. However, Lissak failed to mention the impact of a deteriorated democracy on policies toward the Palestinian citizens of Israel (not to mention their impact on the '67 occupied territories).

Lissak likened the Israeli extreme Right to Jorg Haider's racist party in Austria. In Lissak's reading, both the Israeli and Austrian Right reject the basic principles of democracy. They support the strong rule of the executive authority, its alienation from the parliament and public opinion, and seek a semi-dictatorial regime. Nevertheless, the calamity that abolishing democratic institutions might inflict upon the Palestinian citizens of Israel is not mentioned. Lissak refers in passing to the "exclusion of entire groups which oppose it," his only nod toward the lot of Palestinians. Instead, Lissak is more concerned with how the extreme Right rejects the Zionist Left view that Israel can be both Jewish and democratic. "They also put Judaism above any criterion—on the account of democratic values, and are characterized by military militancy."[17] Shlomo Avineri argues that the nation-state of Israel is entirely similar to other Western liberal democracies "in which some of their symbols and laws represent the culture and interests of the dominant ethnic-national group." Their national hymns may include "motives which are not shared by part of the population, such as [the Israeli/Jewish national anthem] *Hatikva*, the British *God Save the Queen*, and the French *Marseillais* and many [of these

democratic nation-states] hold immigration laws which are similar to the Israeli Law of Return." Avineri continues:

> One can understand the difficulty that Israel's Arabs have in identifying with
> the blue and white flag with the Star of David on it. But on flags of many dem-
> ocratic states there is the sign of the cross: Switzerland, Denmark and Norway
> and of course, the double cross of England and Scotland on the British flag.
> Does this [fact] prevent a Jew who is a citizen of one of these states to swear
> loyalty to the flag? It is indeed difficult for him, because even in a democratic
> state it is difficult to be a minority. On this symbolic level, Israel's Arabs are in
> good company. In any case there is no democratic norm under which it is
> obliged to change the nature of a nation-state's symbols.[18]

In his efforts to compare Israel with other presumably exclusivist democracies, Avineri reduces the issue of national identity to one of symbols. Thus,
he ignores the fact that these symbols do not imply unequal citizenship of the
ethnic-national majority versus the minority, nor of granting prerogatives to
the former. But the very Jewish identity of Israel, and the Zionist aims it is
charged with implementing, expose discrimination against Palestinian citizens. Moreover, the Palestinian minority is a remnant of the indigenous residents who were expelled in 1948 and then marginalized in their homeland.

Avineri's self-proclaimed commitment to the principles of human rights and
democracy is misleading. In actuality, he adheres to Israel's hegemonic political
culture that places the state's security ahead of any other consideration, including
those of absolute human rights. Avineri joined with others in the Zionist peace
camp who expressed disappointment with the Oslo peace process after both the
2000 Camp David Summit failed and the second Intifada broke out in September 2000. Accepting then-Prime Minister Ehud Barak's characterization that
"there is no partner for peace," the Zionist Left helped to legitimize the whole-
sale war declared on Palestinians as part of the US "war against terror."

Based upon US practice in the wake of the 9/11 attacks, Avineri supported
the suspension of any rights that interfered with "defending democracy":

> When a democracy sets out to war, its public discourse changes. For instance,
> the issue of human rights. Since 11 September 2001, people in the United
> States have been in prison under administrative detention. Their names are not
> known. [Some] of them have no access to a lawyer and those who are permitted
> to meet with a lawyer, the court allows listening-in on them [by the FBI]. The
> American public does not take to the streets in order to defend these people.
> The Americans are also changing the immigration laws in a way which clearly
> goes against people of Muslim origin, and the public accepts it.[19]

Those on the Zionist Left who do not ignore discrimination against Palestinians, and even see it as built into the state, continue to characterize Israel as a democracy. As mentioned before, they consider the official rights granted to Palestinians in Israel, such as the right to politically and socially self-organize, and the right to participate in general elections and to be represented in the Knesset, as key elements in defining Israel as democracy.

Hence the wide consensus among Zionist Left intellectuals that freedom and autonomy for Palestinian citizens exist within the framework of the Jewish state, despite the dominance and prerogatives of the Jewish majority. However, they accept the misleading claim that formal civil and political rights granted to Palestinians mean that the inequality Palestinians face is no different than that experienced by members of ethnic minorities in other democratic nation-states.

"Ethnic Democracy"

Sociologist Sammy Smooha has analyzed known models of Western democracy and the extent to which they apply to Israel. He concludes that Israel does not fit any of them because the cornerstone of its being is not the citizen or the community of citizens but the ethnic-religious Jewish nation: "Israel declares and actually is the state of the Jewish people and not the state of its citizens." Smooha attributes the central feature of liberal democracy to the state's neutral approach to ethnic groups within it. The state treats the majority and minority similarly, thus creating one nation comprised by all its citizens. Theoretically, all its citizens are equal.[20] However, the lack of an available model of democracy that "accommodates" the admitted structural discrimination against Palestinian citizens does not prevent Smooha from concluding that Israel is not a democracy. Instead he defines the regime as an "Ethnic Democracy."[21]

Unlike a liberal democracy, an Ethnic Democracy is not a neutral state, and concentrates on maintaining and fortifying the rule of the majority group.

> The state of Israel explicitly declares that we are a tool in the service of the Zionist movement, for implementing its aims . . . In a liberal democracy there is full equality among all citizens. In an Ethnic Democracy, there is no such pretension. There are citizen rights, but there is no equality, but dominance. You cannot present Israel as the beautiful *Eretz Israel*, and at the same time put governance in the hands of the Jews so they can determine how to budget [state resources] and what will be the [state's] symbols. Nevertheless, the intellectuals and social scientists in Israel present the state of Israel as a full Western liberal model. They distort reality.[22]

Smooha epitomizes the Zionist Left's attempt to accept Israel as both Jewish and democratic. Ethnic Democracy is but another name for "Jewish democratic state":

> Within Ethnic Democracy exist two contradictory principles; [On the one hand] there are citizens who are granted citizenship and political rights without connection to their [ethnic] origin. On the other hand is the principle of dominance of Jewish governing. The essence and dynamics of this model is the contradiction between the principle of equal rights and the principle of dominance. If you say that Israel is not democratic you have cancelled this contradiction— "The Jews govern, they do what they want." [But] I say: This is not the case. There are restraints forced on Jews which are connected with the democratic rights granted to all citizens, including the Arabs of Israel.

Noting the democratic rights of freedom of opinion and organization granted to Palestinians, Smooha points out that since the 1970s, Palestinian citizens have established around 300 NGOs, including the Higher Follow Up Committee, which acts as the unofficial leadership of Palestinian citizens in Israel's civil society.[23] Smooha then asks: "Are they futile? A body decides on a general strike in the Arab sector. Isn't this an [indication of a] democratic state? And when they strike, do the authorities put them in jail?"[24]

Challenging Smooha's views, Azmi Bishara argues that the very depiction of Israel as an "Ethnic Democracy" accepts a notion that is the antithesis of democracy: "Since there is no liberal democratic model which can include within it the state of Israel, Professor Smooha turned Israel into a model. It is simply unbelievable. Here comes a scholar and turns what is happening in Israel into a model instead of suggesting a theory which criticizes this reality. You can't turn a unique case into theory."[25]

"The invention of this 'theoretical model,' adds Bishara, confers legitimacy onto Israel's undemocratic regime. 'Ethnic Democracy' is one of the models used to explain the existing situation between the Arab population and the state of Israel. Perhaps it is even the most developed among them and, therefore, the most dangerous. It perpetuates an existing reality and does not criticize it."

Republican Democracy

Tel Aviv University political scientist Yoav Peled made an attempt to develop a more coherent theoretical basis for forsaking the liberal democratic model as a criterion for evaluating Israel.[26] Since Peled, a self-professed "post-Zionist," is identified as inhabiting the most radical edge of liberal opinion, his discourse tellingly demonstrates how far even the most critical Leftist will go in formulating theories that obscure the nature of Israel as a settler-colonial state, to which theories on Western "nation-state" democracies don't apply. First, Peled's theoretical justification for the definition of Israel as a "republican democracy" is considered. This characterization belittles, and even whitewashes, the structural marginalization of the Palestinian citizenry.[27] And another theoretical bias common to Zionist Left academics, that the state of Israel is the embodiment of "modernity" and progress, is shown to merely enable the Zionist Left to violate Palestinian citizenship rights.[28]

In principle, Peled accepts Smooha's description of Israel as an "Ethnic Democracy." Unlike the majority of Israeli academics and legal scholars, he does not deny that the Jewish identity of the state prevents it from being a liberal democracy.

However, Peled challenges Smooha's conviction that the conceptualization of Israel's regime as an Ethnic Democracy can solve "the tension between two political commitments which prevailed already in the Declaration of Independence: the commitment to preserve the nature of Israel as a Jewish state and the commitment to democracy and equality before the law."

The dichotomy between liberal democracy and Ethnic Democracy is incapable of explaining the issue of citizenship in Israel. Instead, Peled characterizes Israeli political culture as a combination between three "constitutional principles or bases of legitimation": republicanism, liberalism, and ethno-nationalism. He thus adds a new category characterizing Israel as another variant of liberal democracy: a Republican Democracy—a "Republic for Jews and Democracy for Arabs."[29]

Of the three constitutional principles Peled enumerates, the dominant one is certainly the "republican principle," which grants moral preference to the common social good over individual rights. Its Israeli version includes both ethno-nationalist and liberal foundations. The power of the republican principle derives precisely from its ability to mediate between Jewish ethnic nationalism and the liberal-universal foundations of Zionism. "'Cutting' through these three constitutional principles," Peled argues, "has brought about in Israel the establishment of a republican democracy and not a liberal democracy. In this [brand of] democracy there are two types of citizenship: republican citizenship for Jews and liberal citizenship for Arabs. Thus, while both Jews and Arabs officially enjoy equal civil rights, only Jews can implement their citizenship in practice through participating in defining the common good. Nevertheless, the civil rights enjoyed by the Palestinian citizens don't lack [any] significance."[30]

Peled contends, during the years since the establishment of the state, the Palestinians' citizenship status has crystallized to the extent that, unlike the case of the Palestinians in the occupied territories who lack any rights, it enables them to implement their political aspirations within the existent legal framework.

Liberal citizenship, Peled believes, refers to a system of rights that are first and foremost designed to defend the private interests of its membership from being harmed by other individuals and, especially, by the state. Citizenship rights are essentially universal and equally granted to all citizens independent of ascribed ethnic, religious, family, or other affiliations. This definition of rights stems from the basic liberal assumption that society is composed of separate individuals who are, in essence, autonomous, rational, and equal. They group together only in order to advance their private matters.

Republican citizenship, on the other hand, is built on a philosophy of moral utilitarianism. A supreme value system that judges the "extent to which the citizens participate in creating the social good" characterizes republicanism. Minority groups, by definition, are excluded from creating the common good. Hence, they also lack the rights and social status that are granted to the participants in creating the common good, because the minority "cannot or do not want to participate in its creation."[31] Peled refers to the republican tradition as "a democratic tradition much older than the liberal tradition. Its recent revival in the form of the 'communitarian movement' in the U.S. provides a sharp counterpoint to liberal democracy."

Communitarian circles accuse liberal democratic societies of being morally inferior, as these societies favor the self-interest of the individual to the collective social well-being, or "collective good." However, they claim, human society is not primarily a mechanism to defend private interests, but it is a moral community with a common goal. "The existence of such a community is connected in an essential bond to the premise of the moral priority of the collective social good upon any private preferences."[32]

State-Centered Approach as "Democratic Republicanism"

The concept of the "common good," as applied to Israel, determines that identification with Zionist goals constitutes the criterion for the "civic virtue" that grants full membership in the Jewish community. The contribution to the "common good," which has been defined by the Zionist vision, forms the basis

for the evaluation of individuals and groups.[33] Palestinian citizens, by definition, cannot participate as a group in determining the common good of Israeli
"society" and cannot belong to the Jewish community. As such, they cannot
enjoy the benefits of "republicanism" and must suffice with "democracy." This
leaves them in a permanent state of "limited citizenship." Palestinians enjoy, at
least officially, equal democratic citizenship rights as individuals. These individual rights are supposedly sufficient in regard to their basic rights as human
beings and as citizens.

Peled does not mention the political and ideological factors that create the
conditions by which the minority "cannot or doesn't want" to participate in creating the "common good." This omission is in line with Peled's uncritical presentation of the discriminatory nature of "republicanism," and the republicans'
self-professed moral supremacy over liberalism. These euphemisms seek to blur
the unequivocal historical facts of the dispossessionist policies of Zionist settler
society, and the discrimination built into "republicanism for Jews" in the pre-
state period and thereafter.

The description of the aims and values of the Zionist colonial project, in
terms of a "common good," belittles how severe the denial of rights and benefits to Palestinian citizens is. "Their *a priori* removal from the political republican community does not mean the absolute denial of the citizenship of
Palestinians in Israel. The republican element which exists in the ethno-republican combination is a democratic element. It would not grant legitimacy
to the existence of a small, permanent population denied of rights within the
borders of the state."[34]

However, as previously discussed, the privileges enjoyed by those who "contribute to the collective aims" cannot be analyzed separately from the "democratic rights" granted to Palestinians. The very prerogatives of Jews are based on
the systematic oppression and marginalization of Palestinians, not just curtail-
ment of some of their rights.

This offhanded mention of the aims of Zionism in the context of "republicanism" places the Zionist Left narrative at the center of Peled's discussion. He
locates the Jewish community's "common good" in the supreme values of the
pre-state Yishuv. These collective goals consisted of: "Pioneering, reciprocal redemption of the nation of Israel and the land of Israel by means of physical
labor, agriculture settlement and self-defense."[35] However, Peled fails to mention
that these goals were euphemisms used to describe to the Zionist missions of
colonizing the land, adopted by the Zionist Labor movement in their ideology

and praxis of dispossession. Using the concept of "common good" to describe the hegemonic, state-centered political culture of Israel, replacing the "pioneering" value system of the Yishuv, is misleading. Peled presents the moral subservience of the individual's rights to the Zionist collective goals without noting the fascist nature of this value system.

In adopting this analysis, Peled joins mainstream sociology in Israel, whose founders, headed by the world-famous Professor S. N. Eisenstadt of Hebrew University, were committed to the ideology of the Zionist Labor movement and the state as the embodiment of Zionism. This school of thought adopted the structural-functionalist paradigm that was elaborated upon by the late renowned American sociologist Talcott Parsons. Although it incorporated reforms over the years, this school prevailed until the appearance of the "critical sociologists" in the late 1980s and early 1990s.[36]

According to Parsons's early theory,[37] society is a "system" characterized by cultural-ideological integration and a functional-structural division of roles and statuses, which act to preserve the existence of the system itself within an environment external to it. This theoretical framework suited the state-centered orientation of Labor-influenced mainstream sociology. Mainstream sociology saw in the Zionist state the embodiment of the "collective" orientations and goals of Jewish society, the commitment to which overrode any "individual" value or interest.

Underlying the perspective of "the supremacy of collective goals," adopted by mainstream sociology until the early 1980s, is the assumption that the state's ideology and policies are but the expression of the common will of its entire Jewish-Zionist citizenry. This perspective ignores class or other social conflicts, as well as the related forces that determine who will rule the state and the nature of its regime. Mainstream sociologists who supported the Zionist Labor movement thus conferred legitimacy on the state-centered, semi-fascist approach that has prevailed in Israeli political culture. There, "the primacy of the liberal principle of the individual upon the collective good had a weak anchor."[38]

Generations of sociology students were educated to see the moral superiority of Israeli society in which "collective" values and goals top the ladder, rather than the "instrumental" values of "personal achievements," which are encouraged in the United States. Eisenstadt's famous course on Israeli society in the 1950s did not include any reference to the Palestinians who were then under military rule and had lost 75 percent of their land by confiscation. The class thus initiated and propagated the analytical approach that portrays Palestinians as "external to the social system," which has been defined as exclusively Jewish (see chapter 7). By the same token, there was no attempt to deal with the concepts of "collective" goals and "instrumental" goals as they related to the essence of liberal democracy. Nor did Eisenstadt elaborate on any of the negative consequences of favoring the supremacy of "collective values" over the notions of individual autonomy and the universal application of human rights.[39]

A Permanent Limited Citizenship

Peled's discussion of the 1950 Law of Return reveals his acceptance of the cornerstone of the "republican democracy" of the Jewish state. He attributes the "republican" interpretation of the Law of Return to Israeli Prime Minister David Ben-Gurion. "Ben-Gurion's argument that the state of Israel is committed to implementing the primordial right of Jews to return to their homeland—a right from which the state draws the very meaning for its existence—is a typical republican argument which contradicts principles of liberalism."[40]

This law, however, as Azmi Bishara points out, deviates from any modern nation-state citizenship, let alone a democratic citizenship.

Though Peled acknowledges the "republican" Law of Return as contradictory to principles of liberalism, he does not directly confront its (im)moral essence. Like his other colleagues on the Zionist Left, he prefers to deal with the Law of Return in the context of "immigration laws," claiming that it is comparable in part to other immigration laws in Western nation-states.[41] Peled does not disclose his own judgment, however. Instead, he relies on the positions of liberals in other countries: "The liberals indeed recognize the right of a community to design its cultural image or constitute a sanctuary for its ethnic relatives since if not, only few immigrant laws would receive legitimacy from a liberal perspective." Peled summarizes his discussion of this fundamental law by emphasizing his "neutral" stance: "Ben-Gurion's argument regarding the moral commitment of the state to advance a common good which precedes its very existence—which justifies making distinction between the rights of different groups of citizens—cannot be acceptable by liberal political theory but is absolutely an acceptable argument from a republican perspective."[42]

But, as emphasized before, this comparison between the Law of Return and other immigration laws is misleading. Underlying it is the fallacious position that Palestinian citizens are immigrants. This is wholly incorrect, as Palestinians are the indigenous residents of the land. Furthermore, in democratic states immigration laws do not condition the right to immigrate and qualify for citizenship on religious/ethnic criteria, as does the Law of Return.

To these misleading comparisons, reflecting his inclination to downplay the inherent discrimination in excluding Palestinian citizens from participating in the "common good" of the "ethno-republican" political culture, Peled adds a rather peculiar comparison. Namely, comparing the situation of Palestinian citizens of Israel to that of their brethren in the '67 occupied territories. He claims that, while the 1967 Palestinians have no rights, the Palestinian citizens of Israel enjoy secondary, "like liberal" (*kemo*) citizenship status alongside the "central political community." Peled's description of this deformed citizenship is nothing less than sarcastic:

> One can describe graphically the supremacy of the ethno-republican principle for defining the citizenship status of the Palestinian citizens over the liberal and ethno-nationalistic ones, as building a defensive wall around the Palestinian citizens in Israel. This wall separates the Palestinian citizens both from the Jewish citizens, who can participate in designing the common good, and the Palestinians in the occupied territories who are denied citizenship, who lack even elementary human and civil rights. Within the boundaries of the wall, the Palestinian citizens in Israel can safely enjoy (at least officially) liberal citizen rights; but they are forbidden to challenge the very existence of the wall.[43]

But accepting the "wall" means renouncing their national identity. This includes their history, the Nakba, and their separation from the rest of their people. As a result, the "liberal" rights they have in Peled's reading are emptied of any real meaning.

By 2006, however, Peled abandoned his blurry analysis for more explicit terms. Like other "post-Zionists" he began to support a Jewish state that would retain "free access to Jewish immigration and to land—as a condition for resolution of the conflict."[44]

Ethnocracy

Peled's and Gershon Shafir's 2005 book *Who Is Israeli?*[45] morally rejects Israel's built-in discrimination against Palestinian citizens, and refrains from unequivocally categorizing Israel as a variant of democracy. The authors elaborate on the specific brand of Israel's democracy. They emphasize that Israel is a state with characteristics of a democratic regime but with different kinds of citizenship granted to different social sectors. Each sector is interpreted and supported by three distinct discourses on citizenship: the republican (identified mainly with the Zionist Labor movement and the Zionist Left until the 1970s); the ethno-nationalist (identified mainly with religious and secular members of the "nationalist camp"); and the liberal (which, since the 1970s, has been identified in part with the Likud, the Labor movement, and the Zionist Left).

Although admitting that the colonial settlement pattern was never forsaken, the authors argue that this pattern existed alongside a fragmented process of liberalization. These two processes and the separate citizenship discourse that developed within them—ethno-national and republican-colonial on the one hand, and civilian-liberal on the other—have been in continual competition. At different historical stages, each received a different political expression. Since 2000, however, the political regime of Israel has changed into an "ethnocracy," a concept first proposed by Oren Yiftachel, a professor of political geography at Ben-Gurion University of the Negev.[46]

Although opposing attempts to define Israel as a democracy, Yiftachel's analysis remains within the conceptual framework that sees "ethnic groups" as central actors. This viewpoint obscures the true colonial nature of Israel's regime. That is, Yiftachel prefers to see in Israel an "ethnic" majority and minority, rather than a colonizing majority that aspires to eliminate both the national identity and struggle of the indigenous Palestinians.

Yiftachel suggests that formal democratic characteristics of Israel cloak an ethnocratic body. That is to say, Israel is a regime in which governing is concentrated within one ethnic group, and not in the hands of the *demos,* the entire citizenry, as is required by a genuine democracy. The ethnocratic regime in Israel is designated to ensure and fortify the Jewish majority by dispossessing the Palestinian minority of more and more resources, especially land. Hence, unlike Peled, Yiftachel determines that the ethnocratic project has existed since the onset of the Zionist enterprise, despite changes that took place in forms of governing regarding Palestinians on both sides of the Green Line. These changes, however, have only been variations to Israel's fundamental ethnocratic structure, which has remained the only permanent category of Israel's regime.

Peled's inclination to refrain from depicting Labor Zionism as the creator of both the state and its hegemonic, semi-fascist ideology is repeated here as well as in his later works. He avoids attributing responsibility for Israel's ethnocracy under Labor governments who ruled until 1977. Also, he claims it was the right-wing government, headed by Sharon in 2001, that introduced a new approach of marginalizing Palestinian citizens and limited the democratic defenses the preceding Labor regime had provided for them.[47] The silence about the atrocities committed by Labor governments on both sides of the Green Line, and later,

Labor's support for and participation in right-wing governments, is in line with the role played by Zionist Left intellectuals. They serve to manufacture consent around the Zionist Labor movement's most appalling policies.

"The Modern Enlightened State of Israel" vs. the "Traditional" Palestinian Minority

In regard to Palestinian citizen eligibility for cultural, let alone political, autonomy, Yoav Peled wrote an article with J. Bruner of Tel Aviv University School of Law.[48] The piece continues the trend of applying theoretical debates over Western democracies to the case of Israel, while at the same time ignoring Israel's distinct nature as a settler colonial state. Peled and Bruner's article deals with the rights of states to intervene in the ethnic minorities' ways of life, as seen through the lens of the educational autonomy of the Palestinian citizens in Israel. The authors accept Israel's authority to deny Palestinian citizens even minimal cultural autonomy if the Palestinians' "traditional way of life and values" blocks prospects for Palestinian students to succeed economically and socially in a modern state like Israel.

Bruner and Peled's conclusion is contradictory to political philosopher Will Kymlicka's unequivocal support for the implementation of collective rights of an indigenous group in a liberal democratic state.[49] Kymlicka believes that these rights, which include autonomy over most aspects of life, are absolute and not conditioned upon the liberal state's assessment of the progressiveness or liberalism of the minority community's culture. Furthermore, Kymlicka differentiates between indigenous minority groups and groups of immigrants or other minority groups, regarding the state's role in defending culture and traditional ways of life. Kymlicka argues that, for immigrants who willingly left their country and intend to integrate into a new culture, their new states of residence are obliged to provide only a minimal defense of their culture. On the other hand, homeland minority groups have absolute rights that oblige the state to defend them, even if it implies issuing rules that limit the freedom of contracts and movement of the governing majority.[50] Among the collective rights of national minorities, Kymlicka includes the rights to self-govern and to veto any legislation that addresses the essential interests of the indigenous residents.[51]

In contrast, Bruner and Peled argue for the need to limit the state's defense of "non-liberal cultures of ethnic minorities." According to the authors' conception, these cultures "do not allow for the autonomy of the individual" and do not "prepare the individual to cope with the demands of modern life. [Instead, these cultures] insert forms of understandings and positions which alienate them [ethnic minorities] from the society around them, thus leaving their members weak in terms of their capacity for autonomy."[52] Two other liberal Hebrew University philosophers, Avishai Margalit (founder of Peace Now) and Moshe Halbertal, join with Peled and Bruner. They stress that it is the obligation of the modern liberal state to deny eligibility of "rights in the public space" for ethnic minorities with "non liberal" cultures ("particularistic cultures") and traditional social structures "which lack the capability to strengthen the personal autonomy or liberties of the individual."[53]

In this analysis, under the misleading Orientalist equating of modernism with liberalism, and of traditionalism with authoritarianism, Western democracies are thus granted legitimacy to discriminate against their non-Western minorities. In essence, they argue that non-European minorities may not have the capability to implement the "enlightened" values and norms that the authors attribute to the states in which they reside. Non-Western minorities are thus assumed to be limited in their capacity "to strengthen the autonomy or liberation of the individual,"[54] ignoring the fact that it is often precisely those "liberal" states, representing the interests of the majority group, that strip the minority of these capabilities. This paternalistic approach regarding the culture of national and ethnic minorities dangerously approaches the moral "slippery slope" down which, political theorist Isaiah Berlin warned, authoritarianism and oppression can result. Despite the good intentions of liberals, Berlin warned, such an approach has the potential to turn the concept of liberty into an idea that permits oppression and violence.[55]

Berlin's warning was substantiated by Bruner and Peled's approach to Arab autonomy in Israeli schools. The authors choose this issue to demonstrate the negative influence that cultural autonomy may have upon the "capabilities" of Palestinians to integrate into the "modern life" of Israeli society.[56] They even criticize the "limited autonomy" enjoyed by Palestinian citizens, and particularly what they consider its most important aspect: "the fact that Palestinian children learn in separate state schools in Arabic up until the end of high school." They claim that the students' insufficient mastery of Hebrew diminishes the prospects for "their social and economic success, as indicated in the fact that only 50 percent of them are employed in the Jewish labor market."[57] The authors acknowledge, however, that although the language issue is an important reason, it is not the only one that accounts for the meager social and economic achievements of Palestinians in Israel.

The absurdity of attributing the marginal social and economic status of Palestinians to their poor Hebrew, even if it is admittedly not the only reason, cannot be understated. The systematic Zionist policies of derailing the Palestinian economy, and the official and unofficial exclusion of Palestinians from the Jewish public and private sectors, make the mastery of Hebrew entirely irrelevant (particularly in light of the fact that Arabic is considered an official language of Israel). Moreover, Bruner and Peled overlook the ongoing campaign of the Palestinians demanding full autonomy from the ministry of education. Since the first years of the state, the ministry enforced the inclusion of Jewish and Zionist subjects into the curriculum, while excluding Palestinian national collective memory and their national and cultural identity. But acknowledging these policies would have compelled the authors to question their implied trust in the state's education system.

In so doing, they ignore the political and ideological context of the recent demand of Palestinian citizens, to establish a Palestinian Council that can replace the current educational system. Bruner and Peled paternalistically argue that it is doubtful if such a council would bring the required change to the present situation. "Still one may wonder if this Palestinian Council [if established] would empower the teaching of Hebrew at the expense of Arabic."[58]

The slide down the "slippery slope" toward explicitly supporting policies of "oppression and violence," in accordance with Isaiah Berlin's warning, is not too far away from Peled and Bruner's analysis. They continue by arguing that, in certain cases, those who adopt the democratic, multicultural approach are compelled to eliminate the presumed educational autonomy of Palestinians. They clarify:

> If the Palestinians acquire sufficient command of the richness of Arabic language and culture, but suffer from inability to socially and economically function and integrate within the society around them; and if it becomes clear that this imbalance can be offset by the state taking over their schools; then any self-described democratic, multicultural individual [themselves included] should support a return to full state control over the Arab-Palestinian school system. This must however be carried out on the condition that their "Arab character" be preserved as much as possible, without damage to the development of replaceable occupational and cultural capabilities.[59]

A careful but critical reading of these intellectuals leads one to a state of disbelief, to say the least. The Jewish-Zionist state is assumed to be the bearer of "progress" and is entrusted with the legitimacy to determine whether Palestinian citizens should be stripped of the meager autonomy they hold today. The fact of the matter is, the supposed "particularistic"[60] culture of Palestinian citizens does not "fit" into the state of Israel, where citizenship is based on the most particularistic criterion: belonging to the Jewish people as determined by the Halacha. Moreover, the fact that every sector of Palestinian life, including the education system, is subject to the control of Israeli security services does not dissuade these intellectuals from portraying Israel as a "modern," "universalistic" state.

CHAPTER 6

Post-Zionism—a Failed Departure from Zionist Left Discourse

This chapter is an introduction to chapters 7 and 8, which deal with a wide variety of critical "post-Zionism" writings that emerged around the end of the 1980s. These writings challenged some of Zionism's hegemonic narratives inscribed in the Israeli collective identity. The narratives primarily represent the established version of Israeli history regarding the Zionist colonization of Palestine, the circumstances that led to the 1948 Nakba, the construction of the state of Israel, the state's claim to be both Jewish and democratic, and the state's policies toward the Palestinian people. For decades these narratives were cultivated by historians and social scientists in the academy and intellectuals outside of it, many of whom identified with the Zionist Left. The post-Zionist writings also disclosed the mechanisms the political and intellectual elites used to silence any dissidence in Israeli discourse on both the levels of theory and of empirical research.

Post-Zionism, however, has failed to bring about a change in the overall commitment of Zionist Left intellectuals to the premises of Zionism and to the leading themes of its history. Previous chapters have explored the Zionist Left's attempts to justify the "Jewish democratic state." Most of the analysis and polemics presented in those chapters took place after post-Zionists began to publish their works, signifying a fissure in the dominant Zionist doctrine. The majority of Zionist Left intellectuals continued to articulate the ideological, scientific, and moral legitimation of the "left" brand of the Zionist project while ignoring the new evidence and analysis supplied by post-Zionists. Moreover, many of them joined the widespread condemnation and accusations against the emerging tide of criticism. Very few bothered to base their attacks on solid theoretical grounds or to use methodical arguments against post-Zionism.

The upcoming chapters attempt to disclose the main themes of post-Zionism that were perceived as threats to the essence of the individual and collective identity of the Zionist Left. The chapters also discuss the Zionist Left's forceful attack on post-Zionism, and how they closed ranks around a strengthened commitment to the Jewish-Zionist state. Both post-Zionist challenges and the violent reaction to them are rooted in the multifaceted social and political circumstances.

The Sociopolitical Background of Post-Zionism's Emergence in the Late 1980s

A combination of factors created, directly and indirectly, the relatively liberal atmosphere that permitted deviation from the dominant narratives.

The first was the long process that unfolded after the electoral upheaval of 1977. After decades of comprehensive Labor Party rule over the Zionist Movement and state, the right-wing Likud Party, headed by Menachem Begin, came into power. This change disrupted the traditional relationship between left intellectuals and the state. For the first time, the overlap between their central role in articulating the hegemonic discourse on Zionism and its history and their legitimation of current state policies under Labor governments had dissolved. Begin's approach to the Palestinians, while not essentially different from those adopted by Labor, could now be criticized more freely. This in itself created the first cracks in the academic community's conformism. Many Zionist Left intellectuals joined the protest movement against the 1982 right-wing government's assault in the Lebanon war, albeit at a later stage. The protest movement against the bloody assault in Lebanon and the mass killing of the Lebanese population was led from the beginning by radical groups in the Israeli "peace camp": the Committee for Solidarity with Bir Zeit University and the Committee Against the War in Lebanon. The Zionist Left headed by Peace Now joined the protest movement only after the September 16–18 massacre in the refugee camps of Sabra and Shatila.[1] The assault on Lebanon was an attempt to do away with the PLO and Palestinian refugees and to establish a collaborationist pro-Israeli government in Lebanon. The Zionist Left grew more and more opposed despite the fact that collaboration between Israel and the fascist Lebanese Phalange Party, whose militia soldiers committed the aforementioned massacre, was initiated long before by the Labor Party security establishment. Besides the Lebanon war, escalating oppression in the '67 occupied territories, and growing resistance that led eventually to the first Intifada in 1987, demonstrated for some Zionist Left intellectuals the futility of their trust in an "enlightened occupation." The Intifada shattered the illusion that the occupation was external to Israel's "social system" and "democratic" political regime. A number of Zionist Left intellectuals gradually came to recognize the Israeli-Palestinian conflict as central to Israeli history and the formation of Israeli society.

The first young scholars who defied the prevailing theoretical/ideological approach in the academy were not graduates of Israeli universities; they were students who had completed their advanced studies in universities abroad. Furthermore, they did not experience the 1948 war as most of the older generation had. On both the personal and ideological level, they were relatively free of the glorification of 1948 as the creator of the Jewish people's "national resurrection." While studying abroad, they became familiar with a variety of postmodernist cultural and theoretical trends that broke away from traditional national ideology, like variations on the "politics of identity." These post-nationalist schools of thought had an impact on the emerging critiques of the official Israeli/Zionist historiography. A "secularization" of this historiography began to set in.[2]

Scholars who have studied post-Zionism[3] tend to attribute its emergence to the prospects of peace with the Arab states and the Palestinians. Beginning with the 1979 Egypt–Israel Peace Treaty, an atmosphere of compromise eventually led to the 1991 Madrid conference, the 1993–95 Oslo Accords, and the "peace process" that lasted until 2000. It is assumed that these events reduced the pressure for "security" in Israeli society, permitting a liberalization process that later allowed for challenges against the establishment's body of knowledge.

However, we must recall that these peace processes did not encourage the acceptance of Palestinian national rights. As a result, they had limited impact on changing the Israeli political regime and culture. The Oslo Accords were the product of US-Israeli dictates and allowed both the continued building of settlements and the reinforcement of Israel's control of the '67 occupied territories. In fact, a dispute over the '67 occupied territories led to a halt in the "peace process" in 2000.[4] Israel's continued expansionist colonialism perpetuated the hegemony of "statism" and the supremacy of "state security" over human rights in general, especially Palestinian rights. The Zionist Left's attack on "post-Zionism" stemmed from its commitment to the prevailing semi-fascist political culture.

The opening of archives and other classified files in Britain, the United States, and Israel at the end of the 1970s revealed documents on the 1948 war. The establishment academy ignored most of the documents, but for critical historians and social scientists, these archives supplied solid evidence for their research. The works of these critical scholars have confirmed some of the arguments and analysis made by Matzpen, the socialist organization in Israel, whose clear voice has been ignored until the present by the majority of academics and intellectuals.

Matzpen has consistently identified Zionism as a settler-colonial project that has impacted all levels of Israel's state and society. Contrary to all streams of the Zionist Left and post-Zionists, Matzpen has adopted a distinctive regional perspective that places the root cause of the conflict (and its ultimate resolution) outside the "Palestine box." Namely, Israel, created and supported by Westen imperialism, is the problem. Hence, the resolution of the conflict is contingent on the collapse of Western imperialism in the Middle East and, subsequently, the democratic transformation of the Arab world.

Some of the post-Zionists have partially adopted Matzpen's insights regarding the colonial nature of Zionism and the state of Israel. However, by taking them out of the context of Matzpen's regionalist perspective—including its anti-imperialist and class analysis—and placing them under the rubric of post-colonial identity politics, the post-Zionists have entirely distorted Matzpen's approach.[5]

Matzpen—a Systematic Rejection of Zionism

Matzpen was founded in 1962 by a group of about fifteen people, four of whom were expelled from the Israeli Communist Party (MAKI): Moshé Machover, Akiva Orr, Oded Pilavsky, and Yrmiyahu Kaplan.[6]

In 1964 Matzpen was joined by a group of people, some of them Palestinian Arabs who had abandoned or been expelled from MAKI (among them was Jabra Nicola—a Palestinian Marxist). Their joining was based on common principles: "Rejection of Zionism, an unequivocal reliance on the basis of revolutionary socialism, opposition to the Soviet Union cult and its implied ideological and political conclusions, an absolute negation of Stalinism, support of truly international solidarity, support of the integration of Israel in a future Arab Socialist Unity which would be based on recognition of the right to self determination."[7]

In the next few years Matzpen developed a consistent anti-Zionist approach, which made it the first distinctly Israeli organization to explicitly reject Zionism on the grounds that it was a settler colonial project enmeshed within the state of Israel. However, while other settler colonial states ended the colonization process once they'd taken over the territory and subdued the indigenous population, this was not the case of Israel. As Matzpen's founder Moshé Machover notes, "Israel is not only a product of the Zionist colonization but also an instrument for its further extension and expansion . . . . Colonization continued between 1948 and 1967 in the territory ruled then by Israel, within the Green Line. Lands belonging to Palestinian Arabs—including those who remained within the Green Line—were expropriated and given over to Zionist colonization. Soon after the 1967 war, colonization continued in the newly occupied territories under all governments: Labor-led, Likud-led, and grand coalition governments [of both parties]."[8] Moreover, "Zionism is the actual implementation of colonization by the Jews of all areas of the Land of Israel. Hence any partition of Palestine, any 'green line,' any accord or treaty that shuts off any part whatsoever of the 'Land of Israel' to Jewish colonization, is, from the viewpoint of Zionism, at best, a transient accommodation—accepted temporarily for tactical or pragmatic reasons, but never regarded as final."

Popular Arab solidarity with the Palestinian cause, and its resistance to US-Israeli policies and their corrupt regimes, necessitated, and will continue to necessitate, the expansion of Israel into neighboring territories. The purpose of this expansion is for Israel to defend its occupations, which in turn requires additional occupations to defend the previous ones. This expansionist drive engenders other forms of domination throughout the Middle East, and is part of the Western imperialist strategy for economically and politically controlling the region.

Matzpen's understanding of Zionism as a settler-colonial enterprise was studied through the prism of the founders' revolutionary, Marxist, anti-imperialist, and class analysis. According to this perspective, Zionism was designed from its onset to be both an outpost of Western imperialism in the Middle East and the most reliable enforcer of Western interests in the region—first those of Great Britain, later France, and since the mid 1970s those of the United States. Most significantly, Israel has helped to eliminate political forces that have threatened the West. This includes secular Arab pan-nationalism, which has yet to recover from its defeat in 1967. Since then, Israel has sought to crush any buds of mass resistance, secular or religious, which aspire to overthrow imperialism, Zionism, and the dictatorial Arab regimes.

Matzpen has linked the struggle for the liberation of Palestine with the larger struggle for the liberation of the entire "Arab East," which is dominated

by imperialism and Western-favored Arab rulers and regimes. Zionism's determination to crush the Palestinian national struggle and to subdue the Palestinian
people is aligned with the comprehensive imperial strategy for sustaining regional rule.

The expulsion of the Palestinians was Zionism's main goal from the outset.
All settler colonial projects, writes Machover, involve the dispossession of indigenous people and brutal measures to suppress resistance. But the projects
differ, broadly speaking, in terms of whether the colonizers exploit the indigenous population as a labor force, or whether the indigenous population is to be
excluded from the settlers' economy, exterminated, or expelled.

For example, as mentioned earlier, South African Apartheid was based on
white settler exploitation of the colonized Black majority's vital labor power.
Black workers remained part of the economy while being denied civil rights.
Alternatively, in North America's colonialist history, the indigenous "Indian"
population was to be exterminated. The Israeli economy, however, from the inception of Zionist colonization, was not dependent on Palestinian labor in the
same way that South Africa's capitalist mining and industry needed Black
African labor. Hence, "Zionism deliberately, consciously and explicitly chose
the colonialist model of North America. Use of indigenous labor power was to
be avoided. The Palestinian Arabs were not regarded as a useful exploitable
source of surplus labor. They were to be ethnically cleansed or—in Zionist parlance—'transferred.'" On the whole, Machover concludes, "Zionism and Israel
adhered to this model of minimizing reliance on Palestinian labor, with only a
partial and brief deviation in the 1970s and 80s." The completion of the 1948
mass expulsion had to be delayed for the right circumstances, such as a regional
war or any provocative actions taken by Israel, which could be used to garner
the support of the international community.

As a settler colonial project sustained and consolidated by Western imperialism, Zionism is "the specific form of capitalist rule in Israel."[9] Matzpen rediscovered the position of the Palestine Communist Party (PCP) in its early years
regarding the false "socialism" and "Marxism" that the Zionist Labor movement
and the Histadrut used to disguise themselves in the pre-state period. Matzpen
pointed out how the Zionist Labor movement, in the service of both Zionist colonization and the interests of the nascent capitalist class, helped to prevent the
empowerment of Jewish workers. Matzpen also emphasized that, since the establishment of the state, Zionist Left governmental and Histadrut policies sustained and fortified the developing capitalist class in Israel. Matzpen unmasked

Zionist Labor's false claims that the Histadrut represents the interests of Jewish workers. Palestinian workers were never on the agenda (see introduction).

Three decades after Matzpen had clarified its perspective of the Zionist Left and the Histadrut, Zeev Sternhell elaborated on the nature of Zionist labor "socialism" in the pre-state period. As discussed in the introduction, Sternhell depicted the ideology of "Constructive Socialism," created by the Zionist Labor movement as the local version of National-Socialism—which retained the main tenets of organic nationalism within a "socialist" framework. "Constructive Socialism" called for Zionist labor and the bourgeoisie to collaborate in the Zionist colonization project—that is, to join efforts in establishing the exclusive Jewish state. Sternhell studied the role played by the Histadrut, how they enlisted Jewish workers in the colonization project while putting aside their socioeconomic interests. Sternhell, however, refrained from incorporating an imperialist-capitalist argument into the context of his analysis.

Matzpen's original analysis—linking Zionism, imperialism, and the construction of a capitalist Jewish state—has been mostly left alone by Israeli Left intellectuals. It was Adam Hanieh, a Marxist political economist currently at the School of Oriental and African Studies (SOAS) who elaborated on this link, basing his analysis on economic research. He studied Zionism's capitalist dimension and its increased role in the political-economic agenda of US imperialism in the region. First Hanieh concentrated on the Histadrut's role in developing Israel's economy as it shifted toward neoliberalism in the mid-1990s. A Labor government, in cooperation with the Histadrut and following IMF "advice" introduced neoliberalism onto the political and economic scene in Israel.[10] The shift destroyed features like welfare and what remained of organized worker power in Israel. The policies of privatization and of transferring resources to the business sector gave rise to private capital independence from the state and its influence. The Israeli economy thus abandoned the old system in which the state sheltered and promoted capital accumulation within big conglomerates that had originated in the pre-state colonization period (and that had been linked to the Zionist Labor movement). The new "free market" economy and the consolidation of the independent capitalist class formed the last stage in the long process through which the traditional pro-capitalist approach of Zionist Labor was openly revealed.

This course of action inside Israel has complemented the US imperialist strategy. While trying to control access to the Middle East's oil resources, the United States has pursued a policy of integrating its regional bases within a single neoliberal economic zone. This has been accomplished over the last two decades through a series of bilateral trade agreements tied to the United States. Hence, Israeli-US peace plans since Oslo, initiated by the Zionist Left, have tried to stabilize the area. These efforts become even more significant in light of Israeli capital's central role in the regional neoliberal project.[11]

Matzpen's emphasis on the tripartite connection of Zionism, capitalism, and imperialism made clear that no socioeconomic struggle can succeed without a fight to abolish Israel's Zionist essence. Consequently, the daily resistance of Palestinian citizens against their national oppression, as well as solidarity with anti-imperialist movements throughout the Arab world, are critical in this context. Of course, the Zionist Left in Israel has never adopted this position, ever captive to Zionist hegemony.

Matzpen, a pioneer in the movement against the 1967 war and occupation, repeatedly applied its political principles to the roots of the conflict and its solution.

On June 8, 1967, three days after Israel opened war against Egypt, a joint Arab-Israeli declaration on the Middle East crisis was published in the *London Times* and signed by the representatives of the Democratic Front for the Liberation of Palestine and Matzpen. The declaration, which was written and signed on the eve of the war, details the conditions for a desirable solution to the conflict. "The abolition of the Zionist character of Israel, the return of the refugees to the territory of Israel; an Israeli agreement for the establishment of a Palestinian state, if the Palestinians choose it and [Israel's] readiness for territorial concessions for it [the Palestinian state]. The new non-Zionist Israel would strive to integrate the Israelis and Palestinians in a federal and socialist, non-national state, which participates in the process of the political and economic unification of the Middle East."

Matzpen's analysis has not been adopted by Israeli masses. The power of the Histadrut, backed by the state and the capitalist class, has prevented the emergence of any genuine Left that could develop an independent working-class movement, much less engage in solidarity with the Palestinians in their fight against structural discrimination and marginalization. The hegemonic state-centered political culture, nourished by Zionist Left intellectuals, has been an efficient tool in blocking these developments.

The overlap of ethnic origin and socioeconomic class in Israel—where Mizrahim occupy the bottom of the socioeconomic ladder of Jewish society (albeit above the Palestinian citizens)—bolstered these trends. Contrary to Matzpen's depiction of the oppression of Mizrahim in terms of class, the prevailing discourse about the nature of Mizrahi oppression and expressions of their resistance have been infused with cultural identity rhetoric.[12] As we shall see in chapter 8, postmodern post-Zionists contributed to this by burying the prospects for class analysis in the realms of identity politics. Post-Zionist analysis also impeded a full understanding of the national oppression and resistance of Palestinian citizens, thus diminishing what they appeared to learn from the Matzpen publications.

"Post-Zionism": The Meaning of the Concept

The meaning of post-Zionism, as used in political-intellectual discourse in Israel, is not clear cut. Post-Zionist adherents have different positions on Zionist colonialism, colonialism's embodiment in the Jewish state, and the dispossession of Palestinians, both before and after 1967. This disparity leaves the concept without clear boundaries. Consequently, categorizing what can be classified as "post-Zionism," and which scholars qualify as "post-Zionist," is difficult. Critics of post-Zionism thus group a wide range of authors together, almost all of whom are accused of violating two central principles of Zionism: conceptualizing Zionism as a colonialist project rather than as a national movement; and challenging the Jewish definition of the state. These are lines that the majority of the Zionist Left does not cross.

Because of the Zionist Left's ubiquitous critique and the imprecise definition of post-Zionism, virtually any critical writing may be labeled as de-legitimizing Zionism and the Jewish state. Consequently, post-Zionist authors are accused of deserting Israel as it struggles for survival. Some of these authors are called "traitors." Historian Amnon Raz-Krakotzkin of Ben-Gurion University (who claims that he is wrongly considered post-Zionist) notes: "'Post-Zionism' is in fact a kind of a general title invented in order to place in one basket, and for the purpose of general condemnation, anyone who does not identify entirely with the establishment, or has critical thoughts about the way history [in Israel] is taught, or who also sees the large damage Zionism has inflicted upon Palestinians or Mizrahim."[13] Tel Aviv University sociologist Yehouda Shenhav, who spearheaded the post-Zionist, multicultural, and post-colonial approach in the journal *Theory and Criticism*, calls post-Zionism "an empty label." "I think," he says, "that the category 'post-Zionism' should not be used anymore, because people use it in a confusing way."[14]

Even attempts to limit post-Zionism to those who recognize the wrongs Israel has inflicted on the Palestinians since the 1967 occupation leaves the concept unclear.

For who among these scholars and which of their studies actually qualify as a challenge to Zionism and the Jewish state? At issue, then, is whether post-Zionist ideology can oppose the continued 1967 occupation and still adhere to the basic premises of Zionism. As discussed in chapter 2, a rather common inclination among Zionist Left intellectuals is to differentiate between the 1967 occupation, which they condemn, and the actions of the Zionist movement in the pre-state and 1948 periods, which they legitimize.[15] Thus Shenhav rightly determines, "Not all who call for the end of occupation are necessarily post-Zionist. Whoever wants to give back the 1967 occupied lands may be a par excellence Zionist because [the reason for making such concessions is] his conviction that nationalism cannot exist without borders."[16]

Nevertheless, throughout the 1990s and in the first decade of the twenty-first century, Zionist Left intellectuals continued their unrelenting battle against an unidentified group of "post-Zionists." Their role as "guardians of the walls" of Zionism has become even more urgent with the collapse of the Oslo process and their realization that no peace settlement is on the agenda. Hence, the issue of the colonial/national essence of Zionism continues to be a central concern to the Zionist Left.

Political scientist Shlomo Avineri's 2007 attack on the post-Zionists is typical. Avineri depicts post-Zionism as disguised anti-Zionism of "the old brand":

> In recent years a phenomenon called "post-Zionism" has developed in the political-intellectual discourse in Israel. Fundamentally, this is a radical criticism not just of Israel's policy. At its base is a total denial of the Zionist project and of the very legitimacy of the existence of the State of Israel as a Jewish nation-state.
>
> Arguments called "post-Zionist" have various aspects not only political but also cultural. They view Zionism as a colonial phenomenon, not as a national movement that is contending with another, Palestinian, national movement over its claim to the same territory . . .
>
> Those who call themselves "post-Zionists" are simply anti-Zionists of the old sort. The term "post-Zionism" sounds as though it is something innovative, which came after Zionism. However, here lies a grave mistake . . . They do not see Zionism and the State of Israel [only] as a reality that has come to pass, but rather as something that is not legitimate from the outset and that must be eliminated down to its very foundations.[17]

The harsh attack against "post-Zionists" has continued despite the fact that, since 2000, a number of well-known critical intellectuals (who are often described as post-Zionist) have explicitly and publicly voiced their loyalty to the Zionist state. For example, Shlomo Avineri's criticism was published after the sociologists Yehouda Shenhav[18] and Baruch Kimmerling[19] expressed their commitment to Zionism and the Jewish state in interviews given in 2005 and 2006, respectively.

The trend of declaring one's loyalty to Zionism represents a recent phase in the unfolding process of critical thought characterized as "post-Zionist." Throughout the years, self-identified post-Zionists have consistenly avoided taking an unequivocal stance on Zionism, one that would inevitably lead to Matzpen's definition of Israel as the vehicle for implementing, advancing and expanding the Zionist colonial project. As post-Zionists have refused to make this stand, the air has been slowly leaking from their balloon.

So-called "post-Zionist" writings have primarily unfolded along two principle lines, roughly corresponding to chronology: that of the "New Historians" and "critical sociologists" of the late 1980s and early 1990s;[20] and the postmodern, post-national work in the late 1990s and early 2000s. Each has shared in the failure to create alternatives to Zionist theory, ideology, and political worldviews.

Most of the former's research lacked a clear moral stance toward the pre-state settler community's dispossession of Palestinians and the Nakba. Those authors, with the notable exception of Ilan Pappé, refrained from adopting a value-judgment approach to the ideology and aims of the Zionist colonial project. (For the change in Benny Morris's later writings, see next chapter.) Most of them declined to pursue implications on contemporary Israeli state and society, especially regarding the citizenship status of Palestinian citizens and their rights for equality. On the other hand, the second wave of post-Zionists rejected aspects of the Jewish-Zionist nature of the state on the grounds that the state denies equality to both Palestinians and Mizrahim, as well as other "minority identities" such as women. Despite their significant differences, it is common among critics of post-Zionism to see the emergence of the New Historians and critical sociologists as the beginning of academic "post-Zionism," which ostensibly continued thereafter in various streams of "postmodernity."

But lumping both waves together is a mistake. There is an assumption that both waves subvert the foundations of the hegemonic Zionist ideology and the Jewish identity of the state of Israel. However, these two strains of thought differ in the extent to which they actually challenge Zionism—as a movement, ideology, or state. While the first works of New Historians and critical sociologists debunked part of the Zionist narrative, mainly regarding the pre-state period and the 1948 war, it was a postmodern, post-national multiculturalism (and later, post-colonialism) that challenged the nature of the Jewish state and the built-in repression of "cultural/ethnic" minorities.[21] As discussed earlier, however, liberal academics recklessly attacked all "post-Zionists." Their intolerance toward any deviation from the hegemonic narrative signified their continued affiliation with the ideology and policies of the Zionist Left. Ironically, this took place at a time when the Zionist Left's ideas had become so indistinct that the Israeli center-Right had adopted them. By 2009, when Labor and the center-Right were united in the government that launched the massacre in Gaza, and later when Labor participated in the most extreme right government (headed by Likud), the Zionist Left's views on the Jewish state, the Jewish majority, and the peace process were completely mainstream.

CHAPTER 7

Revisionist Social Sciences:
Pre-State Colonization
and the 1948 War

The New Historians and critical sociologists who emerged toward the end of
the 1980s departed from the mainstream and challenged the prevailing historiography and sociography in Israeli academia. They primarily concentrated
on debunking the established Zionist narratives regarding the pre-state colonization period, the 1948 war, and the expulsion of the Palestinians. Until the
rise of the New Historians, the pro-Zionist interpretation of each of these
historical narratives had uncritically enjoyed the "scientific" authority of the
historical and sociological professions.

Hebrew University sociologist Baruch Kimmerling recognized the conflict
that scholars of the established social sciences experienced precisely because of
their loyalty to Zionism. However, he did not hesitate pointing to the misleading alternative they chose:

> This was the paradox which confronted previous Israeli social scientists. Part of
> the Zionist vision required the building of a qualitative science, free from ideo-
> logical dependency. On the other hand a "Zionist science," enlisted science [to
> Zionism's mission], was needed. How did the Israeli social sciences confront this
> paradox? The initial impression is mixed: on the one hand, academic history and
> social sciences had laid down a rather valued infrastructure and even were rela-
> tively critical towards Zionist propaganda as featured in the pamphlets of Keren
> Hakayemet [the Jewish National Fund (JNF)],[1] the [Zionist] youth movements
> and even elementary and secondary school text books. On the other hand, until
> recently they [social scientists] were not challenged by any open joint endeavor
> [like that of the New Historians and critical sociologists] which would oblige

121

them to question their ideological independence. An enlisted science has been created in Israel at least in those parts connected to Jewish-Zionist interests, to interests of the dominant political-social camp (namely the socialist labor and mainly Mapai camp), to their Ashkenazi approach, and to a certain extent, also to the male [chauvinist] approach which ignores gender inequality.

Kimmerling ends his portrayal of Israeli social sciences as "enlisted" to the ideology and policies of Zionist Left, by insisting on his neutrality: "These things are not said as accusations or justifications of one of the sides, but as a description of reality."[2]

A. The New Historians: The 1948 War and the Nakba

The four New Historian pioneers who set off the "historians debate" were Simha Flapan, Benny Morris, Ilan Pappé, and Avi Shlaim.[3]

All except Flapan, who died in 1987, went on to elaborate on their first studies. While Pappé sharpened his accusations against the Zionist leadership for their role in the 1948 Nakba, Morris deserted the liberal New Historian camp.[4]

These four scholars were the first to break through the Israeli academic wall that surrounded the misleading narratives of the 1948 war and the Nakba, which had been widely accepted outside the Arab world. Generations of established Israeli historians ignored the narratives recorded by Palestinian historians.[5] In so doing, they discounted numerous testimonies of both Palestinians and Jews— including those from the scholars themselves or their parents—who could testify about events of the 1948 war and the ethnic cleansing committed by the Jewish army. Their commitment to Zionism and the Zionist Jewish state discouraged them from exploring taboo issues in Israeli historiography. "Sweeping topics under the carpet was and still is one of the enlisted science mechanisms," according to Kimmerling.[6]

The Marxist Mapam leader Simha Flapan,[7] not an academic scholar, was the first historian to challenge the myths surrounding the 1948 war.[8] Most of his theses were confirmed and elaborated upon by the other three historians. The New Historians disclosed how the Zionist leadership nominally accepted the UN Partition Plan but covertly agreed with King Abdullah to divide the area designed for a Palestinian state between Transjordan and Israel. Motivated to prevent the founding of a Palestinian state, Britain and the US supported the extension of the state of Israel into areas that were granted to the Palestinians; furthermore, they encouraged the rule of the Hashemites over the rest of the West Bank.[9]

Another Zionist myth the New Historians refuted was the claim that, on the eve of the 1948 war, the Jewish community was in danger of annihilation. The established historians portrayed the military balance of forces as heavily slanted against the Jews. They endorsed the legend of the "few against the many," which cast Israel's victory as miraculous. As the New Historians demonstrated, however, the Israeli army outnumbered all the Arab forces, regular and irregular, that were operating in Palestine throughout the war.[10] Moreover, in June 1948,[11] due to the import of arms from the Eastern bloc (artillery, tanks, and aircraft), the Israelis possessed more firepower than their opponents. As Ilan Pappé pointed out, the result of the war was in fact a true reflection of the numbers on the ground.[12]

The "David and Goliath" myth of the 1948 war was vital for sustaining the image of Israel as an underdog. Soon after the 1948 war, this myth was employed, directly or indirectly, to justify Israel's violation of the UN partition decision (Israel having expanded the area under its control) and the appalling atrocities committed during the ethnic cleansing of the Palestinians. Later the myth of "David against Goliath" was used to sustain the image of Israel as seeking peace with the Arab states.[13]

For almost three decades, establishment historians ignored the first critical history of the 1948 conflict, written in 1961 by Akiva Orr and Moshé Machover, two of the founders of Matzpen. Their book *Peace, Peace, and No Peace*[14] focuses on policies that led Israel to participate in the 1956 British-French invasion of Egypt. Orr and Machover portray Israel's policies as serving the interests of colonial superpowers in the region, rather than striving toward a peace settlement with the Arab states. They discuss the events leading to the 1956 war, including the 1948 war, and the agreement with the Hashemite Kingdom to divide Palestine between Israel and Transjordan. The authors lacked access to classified archival files, but based their research on scattered published information in foreign and Israeli newspapers and political magazines. Nonetheless, they prove that Israel repeatedly rejected Arab states' concessions and attempts to reach peace agreements, and also initiated provocations that led to the 1956 attack on Egypt.[15] Their breakthrough study reached only a small circle of Left activists and made no impact on Israeli scholars. Even after state archives on the period were opened, and despite well-substantiated academic work carried out by internationally acclaimed historians, Israeli historians (led by professors like Anita Shapira, a self-identified member of the Zionist Left) continue to cultivate the image of Israel as a peaceful state that engages in war only when war is inevitable.[16]

The publication of Benny Morris's *The Birth of the Palestinian Refugee Problem, 1947–1949* sparked the most heated confrontation between old and New Historians. Morris's book tackled the issue of the 750,000 Palestinian refugees of the 1948 war, acknowledging partial Israeli responsibility for their creation.

As emphasized by Stanford University historian Joel Beinin,[17] *The Birth of the Palestinian Refugee Problem* is "the single most significant revision of the previously prevailing Israeli historical consensus on the 1948 war. Morris's book cut to the heart of the Zionist narrative, the part that sustains its humanist image. It challenged the justness of Zionism's cause."

The official position on the 1948 Nakba was that Palestinians willingly left the country following orders broadcast over the radio by Arab and Palestinian leaders, calling for people to move to safer places in anticipation of the triumphant Arab armies. Supposedly others fled due to their baseless fears of the Jewish army. The misleading official Israeli position led to the widely accepted conclusion that refugees should be settled in the Arab states, given that they (the Arabs) started the war and created the problem in the first place; thus, they should pay for the consequences. Since the late 1950s, the Israeli narrative has been refuted by historians like Walid Khalidi and Erskine Childers.[18] These historians disproved the Israeli contention that official and unofficial bodies in the Arab world, including Palestinian groups, called upon Palestinians to stay in their homes, and even threatened to punish those who left.[19]

Although Morris agrees that Israel's official reasons for the Nakba were misleading, he does not accept the evidence brought forth by Palestinian and other historians showing that the expulsion was based on decisions of the Zionist political leadership, and that there was a master plan for it.[20] Instead, Morris emphasizes the expulsions conducted by local commanders took place independently and spontaneously as a result of existing operational exigencies on the battlefield, in accordance with the military and strategic requirements of each case. All in all, the Nakba happened through circumstances in the fog of war. Therefore, there was no Israeli accountability or direct responsibility for the creation of the "refugee problem."

In articles that appeared after the publication of *The Birth of the Palestinian Refugee Problem*, Morris attributes more responsibility to the Jewish side for creating the "refugee problem" than in his 1988 book. He maintains that even if there was no national political decision to expel Palestinians in 1948, the number of regional expulsions was greater than reported in the first edition of his book. By 2001, Morris even argued that, although he still could find no document ordering a blanket expulsion of the Palestinian Arabs, the consensus around the concept of transfer was so wide in 1948 that Zionist political and military leaders were convinced that it was essential to the Jewish state's survival.[21] Hence, there was no need for explicit orders from the political leadership, as the commanders in the field knew what was expected from them.

The attack waged by the academic and intellectual elites against Benny Morris was extremely severe, in part because he violated the academy's silent complicity regarding the horrors committed by the Zionist army in 1948. "There was nothing new in the historical details that he [Morris] revealed," says Baruch Kimmerling. "It was well known to all historians who studied the history of modern Israel and the Middle East and not only to historians. [They] knew exactly what happened to the Arabs of Palestine and how most of them were expelled and how and why most of them were prohibited from returning."[22]

In the expanded second edition of his principal work, re-titled *The Birth of the Palestinian Refugee Problem Revisited*,[23] Morris withdrew into the warm embrace of the established historians of the Zionist Left, with whom he had originally been associated. Yet Morris was loyal to his academic commitment to systematic, empirical research. He admits that there was a master plan for ethnic cleansing, and agrees that transfer was a central idea among the Zionist leadership after 1936. And Morris subscribes to the Palestinian historians' interpretation of Plan Dalet, drawn up in 1947 by the Zionist leadership:

> The essence of the plan was the clearing of hostile and potentially hostile forces out of the interior of the territory of the prospective Jewish State, establishing territorial continuity between the major concentrations of Jewish population and securing the future State's borders before, and in anticipation of, the invasion [by Arab states]. *The Haganah regarded almost all the villages as actively or potentially hostile* [emphasis added] . . . [Plan Dalet] constituted a strategic-doctrinal and carte blanche for expulsions by front, brigade, district and battalion commanders (who in each case argued military necessity) and it gave commanders, post facto, formal, persuasive cover for their actions.[24]

In 2006 Pappé unequivocally outlined the comprehensive political goal of Plan Dalet, which was to cleanse Palestinians from the entire expanded area of the future state. "[It was] a blueprint which spelled it out clearly and unambiguously: the Palestinians had to go . . . . The aim of the plan was in fact the destruction of both rural and urban areas of Palestine."[25]

Returning to Morris, he actually supports the mass expulsion. In an interview with *Haaretz* a month before the publication of his 2004 book, he summarizes at length both his new findings on the 1948 ethnic cleansing, and his moral approval of it.[26] He contends that Israel's first prime minister and defense minister, David Ben-Gurion, made a mistake in failing to complete this project, as too many Palestinians were left in their homes. Expelling all Palestinians could have resolved once and for all the continued Israeli-Palestinian "conflict." He hints that the job might still be completed under "certain circumstances." Historian and journalist Tom Segev asks Morris whether he supports the "transfer" of all Palestinians, to which Morris replies,[27] "In the future either the Jews will be transferred or the Palestinians. There is no place for two nations in the area between the Mediterranean and the Jordan river." In returning to the established historian community, he shared their Orientalist views. Morris views Palestinian culture and values as essentially different from those of the enlightened West, to which Israel belongs (namely, the values of humanism, democracy, openness, and creativity). To Morris and his establishment colleagues, the Palestinians are assassins and barbarians who don't value human life and who deserved and still deserve to be expelled.

The research of New Historians failed to bring about an essential change in the commitment to Zionism and the Zionist state among the Israeli Jewish academic and intellectual elite. "Their research, which did not point to Israel's moral responsibility to the question of the Palestinians' refugees," comments historian Amnon Raz-Krakotzkin, "has not led to a renewed discussion on the nature of the conflict and the ways of solving it, but has been represented as an expression of the capability of Israeli society to 'look bravely upon its past.'" However, he adds, "in the meantime, it has been clarified that the refugee question is not only one that relates to the past, but is a central question to the present."[28]

Historian Gabriel Piterberg clarifies the centrality of the refugee question and its implications for the essence of the Zionist state. "The implications [of the expulsion] have decisively molded the lives of both Palestinians and Jews, inside and outside of Israel. Until today, what structurally defines the character of the state of Israel are the return of the Jews and the non-return of the Arabs to Palestine. If this dynamic of return/no return disappeared, the Zionist state would lose its identity."[29]

Certainly the rejection of the Right of Return is not just an esoteric political issue around which all streams of Zionism are united. In many cases it is connected to all aspects of the Jewish state, including the enshrined principle of a Jewish majority and the ideology and policies directed toward the Palestinians on both sides of the Green Line. Most of all, it indicates how many among the

Zionist Left intend to resolve the conflict by way of a distorted two-state solution that negates the national rights of the Palestinian people.

B. Critical Sociologists: Colonization Perspectives on Pre-1948 Society

The critical sociologists emerged at the same time as the New Historians. These academics departed from the prevailing beliefs, held by the established sociology, regarding the nature of the Zionist settlement of Palestine. The established sociologists had accepted Zionism as a national movement motivated by the aspirations of the Jewish people to return to their homeland. They hardly alluded to the expense of the indigenous Palestinian inhabitants as a result of this process. Their position thus confirmed the basic premise of Zionism—which the entire academy and Zionist Left vehemently clung to—when confronting the colonial perspective attributed to "post-Zionism." Their narrative also adopted a "dual development" perspective to portray relations between the pre-1948 Zionist settler society and indigenous Palestinian society. That is, the sociological establishment assumed that modern Jewish settlers existed side by side with a backward Arab society and, except for some economic relations, developed separately, with both groups enjoying much autonomy.[30] The appearance of the critical sociologists marked the first time in Israeli history that Zionist colonialism became a topic of Israeli academic research and examination.[31]

Colonizing Necessities: Exclusion and Dispossession

As early as 1983, sociologist Baruch Kimmerling applied the colonial paradigm to the pre-1948 Zionist settler project in Palestine, and to Israeli society thereafter. Six years later, Gershon Shafir, elaborated on Kimmerling's studies, confirming the colonial-settler model.[32] As Kimmerling put it, "I have constructed a different conceptualization of Israeli society, namely as an immigrant-settler society—a conceptualization which brought Zionism closer to a certain species of colonialism. This made the works of the majority of [Israeli] researchers irrelevant and threatened their reputation."[33]

As mentioned, the predominant belief in Israel and abroad, both popular and academic, was that the Zionist Labor movement was led by a socialist ideology in its project to settle the land. Accordingly, it was assumed that the noble value of social justice motivated the Jewish exclusivist and collectivist economy and labor policies adopted by the Yishuv.[34] Kimmerling and Shafir challenged this perspective, arguing that, in comparison to other colonization movements in the modern world, what uniquely characterized the Zionist project was the struggle to purchase lands and the endeavor to occupy labor markets. The collectivist patterns and the exclusivist nature of Zionist colonization were a result of settling in a land that was relatively densely populated (in comparison to North America and Australia). Hence, emphasized Kimmerling, the purchasing of lands was not done privately but through collective means and the central institutions of the Zionist movement.[35]

In his study of the labor market, Shafir shed light on the reasons for the emergence of the collective settlements known as Kibbutzim and Moshavim. Historically this facet of Zionist colonialism was perceived as having embodied the ostensibly socialist ideology of the Zionist labor institutions, with lands placed under the ownership of the nation for Jews to settle and cultivate. But this model was not derived from any affinity to socialist values; rather, it proved to be the only practical model for the creation of functional settler colonies. In trying to prevent free competition with cheaper Arab-Palestinian labor, Kibbutzim supplied workplaces for Jews only. This substantively contributed to the success of the "Hebrew labor" slogan by excluding Palestinians from the Jewish labor market. In effect, the market was sliced in two: a Jewish market and an Arab market, with different wages and labor defense strategies. Buying only "Hebrew produce" reflected the policy of excluding the Palestinians from the marketing sector of the economy as well.

As noted, the depiction of Zionism as a colonial project signified, albeit partially, a revival of the long-silenced analysis of Matzpen.[36] Shafir's work confirmed Zionist colonialism's relationship to the indigenous population—a relationship that Matzpen identified over three decades earlier. Shafir emphasizes that Zionist colonialism is best understood as a settler colonialism similar in incentive and derivation to that of North America, Australia, and New Zealand, which preferred to exterminate the indigenous population—or what Shafir calls "pure settlement colonialism."[37]

The writings of Kimmerling and Shafir in the 1980s adhered to the above-mentioned scientific neutrality that also characterized the first works of the New Historians.[38] They refrained from making direct moral judgments of Zionist colonization and its dispossession of the Palestinians. They also avoided criticizing the ideological biases of their colleagues and the theories and methodologies they used. The ferocious attack against them and the New Historians—all of whom were lumped together as "post-Zionists" and "traitors"—brought Kimmerling and Shafir to change their approach toward the established social sciences. They set out, together and with others who joined them, to sharply criticize the theoretical and methodological tools their colleagues used in servicing the hegemonic ideology.[39]

The Historians' Dispute

The debate between the New Historians and the critical sociologists on one side, and the social scientists of the establishment on the other, broke out less than a year after the Oslo Accords were signed. The first salvo of what came to be known as "the historians' dispute" was in a 1994 article published in *Haaretz* by author Aharon Meged, a longtime supporter of the Zionist Labor movement. In the article he accuses the post-Zionists of rewriting history "in the spirit of its enemies."[40] He claims that the post-Zionists had signed up to support the aims of "the Arabs" by constructing an anti-Zionist historiography that reproduced "the old communist and Soviet propaganda which presented Zionism as an imperialist-colonialist movement." Meged claimed that this was the result of an innate suicidal instinct amongst the post-Zionists who know that denying the justification of Zionism will bring about the destruction of Israel. Hence, he overtly called for a social science whose role is to confirm the central tenet of Zionism.

Escalated Criticism on "Established Sociology"

Throughout 1994 and 1995—what might be described as the peak years of the Oslo peace process—the debate over the new "post-Zionist" scholarship rapidly escalated in daily newspapers[41] and academic journals, as well as in books and anthologies.[42] The established social sciences were critiqued as an "enlisted science" that played the role of supplying scientific justification to the ideology and policies of the pre-state Zionist Labor movement and its successors in Israeli government.[43] As sociologist of Hebrew University Michael Shalev notes, "All critical scholars are united around questioning the assumptions and determinations which the justification of Zionism was based upon, and which served as sources of legitimacy for the claimed authority of Israeli elites."[44]

The theoretical framework utilized by the "enlisted" social sciences in the study of Israeli society was the functionalist-structuralist paradigm that, as discussed in chapter 5, predominated for decades under the leadership of S. N. Eisenstadt.[45] The assumed existence of closed integrative social systems was applied to the analysis of Israeli society, which was seen as a society whose characteristics were affected by neither the wars with the Arab states nor internal "conflict." This theoretical framework was used to justify the exclusion of Palestinian citizens from the paradigm of "Israeli society" because they were considered "external" to the social system, which was perceived as embodying Jewish society alone. "In this way," writes Kimmerling, "Israeli scholarship tends to confirm the political and legal perception of Israel as the state of the Jewish people residing both within and outside its boundaries, rather than as the state of its citizens (which would also include Arabs)."[46]

However, the idea that Zionism was a colonial project clarified the need to place the Palestinian-Israeli "conflict" within the center of sociological analysis of Israel society. Kimmerling and Shafir condemned mainstream sociology's disregard for the 1967 occupation and the Palestinians inside Israel. They emphasized the necessity to include both in the analysis of Israeli society.[47] They insisted that during most of its history, Israeli society was best understood in terms of the broader context of Israeli-Palestinian relations and not through existing inward-looking interpretations. "The many taboos on the Arab question," Kimmerling claims, "have prevented the established sociology from raising the important question which it should have confronted: how has the Jewish society both in the 'Yishuv' period and after the erection of the state, been formed, molded, through its contacts with the Arab society."[48]

Another challenge to the ideological bias of established sociology is of the prevailing supposition that Jewish history and the settlement of Palestine were unique and thus incomparable to other cases of colonization. The commitment to Zionism and its predominant narrative allowed mainstream sociologists to avoid applying a comparative approach to the study of the Jewish-Israeli society—an approach they used in their research of other societies. "And not by accident," says Kimmerling. "The reason is almost self-understood: Such a comparative research would have placed Israeli society within the category of immigrant-settlers, similar to North America, South America, Australia, New Zealand, Rhodesia and Algeria, as indeed it is presented in the research of the two sociologists considered critical—Gershon Shafir and myself."[49] Radical historian Shlomo Sand adds, "Contrary to the established historians, Kimmerling and Shafir succeeded by means of comparative methodology, to lay the foundations for the beginning of 'secularization' of Zionist history. What is attractive about this is the fact that precisely [their use of] typical sociological ways of expression—relying on models and patterns—has granted an academic legitimacy to repealing the uniqueness attributed to Jewish history by traditional historians."[50]

The Response of Zionist Left Academics: Sociologist Moshe Lissak

How the established social sciences (identified with the Zionist Labor movement) responded to the New Historians and critical sociologists is summarized in an article published in 1996 by Moshe Lissak, a professor from the department of sociology at Hebrew University. As a first generation student of Professor Eisenstadt, and a senior scholar of Israeli society, Lissak can be seen as representative of the approach shared by most others in his profession (in the mid-1990s) and as an inspiration for criticism of post-Zionism into the present.[51]

Lissak primarily attacks the colonialist perspective adopted by critical sociologists, which he attributes to their ideological anti-Zionism. "Of course the use of the concept colonialism [by the critical sociologists] is not by chance: What we have here is an explicit intention to morally condemn [Zionism]." He adds sarcastically, "Isn't it [the case] that the Zionist movement and the state of Israel were born in sin [as they argue]?"[52]

But defining the critical sociologists as anti-Zionist is baseless, contends sociologist Michael Shalev. "Whoever examines the participants in this dispute will immediately discover that this is untrue. The common denominator of the partners to the critical community is not the rejection of basic assumptions of Zionism (indeed some do reject them—others don't)."[53] A better description of this common denominator (one which Shalev applies to himself) is the "disappointment" these new social scientists experienced when they realized that the Zionist myths they sustained were wrong.[54] Anthropologist Dani Rabinowitz of Tel Aviv University—who, to Shalev, represented even more explicitly the motives of the critical social scientist—shared this disappointment. Rabinowitz described his own radicalization process when he realized in a relatively later stage of his education that the educators and the authorities who were responsible for his Israeli socialization distorted the facts and lied in regard to essential matters related to Israeli society and its past.

Rejecting the assessment that the established sociologists did not employ comparative methods, Lissak argues that these methods were used precisely to disclose that no "colonial situation" emerged during the settlement years of the Yishuv. Comparative research confirmed that the Zionist settlement was a unique phenomenon in two main respects: 1) the national liberation motives of the Zionist immigration to Palestine, and 2) the social-economic ideology, policy, and institutions adopted and built by the Labor Party.

National Liberation Motives

Lissak uncritically accepts the basic Zionist assumptions, which he describes as a liberation movement. "The erection of the nation-state also meant the 'return to history,' namely to stop being a passive factor in the regional or world game of political forces and to become an active and influential fact." This goal is what made the Zionist movement a unique phenomenon: "It has never characterized other liberation movements and where it did (like in the Balkans) it did not reach the same extent, intensity and strength as in Zionism."[55]

Lissak represents the subjective idealistic worldview shared by many Zionist Leftists when discussing the nature of the Zionist movement. He focuses on the intentions of the Zionist colonizers and the ideology of the Yishuv to explain the Zionist movement's ostensibly unique characteristics and to refute its colonialist image. He pays almost no attention to the political-economic interpretation of the ideology of the Zionist Left movement and to its policies, which had been developed by Shafir and Kimmerling. The propensity to concentrate on subjective consciousness rather than looking at historical and economic social reality is most evident in the significance Lissak attributes to the self-identification of the settlers "who never saw themselves as colonizers."[56] Accordingly, the very colonial policies carried out by the Zionist Labor movement are described as though they were activated by anti-colonial motives, thus whitewashing them. Kimmerling had already rejected this stance two years earlier in his response to the aforementioned Aharon Meged. "The two thousand years of Jewish longing to Zion are indeed a cultural and political fact, and are truly a part of the way the 'story' should be studied. But they don't change in any way whatsoever the colonial reality." That is, "a situation in which groups of people from different parts of the world, immigrate to a certain place, build a society and state on the ruins of another society, though they did not succeed in eliminating it. At the same time, the local society [Palestinians] did not manage to expel them [the settlers], as happened in other very well known cases." Indeed, claims Kimmerling, there is nothing unique in the self-identity of the Zionist settlers. Like most settlers in North America, South Africa, and Algeria, the Zionists did not see themselves as colonialist, but as "builders of a new and more moral society, than that of their country of origin . . . Zionism also always stressed its good intentions towards the local population, and preferred to ignore the consequences which it brought about for them."[57]

Ideology, Policy, and Institutions

According to Lissak, the socialist worldview of the Zionist Labor movement was expressed in the relationship of the Yishuv with the indigenous Palestin-ian-Arab population, and in the collective nature of its economic and social frameworks. In developing his debate with the "critical sociologists," he com-pletely ignored even a "loyal" Zionist Left member like Zeev Sternhell, who a year earlier had published his study uncovering the false socialist motives and ideology of the pre-state Zionist Labor movement.

The Zionist Labor movement, says Lissak, had never thought to develop a colonialist project constructed upon the desire to exploit the Palestinians as a source of cheap labor. The "enlightened" alternative that the "socialist" settlers preferred was the policy of "one beside the other," and not "one which replaces the other." The separation of the two populations was to lead toward the parti-tion of the land between two nation-states, one Jewish, one Arab. The Zionist Labor project preferred to disconnect almost entirely from the "Arab sector" and to build an autonomous system, an economic, political, and cultural struc-ture that would not depend on the Arab population.[58] Lissak admits that the policy of separation as well as the collectivist/socialist dimension of the Jewish settler society also served practical reasons, as demonstrated by the critical so-ciologists. For example, the systematic policies of eliminating Arab labor from the Jewish employment sector were intended to provide work exclusively to Jewish laborers. However, he insists that the main driving force for the adoption of exclusivist/separatist strategies was the Yishuv's ideological striving for a so-ciety that would implement democracy and equality.[59]

Another positive function of the separation strategy, argues Lissak, was its success in weakening the "friction" between the Jewish and Arab communities for an extended period of time. The critical sociologists, Lissak argues, mislead-ingly emphasize the struggle in labor and land markets as proof of the colonialist nature of the Zionist settlement. However, the competition between Jews and Arabs in the labor market had weakened since the early 1930s due to "structural differences" between the Jewish and Arab labor forces.[60] Moreover, the impact of the limited exclusion of Palestinian laborers was not too severe because these Palestinians were peasants who took jobs in the Jewish sector only as "an additional income for improving their level of life"—they had an economic base in their villages, albeit a poor one.

The systematic effort to obscure the dispossessive colonial dimensions of Zionist policies is also demonstrated in the way Lissak tackles the question of the Zionist institutions' purchasing of Palestinian lands. Land transactions between Zionist institutions and Palestinian absentee landlords, and the forceful removal of peasants, who for centuries resided on these lands, is presented descriptively as an "economic exchange." Namely, as one of the two main "joint economic exchange markets where buying and selling agricultural produce and lands" with the Arab population took place.

In parallel with the process of emptying Zionist policies of their colonial essence, the issue of awakening Palestinian nationalism is completely ignored, as are the reasons for resisting Zionist colonialism and British imperialism. In this context Lissak's off-hand and distorted way of representing the 1936–1939 Great Arab Revolt is amazing.[61] The revolt was in essence an anti-colonial uprising directed largely against the British Mandate and its support for Zionist colonization, demanding the cessation of Jewish immigration threatening to bring about the de-Arabization of the land. However, Lissak ignores the anti-colonial essence of the revolt and the mass popular base of oppressed farmers and workers who ignited the uprising. Nor does he comment on its bloody repression by the British with the help of the Zionist paramilitary units affiliated with the British Mandate police forces.[62]

The way he mentions the 1936–39 Palestian revolt indicates a disregard of its centrality in the collective memory of the Palestinian national movement, as though it was not relevant to understanding the nature of the "Yishuv society." Lissak's commitment to Zionism boils down to blatant sarcasm when he determines that the revolt "helped to reduce competition between Jews and Arabs."

"Another reason [in addition to differences in their labor power structure] that contributed to the great reduction in contacts within the slice of labor market Jews and Arabs were competing—was the *political and security events* [emphasis added] in the second half of the 1930s. As is known, this reduction first followed the general strike declared by the Arab Supreme Committee and second, because of the escalation in the security situation."[63]

Of course, Labor Zionism never envisioned expulsion as a solution in Lissak's eyes. When the 1948 ethnic cleansing is mentioned, the research of the New Historians, which was already well known, is presented in very evasive language. Lissak notes that there are different versions about the number of the people expelled and the extent to which there was a premeditated plan to commit this expulsion.

Based on these evasions, which ignore or misinterpret proven historical facts, Lissak summarizes his approval for the self-righteous positions adopted by ideologists of the Zionist Labor movement. The strategy of the Labor movement, he determines, was to lay down the infrastructure for "symmetric conditions between the Arab society and the Jewish society." Hence, there is no basis to the argument that, because the Labor movement led the settlement (*hityashvut*) project, it was the "spearhead" of Zionist colonialism.

Confirming the "Wrongs," but Clinging to Zionist Narratives: The Case of Biological Warfare

The mid-1990s confrontation with the New Historians and critical sociologists did not bring about any essential change to academic historiography, especially regarding the 1948 war and the nature of the Zionist project. Departments of Jewish history continued to repeat the traditional paradigms of prevailing Zionist narratives.[64] Intellectual circles outside the academy—including even the self-described socialists who belong to the most radical currents of the Zionist Left—also seemed inclined to maintain Zionist justifications for the 1948 war and the "purity of arms."

Arie Aharoni represents this trend. Aharoni is a member of the Hashomer Hatzair Kibbutz Beit Alfa, a literary researcher, and supporter of the "peace camp." He was among the founders of NES—an unsuccessful attempt to transform extra-parliamentary activity into a "Peace List" that competed in the 1969 Knesset elections. Unlike the Mapam Party, which Aharoni's kibbutz was affiliated with, NES called for returning all of the '67 occupied territories as part of a peace settlement. Aharoni wrote a memoir about the pre-state "golden years," when he participated in the Hashomer Hatzair youth movement in Tel Aviv and later in his kibbutz Beit Alfa.[65] In a chapter dedicated to his experience in the 1948 war, he demonstrates the pathetic manner in which the Zionist Left solves the contradiction between its call for both universal human values and loyalty to Zionism. The book was published in 2000 and was likely written during the "liberalizatiòn" period of the Oslo "peace years," when the boundaries of legitimate public discourse were somewhat expanded. Hence, he dares to point out some "wrongs" committed during 1948, but feels limited by his loyalty to Labor Zionism, which led the war.

What bothered Aharoni was the Zionist forces' resort to terror, which included the use of biological and chemical weapons.[66]

As a soldier in the "Negev" battalion, Aharoni himself witnessed the Jewish army's attempt to poison the Egyptian army's drinking water with Typhus microbes.[67] However, he ridicules the entire project by describing it as a stupid, clumsy initiative of a local commander. Aharoni highlights his personal success in ridding his unit of the microbes, but in an unclear and mocking fashion, he also refers in passing to another instance in which the scheme was implemented but failed to cause mass causalities.

Typical to the Zionist Left's emphasis on one's upstanding liberalism, Aharoni declares his commitment to humanist values. "[I] did not ignore and even publicly opposed the wrongs we have done to the Arabs, when the war began to turn to our benefit and protested in the available forums [a reference to a meeting of soldiers who were members of Mapam with their leaders] against the expulsion of the Arab population, the destruction of villages and the robbery of property." He also admits that, since his witnessing of the 1948 war atrocities, he felt the strong need to document and publicize them "when the time is ripe for it, as a kind of a moral message for the coming generations."[68] In 2000, fifty-two years after the events took place, Aharoni considered the time ripe enough. Nonetheless, he felt some trepidation in publicizing his evidence, which may "toss fuel on a fire lit by the abundant works of post-Zionist historians." He tried to distinguish himself from the post-Zionists by joining the fierce attack against them. "The impression their [post-Zionist] studies give to their audience as expressed by the latter's responses in the media is that the entire Zionist struggle in the pre-state period for the establishment of the state, and which peaked in the War of Independence, was born in sin." While Aharoni acknowledges, "No doubt the means of implementing Zionism did not lack manifestations of wrongdoing," he emphasizes that these were only natural manifestations that are seen in any national struggle. Moreover, despite the already well-known facts disclosed by New Historians, he still justifies the Nakba with the typical defense. Namely, that the struggle itself was one of "life or death" and, as such, "it is well known that deeds of extreme cruelty, of terror and bloodshed are committed by those who are pushed to the wall, who have nothing to lose."

Conclusions about the morality of the war, despite the "wrongs" committed, soon appear. "Although it is essential to unequivocally condemn these manifestations, given the long time in which we exist and now that the state of Israel is a fact, one basic thing should not be ignored: that if we would not have won the War of Independence, the post-Zionists would not have been born, and their research which discloses secrets would not be written." While Aharoni admits that the "enlisted" historians did all they could to obscure and belittle the wrongs done, "all their attempts at camouflaging cannot cancel the fundamental fact that the 1948 war was unavoidable, and if God forbidden, we had lost it, it would have been the end of [a] generations' dream to return to Zion." After verifying his loyalty to Zionism and the state, the author wishes that, "after such an introduction, it seems that my below evidence regarding other events [referring to the use of biological weapons] which happened in the War of Independence, will be accepted [by the reader] in the appropriate proportion."[69]

Indeed, the "new history" of 1948 has not weakened the commitment of mainstream academia and Left intellectuals to the hegemonic Zionist narrative. Even admitting some appalling atrocities has not provoked an analysis of the context of the systematic policies and dominant values of Zionist colonialism. But while the stormy "historians' dispute" on the pre-state Yishuv and the Nakba took place, a new critical current began to emerge—a post-Zionist attempt to challenge, both theoretically and morally, the nature of the Jewish state and its built-in discrimination against Palestinians. It adopted different theories and ideologies derived largely from postmodernist approaches, including postnationalist multiculturalism, and postcolonialism, all supporting in various ways identity politics. The Israeli periodical *Theory and Criticism*, founded in 1991 under the direction of its editor, philosopher Adi Ophir, and beginning in 2000, edited by sociologist Yehouda Shenhav, became the main platform for publishing the works of scholars who criticially analyzed the culture and structure of the Israeli state and society.

CHAPTER 8

The Postmodernist Current in Post-Zionism

This chapter focuses on the post-Zionists, who are considered the theoretical and ideological core critics of the Jewish state. This group of intellectuals subscribes to a variety of different postmodernist and multicultural beliefs that influence their objections to the structural, class, and national "inequality" of Israeli state and society.

Israeli post-Zionists shared in postmodern disillusionment with rationalism and the belief in the progress of science, both of which are central to the Enlightenment and modern thought. Postmodernists emphasize the importance of power relations and discourse in the construction of knowledge and the individual's worldview. They also highlight how dominant elites, in order to maintain the political and social status quo, persuade the subordinate social strata to adopt their values and norms.

Postmodernists' rejection of the Enlightenment gave rise to skepticism toward grand, universal narratives and paradigms of modernity, such as liberal nationality and revolutionary Marxism. These grand narratives, the postmodernists claim, no longer explain or justify political and economic regimes and individual norms of behavior. Instead, in a postmodern era, they argue, people organize their cultural life around a variety of more local and subcultural ideologies and myths that mobilize people to struggle for their recognition.

Post-Zionist, postmodernist Israeli intellectuals applied these assumptions in the critical writings that focus on the role of the academic establishment in serving the state's ideology and policies. These intellectuals initially based their criticisms on their claimed relationship between knowledge and power structures.[1] Postmodernism's distinction between reality and representation, and the disclosure of power relations behind representation, was perceived as central to their own role as cultural critics. Consistent with this perception was the adoption of postmodern challenges to "grand narratives," which included a critique of nationalism, defined as "total" and oppressive. According to philosophers Ariella Azoulay and Adi Ophir, the nation is "an imagined group, whose essence, past and designation, precede the characteristics of its members, and are granted to them without their consent."[2] "In other words," writes Ben-Gurion University sociologist Uri Ram, a colleague of Azoulay and Ophir, "nationalism is a structured identity, enforced and limiting, like other elements in the modernity discourse."[3] Accordingly, the postmodernists criticized Zionism for being the Jewish variant of an "imagined" nationalism that carried with it an oppressive discourse excluding the narratives of a variety of marginalized social groups in Israel, both Jewish and Palestinian.[4]

"While post national intellectuals as well as identity politics-influenced post-Zionists rightly questioned Zionism as an 'imagined nationalism,' they refrained from looking more critically upon the depiction of Jewish people as a religious-ethnic group. They thus avoided challenging some of the main Zionist narratives on which the movement bases its justification of the right of the Jewish people to Palestinian land, namely, that of the return to their homeland from exile."[5]

Even the first genuine attempts of post-national scholars to criticize Zionism developed rapidly into versions of identity politics based on the discourse of "difference" and "otherness," which also characterized a large part of postmodernist thought. These versions include post-national theories of multiculturalism and postcolonialism, which have been invariably applied to a variety of Jewish minority groups, like gays and lesbians, feminist women, and the Mizrahim.

Both Palestinian citizens and Mizrahim are perceived as victims of the "Ashkenazi state," which enforces its culture, silencing voices and systematically erasing others' identities. Accordingly, the main dividing line in Israel is that between Ashkenazi-Zionist oppression and the non-European Mizrahim and Palestinian Arabs. However, as justly emphasized by Ein-Gil and Machover, "despite the subjective Orientalist racism of most veteran Zionist leaders, the objective logic of the Zionist project has eventually led to the co-optation of a substantial Mizrahi elite. Moreover, with the passage of time the ethno-cultural aspect of oppression of the Mizrahim—stressed by the Mizrahi identity ideologues—has gradually receded in importance."[6]

Among the leading scholars embracing a political identity approach are Mizrahi academics and intellectuals who have headed Mizrahim political projects that fight for acceptance and equality. [7] Most of them have abandoned a socioeconomic or class analysis of the inferior status of Mizrahim, and have focused almost exclusively on their cultural oppression by the Israeli Ashkenazi elite. In this reading, the cultural discrimination against Mizrahim has been wrongly equated with the national oppression of Palestinian citizens, who are considered to form another minority or "identity group" in Israel. Because the post-Zionist analysis has not identified Zionism as a colonizing project and Israel as an expansionist settler state, the distinct nature of the Palestinians—a nationally oppressed, colonized minority who survived the 1948 Nakba—is ignored.

Unsurprisingly, these post-Zionist currents have failed to provide a theoretical analysis of Israel as a colonial-settler state and one that is inherently oppressive in terms of class and nationality. Thus, the post-Zionists have been unable to replace the Zionist "grand narrative" with a universalist, progressive worldview that envisions a truly democratic regime in Israel. Ignoring the heightened national consciousness of Palestinian citizens, and reducing Mizrahim identity to a simple question of culture, has not advanced the struggle of either.

Before discussing the post-nationalist intellectual and political projects of Israeli post-Zionists, we shall review the history of Mizrahi marginalization and protest and established academic analysis regarding them. [8] This will complement our examination of Palestinian citizen oppression, addressed in previous chapters, and will provide a foundation for assessing the post-Zionist contribution to the democratization of Israel.

Mizrahim: Exploitation and Rebellion

The Mizrahi were brought to Israel from the Middle East and North Africa in order to establish a Jewish majority in the newly founded state, to supply conscripts for the growing needs of the army, and to settle the new areas conquered in the 1948 war. Especially important were areas near the 1949 Armistice Line, which expanded beyond the borders designated by the UN decision for the Jewish state. Settling these areas would establish "facts on the ground" to prevent the possibility of the Palestinians reclaiming their land. The Mizrahim were encouraged to immigrate to Israel only after it was clear that European Jewish immigrants were insufficient in number and could not settle the "empty" occupied territories or increase the Israeli army. From its in-ception, the Zionist project defined itself as a solution for European Jews: es-tablishing a European state in the Middle East to serve as a stronghold of Western "culture" there. Not until the end of World War II were Jews from Arab countries included in the vision of the Jewish state.

The Mizrahi immigrants were in fact dumped in non-populated areas where new towns were built without any real economic planning or productive em-ployment. Thus, the "development towns" were created, destined to become the most neglected Jewish communities in the country. "Emptied" neighborhoods, originally Palestinian or "mixed," were also resettled with Mizrahi newcomers. These turned into pockets of poverty as well.[9]

"Modernization" Theory

In the introduction, we called attention to the Mizrahi immigrants' place in the capitalist class system. Mizrahim came to constitute the bulk of the Jewish working class, and were located mostly in blue-collar jobs, whether "skilled" or not. We also emphasized the Ashkenazi establishment's Orientalist rationale for justifying the entrenched lower position of Mizrahim in the economy and society. During Israel's first two decades, establishment sociology, led by He-brew University's S. N. Eisenstadt, translated these ideologies into "scientific theories." This approach supplied early Israeli governments (all from the Left, and led by Mapai) with the theoretical explanations that directed their poli-cies for social absorption and cultural socialization of the Mizrahi immigrants. According to the "modernization" theory adopted by Eisenstadt and his disci-ples,[10] 1950s–1960s Israel was in an advanced stage of modernization—scien-tifically, technologically, and socially. Mizrahim were expected to be "absorbed through modernization," in essence, to pass through a process of disconnec-tion from all characteristics of "traditional society" and to begin acquiring the "modern orientations" of contemporary Western Israeli society. "In other words," writes Sami S. Chetrit, "erasure of 'backward' identity and culture (de-socialization), and acquiring 'modern' identity and culture by means of imita-tion and assimilation (re-socialization)."[11] The racist perspectives underlying this theory were expressed in different psychological and educational theories adopted, among others, by the Hebrew University Department of Education, which determined that Mizrahim had a limited capability for abstract think-ing or rational planning for the future.[12]

Popular Uprisings

Unfortunately for the Ashkenazi establishment, the Mizrahim did not accept this treatment. Consequently, a few militant social protests took place during the first decade of the state. The most significant of these was the 1959 Wadi Salib Uprising. Wadi Salib is a Palestinian neighborhood at the foot of Mount Carmel in Haifa. The area's original Palestinian residents were expelled in 1948. Their empty houses were settled with immigrants, mostly from North Africa, particularly Morocco. Most of these Mizrahi residents were unemployed and neglected by the Mapai-led municipality and the Histadrut. The uprising came in response to a police shooting of a patron in café where unemployed residents passed their time. Fierce confrontations with the police took place in Wadi Salib. Solidarity demonstrations in other Mizrahi neighborhoods erupted around the country. The police brutally repressed the uprising, and the Labor Party-led state was thus able to earn another decade of "quiet." Mizrahi protests during the 1950s took the form of local outbursts that did not extend into an organized countrywide movement. Nor were they articulated in class or universalistic democratic rhetoric, which would imply solidarity with the lot of Palestinian citizens, then living under a military government. Only the Israeli Black Panther movement raised the slogans of both anti-Zionism and class-consciousness. Crucially, the Black Panthers linked the Mizrahi struggle for social equality with the struggles of Palestinian citizens. The Black Panther movement recognized the Palestinian people's national rights.

1971: The Black Panthers' Rebellion—Anti-Zionism and Class Consciousness

The Black Panther Uprising, which lasted from March 1971 to the end of 1972, expressed second-generation Mizrahim's rejection of the "modernization" notion—that income and education gaps between Ashkenazim and Mizrahim would close with time. Already by the end of the 1960s, it was clear to all that the second generation of Mizrahi immigrants were still socio-economically behind second-generation Ashkenazi immigrants. Their placement in the lower echelons of the economy and society was set in place during the 1960s, as Sami S. Chetrit describes:

> From the 1960s the state adapted its systems to the class-cultural reality, [it became] like a large and sophisticated organization of social workers and welfare officials, who turned the Mizrahim from free people to those who are "taken

care of;" the educational system was adapted to the cultural "needs" of Mizrahi students, in fact creating a separate and inferior education system according to the low expectation level of the state; housing conditions were fitted to the "socioeconomic conditions" and "life habits" of Mizrahim; employment [was] in accord with their position in the new industrial economy, as blue collar laborers, especially after the large economic growth that took place in the wake of the 1967 war, in which Mizrahim did not share in.[13]

In order to keep the Mizrahim as an acquiescent labor force, the state, with the help of the academy, maintained a political culture that totally delegitimized Mizrahi protest. In addition to co-opting Mizrahi activists, the government strengthened its reliance on the work of Mizrahi collaborators, and institutionalized the mechanism of the "local boss" as a vehicle to intercede between the central government and Mizrahi communities.[14]

The second generation of Mizrahim, who spearheaded the Black Panther uprising, were well aware of these developments. They realized that their condition had been created by 1950s Mapai policies designed to entrench the Mizrahim's social and economic oppression. Hence, many of the Mizrahim lost faith in any "peaceful" means that were presumably available.

The uprising burst out in the Musrara neighborhood of Jerusalem, which, between 1948 and 1967, bordered Jordanian-controlled East Jerusalem. This old Palestinian neighborhood was occupied in the 1948 war, and was quickly populated with 650 Mizrahi immigrant families, mainly from North Africa, with a few from Iraq. Only after the 1967 occupation of East Jerusalem, when the neighborhood's dependence for "security" subsided, was the path cleared for socioeconomic protest.

The uprising consisted largely of militant and rowdy demonstrations that sometimes included damage to property symbolic of Mapai rule—usually government, party, or Histadrut institutions. These protests spread to other parts of the country, and were coordinated by a chosen central committee. Thousands of Mizrahi activists and supporters, including a small number of anti-Zionist Left Ashkenazim, participated in the countrywide demonstrations that took place in Jerusalem. The chosen name indicated the perceived similarity between the Mizrahi struggle and the most significant radical movement of Blacks in the United States, the Black Panther Party. However, the central ideological themes of the uprising were nourished by the Musrara youth's class consciousness. This was largely due to the early involvement of members of Matzpen in the development of the Black Panthers movement.[15] Matzpen continued to support the Panthers throughout this period, both politically and logistically, helping to organize their demonstrations, forging solidarity with left-wing Israelis, and defending them against the brutal attacks of the police. The emerging class consciousness of the Black Panthers[16] is reflected in a leaflet distributed at a demonstration in Jerusalem on August 23, 1971:

> To the screwed citizen–
>
>   You are screwed not because—God forbid—you were born that way, but because they are screwing you. Let us assume that you are a blue-collar worker born in Iraq, Yemen or Morocco, and a head of a family with many children. One can guess, more or less, your past: on your arrival to Eretz Israel you were thrown into a Maabara [a transient camp] where you received an exploitation salary. Even more seriously, the fruits of your labor were eaten by them—the labor managers, the owners of the enterprises, the bosses. Until this very day they boast that they built the state and its roads . . . They now hold senior positions in the state that you have built, and you, the true worker, the true builder, remain screwed. After all, you did not immigrate from Moscow or Leningrad, so why should you get a normal apartment?[17]

The Black Panthers' slogans demonstrated the total identification of the state as the source of Mizrahi oppression. "A state in which half of its citizens are kings and the other half, exploited slaves, we shall set on fire." And "Either the cake is for all, or there will be no cake." They argued in clear and direct language that a state employing oppressive economic and cultural policies has no right to exist. As Black Panther leader Kohavy Shemes put it: "I differentiate between the government and the state, but you can not scare me with what happens if we destroy the state because we don't feel that we are partners."[18] Their challenge to state policies thus included a rejection of "security above anything," which the establishment used to silence any protest of Mizrahim.

Long before the New Historians and critical sociologists, the Black Panthers challenged the central narratives of Zionism, including the "ingathering of the exiles" and the "melting pot" ideology. They did not stop at simply criticizing discriminatory policies; they also attacked the Zionist movement, which had seduced Mizrahim to immigrate to Israel with misleading promises.[19]

Already in 1972—years before figures in the Zionist Left took similar steps—the Black Panthers met PLO leaders and recognized the organization as the legitimate representatives of the Palestinian people. The connection between their class identity and solidarity with the Palestinian national struggle was expressed in the Black Panthers' participation in the May Day demonstration of 1972, organized by the radical left groups Matzpen and Siah.[20] The demonstration called for the end of the 1967 occupation and return of the areas

Israel annexed after the war, and they condemned government policies that created and maintained poverty. The police violently broke up the demonstration and arrested around sixty demonstrators.

By the end of 1972, the political establishment had succeeded in silencing the Black Panthers. A smear campaign presenting them as members of a global terrorist network undermined their legitimacy. The state staged mass arrests of their members, and because criminal files were opened—promising heavy punishments if they continued to protest—most members lived in fear from then on. Later, as mainstream political parties tried to blunt the appeal of the Black Panthers, Mizrahim turned to reformist politics. The door was open for regressive forces to solicit the Mizrahim after the state crushed the Black Panther Party.

The accumulated rage of the Mizrahim against Mapai governments eventually found its expression in "the rebellion at the polls" during the 1977 elections, when Mizrahim shifted their allegiance en masse to the right-wing Likud Party. Later, much of this political energy was co-opted into religious Mizrahi parties, which gradually diverted any potential radicalism into anti-Palestinian sentiment. By 2009, the Mizrahi orthodox Shas Party, which at its onset was politically moderate, had become an extremely right-wing, racist party.[21]

A few years after the suppression of the Black Panther uprising, sociologist Shlomo Swirski, then of Haifa University, pointed out how class functioned in the oppression of Mizrahim, emphasized earlier by Matzpen and the Black Panthers (albeit based on a different theoretical framework).[22] Swirski relied upon Dependency Theory to explain the socioeconomic status of Mizrahim. This theory focused on the exploitation of "developing" states by "developed" states, and the interwoven relationships between the world's "center" and its "periphery." Accordingly, Swirski refuted the modernization theory used by established sociologists, who espoused that the "traditional" backward culture of the Mizrahim was responsible for their socioeconomic position in the modern Western society of Israel. Swirski showed how the policies adopted by the Ashkenazi elite in the first years of the state assigned Mizrahi immigrants to lower levels on the economic pyramid as Mizrahim built Israel's modernized economy. On the contrary, the Mizrahim were not "backward." But they were "made" backward by the ethnic division of labor created by Zionist Left governments.

1988: Ella Shohat and the Mizrahim as Victims of Zionist Orientalism

Seven years after Swirski's social class explanation of Mizrahim oppression,

Ella Shohat, a radical cultural critic, published her essay, "The Sephardim in Israel: Zionism from the Standpoint of Its Jewish Victims."[23] After mentioning Swirski's analysis of the class divisions between Mizrahim and Ashkenazim, Shohat discusses the Zionist project as a Eurocentric, Orientalist effort that oppressed its third-world subjects, Palestinians, and Mizrahim alike. Following in the footsteps of Edward Said's *Orientalism*,[24] Shohat emphasizes the need to consider the negative consequences of Zionism upon Mizrahim, in addition to the Palestinians. "The Zionist denial of the Arab-Muslim and Palestinian East, then, has as its corollary the denial of the Jewish Mizrahim, who like the Palestinians, but by more subtle and less obviously brutal mechanisms, have also been stripped of the right of self representation. Within Israel, and on the stage of world opinion, the hegemonic voice of Israel has almost invariably been that of European Jews, the Ashkenazim, while the Mizrahi voice has been largely muffled or silenced." Both Edward Said's book and Shohat's essay made little impact on the established social sciences in Israel. Additionally, Swirski's deviation from the cultural-based analysis of mainstream sociology was completely ignored.

Post-Zionists critically discussed the Orientalist approach that characterized Zionism and Israeli state and society. However, they largely concentrated on the cultural/ideological aspect alone.[25] Like their Mizrahi colleagues they argued that both Palestinians and Mizrahim were excluded from the state narrative and national memory of Ashkenazi Jews. The collective identities of both Palestinians and Mizrahim were oppressed and marginalized, thus allowing them to be grouped together under a category of "others."[26] However, Swirski and Shohat's greatest impact was on the "New radical Mizrahim," who emerged in the 1990s. They adopted a "New Mizrahi discourse" that signaled a departure from that of the Ashkenazi establishment and the Mizrahi leaders themselves.

The 1990s' "New Mizrahim"

A wave of intellectuals, academics, students, and artists introduced a New Mizrahi discourse. They rejected the labels *Sephardim* and *Hanizrach* (Eastern ethnic groups) used by the political and academic establishment. Instead they defined themselves as "Mizrahim," which indicated a new political identity and critical standpoint. Sami Shalom Chetrit was among the first intellectuals involved in the new "movement." He summarizes its radical new discourse that represents a systematic analysis of the Mizrahim as "victims of Zionism," both in class and cultural terms.

The radical innovation of the "New Mizrahim" is their perception of Mizrahim (as defined by Ella Shohat) as the "Jewish victims" of the Ashkenazi Zionist revolution, second to its main victims, the Palestinians, who are perceived by Zionists as enemies. According to this criticism, Mizrahim were tied to the Zionist revolution in circumstances upon which they had no influence, in order to serve as a human power reservoir for the demographic-territorial struggle of Zionism against the Palestinians. As we learned from Shlomo Swirski, they were also brought to Israel in order to erect the proletariat upon which the Israeli modern economy was built, the fruits of which the Mizrahim have not enjoyed.[27]

Chetrit notes the criticism directed at both Zionism's Orientalist ideology and capitalist nature: "[It] focuses on seeing the ideology and the founding movement which governs the state—the Ashkenazi Zionism—as a national European Jewish organization, neo-colonial from the political perspective, capitalist from the economic perspective and Eurocentric-Orientalist and anti-Mizrahi from the cultural perspective."[28]

"In the beginning," adds Chetrit, "it [the New Mizrahi discourse] was indeed promising." Mizrahi activists initiated radical organizations that were connected to the poor neighborhoods and development towns. They tried to empower the neighborhoods and towns and to self-organize around the most urgent needs. These organizations included: Hila, a non-governmental organization that struggled for equality in education in development towns and poor neighborhoods;[29] the radical Mizrahi magazine *Iton Aher* (literally, "A Different Magazine"); and Kedma, an alternative experimental school that was eventually closed down by the Tel Aviv municipality. "There was a good atmosphere around these projects," notes Chetrit, "a feeling that at least a sort of *avant-garde* had emerged. I don't know whether these were mass movements. But what is important is the fact that the activists both worked with the people and were located in the radical and critical fronts in terms of political struggle, Zionism, etc."[30]

Then in 1997 came the attempt to establish an umbrella organization for all these separate community-based initiatives in the form of the Israeli Democratic Mizrahi Rainbow (Hakeshet Hademocratit Hamizrahit, hereafter referred to as *Keshet*). Among the founders of Keshet were activists in "New Mizrahi" organizations, intellectuals involved in these projects, and academics and rank-and-file supporters who came from a variety of other political bases. "It seemed as though this comprehensive self-organization of Mizrahim, combined with a strong political consciousness, might lead to radicalization of the Mizrahim masses. But the academicians among the founders of the coalition, who later became stronger in the movement, took the initiative back to [the academy] and to Van Leer Jerusalem Institute."[31]

Indeed, their multicultural and postcolonial theories, which implied the Mizrahi issue was one of identity politics—heavily detracting from the Black Panthers' politically radical emphasis on social class. In addition, little remained of both Ella Shohat's challenge of Zionist-sponsored Orientalism and its systematic cultural and economic oppression, and Chetrit's attempts to theorize the link between class and ethnicity. By 2011 even Chetrit adopted an approach that strongly emphasized culture and identity. Among the few Mizrahi intellectuals who remained loyal to the class approach were Zvi Ben Dor and Moshe Behae. As we shall see below, solidarity with Palestinian nationalism, which these earlier radical approaches implied, was excluded from Keshet's agenda. Instead, the movement became defined distinctly by identity politics, inspired by its leaders' post-national, multicultural, and postcolonial theories.[32]

Multiculturalism

The multiculturalist perspective as applied to the Israeli social and political scene emphasizes the importance of preserving the different cultures of immigrant minority groups. It is often presented as an alternative to the "melting pot" ideology and policy that aimed to create a unified national identity out of all ethnic groups in Israeli society. Multiculturalists see the state's unification policy as oppressing immigrant minorities who are forced to forsake their cultures in order to integrate with the state's mainstream.

The "melting pot" ethos has existed in Israel since the first decade of the state's establishment. It was a strategy to ensure that new immigrant groups committed to the Zionist, Mapai-headed state.

Yehouda Shenhav and Yossi Yonah, professors of sociology and political philosophy at Tel Aviv and Beer Sheva University, respectively, were the first multiculturalists to critique the melting pot ideology and policy.[33] Their criticism reflected the relatively liberalized discourse of the Oslo years, which enabled marginalized Israeli groups to make their voices heard. Among the groups that took advantage of this atmosphere were feminists, LGBT (lesbian, gay, bisexual, and transgender) activists, and extra-parliamentary peace movements. Each of these challenged some aspect of the dominant political culture in Israel. Nevertheless, the political reawakening of the Mizrahim had the greatest potential to challenge the political regime and hegemonic political culture.[34]

The Israeli political and social establishment closed ranks in defense of the dominant, homogeneous Zionist identity and culture. As in the previous wave of attacks against the New Historians and critical sociologists, the campaign against "multiculturalism" was led by academics committed to the Zionist Left ideology.[35] Cherishing the notion of an "integrated" society, which was expressed in slogans like "ingathering of the exiles" and the "absorption of Olim [Jewish immigrants]," they accused multiculturalism of privatizing Israeli culture and transforming Israel from a "solidarity" society into a "sectarian" society. They expressed concern for the loss of a beautiful, unified Israel and warned of the dangers of fragmentation in apocalyptic tones. As Yossi Yonah and Yehouda Shenhav explain, "The concept of multiculturalism, especially when attached to 'postmodernism' or 'post-Zionism' became 'a red cape' for . . . nationalist Left circles, because it threatens the position of Zionism."[36]

Having perceived multiculturalism as a direct threat to the hegemonic political culture, the state openly intervened in the public debate by funding two reports on Israeli cultural policy that challenged multiculturalism. Two committees of well-known scholars of social sciences and cultural studies, many of whose members were known to be part of the Zionist Left, authored the reports, "Cultural Policy in Israel" (known as the "Bracha Report," published in 1999),[37] and the "Culture Certificate-Vision," (the "Shavit Report," issued in 2000).[38] In both reports, the authors categorically oppose granting legitimacy to cultural pluralism and warn of its dangers. The Shavit committee claims, "recognizing the legitimacy of the 'different' does not mean conferring legitimacy to a fragmenting and dividing cultural reality." The Bracha report declares, "[Israeli] society confronts a real danger of falling apart. Emerging multiculturalism will undermine the dream to bring to life the motivation towards a re-birth of Jewish/Israeli culture. This is a dangerous game."

The authors make the concept of "state" a central focus of the political work of the committees. They call for promoting a common political culture—a "cultural core" engineered by the state, allowing "for mutual solidarity between citizens." Shavit's report suggests "[establishing] a mechanism which will determine what cultural assets deserve to be retained and advanced by the state" and that Israel "consider the erection of one national authority for the cultural assets of the countries of origin."[39] All in all, the content of the suggested hegemonic culture should reflect the Zionist identity of the state and society: "We want the resurrection enunciated by cultural Zionism to continue to nourish the state of Israel which is preoccupied with the question of its identity 50 years since its establishment."[40] The reports thus represent the "statist" political culture of Israel embodied in the structural functionalist school of the 1950s and 1960s. They follow the sociological establishment of the time by providing a theory that sees the state as the embodiment of the "collective" goals of society, one that overrides individual and sub-group rights and interests.

Yonah and Shenhav challenge the "state-centered" approach of the Bracha and Shavit reports:

> They [the composers of the reports] set the state above . . . [They] speak about cultural life of the state not the cultural life of society. Thus [they] seek to strengthen the state's power as the only actor [with] an interest in designing the state culture as mediator, conciliator, organizer . . . [in charge of] allocating of resources. . . . Placing the state above society is based on delineating boundaries between "universal" (state) and particular (society), between modernity and traditional, between rational and irrational, and between legal and illegal. . . . This implies that the social order is fragile, and only the state can save society from anarchy.
>
> [Moreover,] the state is presented [by the composers of the reports] as a rational agent, and culture is presented as an engineered product of the state, and not as a spontaneous phenomenon which grows from the needs of different groups. . . . This image perceives the state as though it is above any social conflicts and not influenced by particularistic interests of social groups.[41]

Yonah and Shenhav draw our attention to the state-worshipping, semi-fascist positions of these "liberal" intellectuals. But unlike Baruch Kimmerling, they do not name it as such. Instead, they correctly point out that the suggested cultural core implies the end of civil society: "It blurs the distinction between society and state, and even seeks to absorb society within it. The [cultural] core is perceived not as phenomenon that grows from below by means of voluntary, reciprocal relations in the civil society, but as an entity planned and engineered from above."[42]

However, the alternative to this state-engineered culture is not the unification of all progressive social forces—both Jewish and Palestinian—in a struggle for the democratization and de-Zionization of the state. Loyal to postmodernism's "mistrust" of grand narratives, Yonah and Shenhav fall into identity politics, which diverts the potential for radicalism among the Mizrahim into ethnic interest groups. They also completely ignore the national awakening of Palestinian citizens, and distort the national basis for its resistance to the Jewish-Zionist state.

Identity Politics

Multiculturalists like Yonah and Shenhav see the post-national identity politics of different "cultural groups" as a challenge and alternative to the coercive, hegemonic Israeli culture. They believe that identity politics in general can subvert the hegemonic culture and, in many cases, undermine the classic nation-state itself.[43] Social groups concentrating on their own cultural identity and how to counter discrimination liberate politics from the old grand narrative (or "fundamental assumptions") and take them into a "new space." Identity politics will hopefully free individual and community identities from the three grand narratives that have dominated social and political thought in modern times: "It distances the system of identities from the liberals' [camp], which [sees] identity as an individual concept distinct from society; from the national [camp], which seeks to contain a unified identity that retains and represents the fundamental nationalist assumptions; and from the class [camp], which seeks to continue speaking in the language of class solidarity."[44] In Israel, they argue, identity politics inspire an objection to the oppression of state-promoted culture and motivates national, ethnic, gender, and sexuality struggles. Each of these social groups strives to achieve recognition and liberation from political oppression.

Criticism of the various dimensions of multiculturalism and identity politics, especially among the Left outside of Israel,[45] is useful in our understanding of the role played by post-Zionists, who adopted these perspectives in blocking the struggle for the democratization of the Jewish state. The first criticized dimension largely relates to the relativistic nature of identity politics, as it emerged in the United States after the decline of the Black Power and women's liberation movements. As Aijaz Ahmad writes:

> Multiculturalism denies the idea that there is a hierarchy of determinations in existing social relations which are the inevitable result of historical formation, far beyond any valuation that any individual may attach to them. It tends to push down, in the scale of priorities, the idea that given the specific history of the United States, given the social structure bequeathed by slavery, the position of the Afro-Americans is *unique* and can not be collapsed into generalities of ethnicity, difference, and "multiculturalism." In other words, this kind of relativism tends towards the obliteration of actual, historically given relations of power in favor of a leveled-out notion of multiplicity and difference in which everyone becomes, sooner or later, everyone else "other" and, by the same token, a member of a minority and even "subaltern" group.[46]

A similar transformation happens when post-Zionist multiculturalists consolidate Mizrahi feminist women, members of the LGBT community, and various immigrant bases into "identity groups." What makes identity politics so crippling as an alternative to Zionism is the claim that Mizrahi and Palestinian citizens are equal "victims of Zionism." As noted, a number of Mizrahi intellectuals accepted post-Zionist multiculturalism and identity politics as conceptual tools for criticizing the state's hegemonic culture from the standpoint of its Mizrahi victims. Thus, they partially adopted Ella Shohat's perspective of Zionism as a colonialist-Orientalist-ethnic (Ashkenazi) project that discriminates against the "internal other," the Mizrahim.[47] This approach, which has found support among anti-Zionist Mizrahim and even Palestinian progressives,[48] was thoroughly criticized by Matzpen veterans Ehud Ein-Gil and Moshé Machover.[49]

In accordance with Matzpen's traditional positions, they recognize the Orientalist nature of Zionism as a historical fact. The Zionist project was initiated and has been led predominantly by Ashkenazim. The authors also reveal the state's aforementioned motivations in bringing in Mizrahi immigrants, as well as the exploitative policies and racist ideologies that characterized the "absorption" of Mizrahi immigrants, who were depicted as "culturally inferior" and treated as colonization fodder by the Zionist leadership.[50] However, Ein-Gil and Machover argue that, with the passage of time, the ethno-cultural aspect of Mizrahi oppression, as stressed by Mizrahi ideologues and postmodern intellectuals, gradually receded in importance, as compared to the socioeconomic oppression of the Mizrahi masses. The Mizrahim continue to face educational and cultural disadvantages, which mostly reflects class barriers justified by racist ideology. This is fundamentally distinct from the national oppression of the Palestinians.

The "identity" discourse thus serves to diffuse and even to belittle the structural oppression of Palestinians, the raison d'être of the Jewish Zionist state. As previously discussed, the very concept of citizenship in Israel is built upon the exclusion of Palestinians from the national Jewish collective. Threats of emptying Palestinian second-rate citizenship of any real political meaning and stripping them of basic human rights are constant. As the absolute "other," Palestinians are always in danger of ethnic cleansing, as the state waits for an opportunity to arise. In contrast, Mizrahim are included in the Jewish national collective and receive full citizenship, even though they are positioned in the socioeconomic hierarchical structure as inferior to that of Ashkenazim. The difference between Mizrahim and Palestinians is essential.

The two groups have significantly different interests in sustaining current Jewish dominance and the prerogatives granted exclusively to Jews. Hence, it is misleading to think that the strengthened national consciousness and struggle of Palestinians is comparable to the Mizrahim. In fact, this conflation diverts attention from the main axis of Israeli oppression. For the Mizrahi masses, socioeconomic deprivation is increasingly the central issue. Issues of cultural discrimination, such as being subjected to contemptuous or patronizing Ashkenazi attitudes, while still very much alive, are gradually becoming less relevant, and tend to be an aspect of class-based cultural antagonism. Ein-Gil and Machover's analysis concludes that framing Palestinians in Israel as another identity group fighting marginalization empties the Palestinian national struggle of its true essence: the democratization of the Zionist state and the dismantlement of its colonial-Zionist nature.[51]

As Aijaz Ahmad has determined,[52] theories of post-national multiculturalism and identity politics fail to distinguish between different kinds of nationalisms: those which are indeed "chauvinist and fascist," and progressive ones that express the will of the people struggling for self-determination and liberation from imperialism and colonialism. The latter very much applies to Palestinians in Israel, who must strengthen their national identification. "They cannot just forgo nationalism," says Ahmad, in regard to anti-colonial national movements. "They have to go through it, transform their nation-state in tangible ways, and then arrive at the other side."[53] The tendency of multiculturalism and identity politics to ignore the strengthened nationalist consciousness of Palestinian citizens of Israel and their challenge to the Jewish Zionist state is consistent with avoiding the fact that Israel is the vehicle implementing the Zionist colonial project, and not just another Western nation. Multiculturalist analysis remains unaware of how central the national oppression of Palestinian citizens is. It has not provided the conceptual or ideological basis that would enlist Mizrahim and other identity groups to join the Palestinians' struggle. This also explains the failure of post-colonialism, which some post-Zionists adopted later as "one of the most radical versions of multiculturalism."[54] It contains similar deficiencies and even weakens the capability of post-Zionism to replace the hegemonic perspective.

The Postcolonial Perspective

The transposition of post-colonial perspectives into Israel can be seen in Yehouda Shenhav and Hanan Hever's 2002 article, "The Postcolonial Gaze."[55] The authors make the analytical distinction between two stages/versions of challenging colonial domination: the "old," anti-colonial approach, which they term "the Third-World perspective," and the new "post-colonial studies," which they themselves adopt as relevant to the analysis of Israel's political and social regime.

The "old" anti-colonial approach, they say, primarily dealt with "questions which relate to the economic and political reality, the flow of capital and labor, class relations, and forms of imperial control, based on Dependency Theory." Unlike the first stage/version, however, post-colonial studies, according to Shenhav and Hever, do not deal with social-economic oppression but with "questions of consciousness, color and self-identity and the dialect of gazes between Black and White, including the phenomenon of imitation." Furthermore, this version of identity politics is also described as a liberating discourse. In this sense, becoming liberated from the chains of colonial language and its structure of knowledge allows one to move to the "softer" terrain of cultural studies—namely, to questions of "body, gender, color, class or other identities."[56] Having abandoned their belief in colonial economics and national oppression, the post-colonialists focus on racialized minorities that are themselves part of Western societies, such as Blacks in the US, England, or France, "in which a meeting between the First and Third world populations takes place."[57]

Indeed, when applied to Western democracies, "postcolonial studies" did play a relatively liberating role, albeit on the level of identity and culture alone. As the authors emphasize, it rejected the ethnocentrism of the Western world, including labeling the "other" as inferior to Europeans, or being backward, irrational, and passive. Moreover, it supplied subjugated people with a language to raise their voices, which had previously been unheard from in Western culture.

However, while the discourse of postcolonial studies may describe the situation of third world immigrant groups in Europe in some respects, its application to the case of Palestinians in Israel is totally misleading. One cannot label Palestinians as an "ethnic identity group" (as is the case with immigrants), because it is they who are the original inhabitants of the land and whose national homeland was occupied by a colonial force. Moreover, the fact that one Israeli regime has emerged throughout all of Historic Palestine confirms the falseness of the postcolonial perspective. Hence, the "old" anticolonialist approach—the "third-world perspective"—in which the colonized people fight for national liberation—applies more accurately to the Palestinian case than does an identity-based, culture-oriented focus of post-colonial studies. Applying the conceptualization of "identity ethnic groups" in a host country to the Palestinian national minority in Israel only adds another dimension to the multiculturalists' disregard of Palestinian national self-definition and struggle.

Shenhav and Hever recognize the importance of lifting the silence on colonial discourse in Israel, including the hidden "events" of the 1948 war and their
meaning. "Silencing the use of the concept 'colonialism,'" they emphasize, "means
silencing history as well." Hence, the purpose of the post-colonialist perspective
is to "re-present the colonial history and read its relation of forces through solving
the practice of hiding."[58] However, after this promising opening, one would expect a thorough analysis of at least the history of Zionist settlements in Palestine,
a clear position regarding Zionist settlements' distinctively oppressive colonial
nature, and some indication of how Zionist colonial oppression has been implemented and embodied in the state of Israel. Instead, they hesitate to define Zionism as a colonial project and when it is mentioned they refrain from
elaborating on it. Avoiding an explicit position regarding the continuity of the
Zionist colonial project, from the pre-state days to the current state of Israel, appears to be a necessary condition for applying the "identity" brand of post-colonialism to Israel. It sanctions the comparison of Palestinian citizens' oppression
with that of non-European minorities in any other Western state, finding them
about equal, thus avoiding the national nature of their oppression.

Why they explicitly avoid the notion that Israel is a vehicle for advancing the
Zionist colonial project is found in an answer to a question they raise: "What is
the relevance of the concept 'colonialism' for the discussion on the society and culture in Israel today?" Their answer clarifies that they are aware of researchers, political figures, and intellectuals within the more radical circles of the Zionist Left
who have wrestled with whether Zionism is a colonial project or a national movement. However, Shenhav and Hever choose instead to concentrate on the time
period when Israel's "colonial dimensions" emerged. "There are [those] who determine that since the beginning of the colonization of Palestine at the end of the
19th century, Zionism acted as a special species of colonialism that peaked in 1948.
Others mark colonialism from the beginning of the Israeli occupation of the territories in June 1967."[59] But Shenhav and Hever refrain from committing to either
position. "In any case, what is important is [that] the post-colonial gaze on the
society in Israel should be a "distanced" gaze which examines the extent of its colonialism and its connection to colonial mechanisms in other places and times."[60]

Playing down the significance of the debate is indeed deceptive. There is an
essential difference between the two perspectives. One sees Zionist colonialism
beginning with the settlement of Palestine. The other sees only the 1967 occupation as supporting the colonization model. Each points to a different set of
historical-political root causes, and to a different perception of the nature of the

Jewish state. Professor Zeev Sternhell, for example, attributes colonialism to the 1967 occupation and beyond that does not challenge the exclusivist Jewish state. This stance is shared by the majority of the Zionist Left and the peace camp. The two-state solution, in its distorted formulation adopted by the Zionist Left, indeed includes withdrawal from parts of the '67 occupied territories. Yet it would leave intact Israel's brand of Apartheid.

On the other hand, acknowledging the colonial nature of the pre-state Zionist movement implies seeing Israel as the embodiment of the pre-state movement. Avoiding an unequivocal stance on the colonial nature of the Zionist movement renders a full understanding of Israeli state and society impossible. It dissolves and mischaracterizes Israel's colonial essence in the present as the product of the Zionist project.

Alongside the authors' hesitancy to "take sides" in this debate is their equal refusal to reject the notion of Zionism as a national liberation movement. Instead, they adopt a misleading conceptualization of Zionism as an ideology and movement, portraying it as nationalism with both liberating and oppressive dimensions. "Zionism served as a central tool for insurrection and for achieving national independence [for the Jewish people]. But at the same time it serves as a tool for repressing Palestinian nationality. Pointing to this duality splits nationalism into co-existing incompatible elements whose accurate composition and reciprocal relations can be described through the post-national 'gaze.'"[61] Writers like Shenhav and Hever assume that Zionism's contradictions can be resolved by implementing the visions of post-nationalist, multiculturalist, and post-colonial currents. But this is impossible: by definition, colonialist projects cannot be liberation movements because they are fundamentally based upon subjugating and oppressing the colonized.

Post-colonialists avoid addressing the fact that Palestinians in Israel do not accept the supposed "contradictory functions" attributed to Zionism. This dualism is fictitious. As Azmi Bishara aptly described, Zionism is a colonial project disguised as a national liberation movement. Like most post-Zionists, the post-colonialists ignore the fact that, by 2002, when Shenhav and Hever's article was published, the NDA and Bishara's democratic nationalist perspective had already spread widely among the younger generation of Palestinians in Israel. This was not what post-nationalists and post-colonialists expected.[62] Unlike Zionist Left supporters who publicly fought against Palestinian citizens' ideas, post-Zionists avoided addressing them and continued developing their multicultural post-colonialist theories. Indirectly, they pulled the rug out from under the nationalist essence of the Palestinian struggle. In fact, they betrayed the Palestinian national struggle in ways that went beyond theory. This is evident in the political activity of Mizrahi intellectuals operating within the framework of the Israeli Democratic Mizrahi Rainbow Coalition—otherwise known as Keshet.

The Fruit of Identity Politics—No Solidarity with the Palestinians

The identity politics of academic leaders of Keshet, like Shenhav and Yonah, have indeed merited Ahmad and Hobsbawm's criticism of identity politics. They see "identity" as impeding the solidarity between various identity groups, most of which fight for their respective goals. Thus, identity politics prevent different sectors of the working classes from building a collective movement beyond their select "identities." Further, it leaves these sectors prey to continued exploitation and marginalization. In the case of Israel, proponents of identity politics who led Keshet refrained from connecting a Mizrahi struggle for equality to that of the Palestinians.

Nor did Keshet view the dismantlement of the Zionist nature of the Israeli state as the condition for Mizrahi and Palestinian equality. Says Sami Shalom Chetrit, "With regards to the most serious test—i.e., their position towards the Zionist question—they failed. One cannot deny it: Keshet at present [in 2003] is a Zionist movement. The language and content of their writings are that of a Mizrahi-nationalist language, a kind of socio-nationalistic version."[63]

A conspicuous example of Keshet's commitment to Zionism, and its lack of solidarity with Palestinian rights, can be seen in its campaign demanding the reallocation of ownership rights to state lands and public housing apartments. In chapter 3, the Apartheid nature of Israeli land laws was presented. Accordingly, the great majority of "state lands" in Israel (93 percent of the total land mass) are Palestinian lands that have been appropriated since the 1948 war. According to the Basic Law of 1960, the Israeli Land Administration (ILA) was granted the exclusive right to determine land policy and land allocation, with the ultimate purpose of ensuring these lands remained in Jewish hands. Based on this law, ILA policy guarantees that state-owned lands cannot be transferred or sold. The ILA can lease these lands on a long-term basis (up to 49 years) but is not allowed to transfer ownership to renters. Leases for agricultural land stipulate that land can only be used for agricultural purposes and, if the agricultural designation of these lands changes, the renters must return them to the ILA.

In the early 1990s, however, agricultural land leased to Kibbutzim and

Moshavim began to be privatized. The 1992 ILA decision 533 allowed agriculturally designated lands leased from the state to be designated for commercial, industrial, housing, or tourism purposes. Many of these lands were subsequently transferred to Kibbutzim and Moshavim (most of which were Ashkenazi-run). In effect, Kibbutzim and Moshavim became the owners of these state lands, or they were granted high levels of compensation for parting with the lands they'd cultivated.

During the same period, the government was also privatizing public housing. Most of the tenants were Mizrahim living in poor neighborhoods of big cities and "development towns." The legal status of the apartments determined that, after the death of the tenant, rights would revert to government-owned companies. Tenants could not bequeath their apartments to their children. Mizrahi tenants demanded ownership rights of 120,000 apartments, for which they had been paying subsidized monthly rent to the state for decades. However, unlike the case of Kibbutzim lease-holders, in which the government supported their demands for ownership of their leased lands, the requests of the public housing tenants were rejected.

Keshet was active in both campaigns against the government decisions. Due to the public housing campaign launched with other social movements, the Israeli Knesset passed the "Law of Public Housing" on October 17, 1998. This law enabled some of the Mizrahi public sector tenants to purchase their apartments. However, the state's response to land ownership rights granted to the Kibbutzim and Moshavim were handled differently. After several previously unsuccessful appeals to the High Court in the 1990s, Keshet made another attempt, along with ACRI. Keshet requested that the privatization settlements made between the ILA and the Kibbutzim and Moshavim be canceled. On August 29, 2002, the appeal was accepted. The ruling determined that the ILA decision had indeed granted exaggerated and unjust benefits. The court based its decision on the violation of the principles of "distributive justice." The ILA, however, quickly circumvented the court's decision. Within a short period, most of the deals that began prior to the High Court decision were cleared. Though Keshet appealed again in 2003, the issue was effectively buried.[64]

In both cases, Keshet fought on behalf of Mizrahim alone. Palestinian rights were not on its agenda. After all, the public housing campaign was focused on a discriminatory policy that excluded Palestinian citizens in the first place. Still, one might have expected post-Zionist theoreticians would take the opportunity to question the appalling Israeli government policies that prevent Palestinians from even building on whatever meager lands they still had. Keshet's demand to share ownership of state lands with Kibbutzim and Moshavim is, in fact, an attempt to share the spoils of the robbery of Palestinian land, which has been taking place throughout the state's history, up to the very present.

Palestinian attorney Jamil Dakwar made clear the betrayal of Palestinian rights as presented in Keshet's appeals to the High Court:[65] "These appeals in fact aim at preserving the *status quo* which existed prior to accepting the ILA decisions regarding the privatization of lands and the change of their designation. Namely, the situation in which the state continues to hold 'state lands' and act in accordance with the discriminatory designations of them. Moreover, since the allocation of lands in the past was discriminatory, the transfer of the ownership to those who benefited from the discriminatory policy means perpetuating the discrimination and even making it more severe." Dakwar ends his article by demanding that the state return all confiscated lands to their Palestinian owners.[66]

In fact, the Keshet made a deal with the government: silence on the Palestinians was rewarded with benefits for Mizrahim. Sociologist Shlomo Swirski explains the nature of this "shameful deal" regarding the privatization of state lands: in order to please Keshet and others who opposed the high compensation granted for the unfreezing of land, government agencies called for establishing a fund for the residents of "development towns" to improve their economic situation. "The designers of this deal will [thus] enable the state to perpetuate the robbery of Palestinian lands . . . [because] as long as these lands are under the ownership of the state (which also keeps the documents that at least in part can prove [Palestinian] ownership), the possibility for demanding compensation from the state exists. But after their privatization it will be very difficult to do so, if not entirely impossible."[67]

Keshet based its demand for Mizrahim rights to state lands and public housing on the same Zionist rhetoric the government and the Kibbutzim used. It claimed that the Mizrahim equally contributed to the Zionist project. In the beginning, this rhetoric was allegedly a tactical means to advance the campaign for public housing tenants. But over time, it became the primary moral claim.[68] Keshet argued that Mizrahim, like members of Kibbutzim and Moshavim, played an integral role in implementing the Zionist goal of settling the country and defending it by populating frontier communities. They also emphasized the pioneering Zionist role their communities played via "population dispersion," a code name for the Judaisation of Palestinian-populated areas, severing their connections. Shlomo Vazana, a Keshet spokesperson, complained at the time that the equal role played by Mizrahim in "defending the state of the Jews" had been ignored. "No one spoke about the immigrants from the Arab countries as heroes, despite the fact that they had been [heroes]."[69] Yossi Yonah, a Keshet founder and one of its central figures, expressed a similar thought: "The Mizrahi immigrants who settled the borders were Zionist pioneers to the same extent as the mythological Zionist agricultural settlers [the Kibbutzim and Moshavim], and even contributed like them to the security of the state."[70]

Keshet adopted the slogan: "These lands are also mine." Nabih Bashir, a Palestinian citizen who had joined Keshet when it was founded, comments:

> I cannot accept the slogan "these lands are also mine," even when it is justified as a semantic-tactic used to find an "acceptable language" that can hopefully create dialogue between the *Keshet* and the [Jewish] public. Behind it hides "our" perception that the settlement of neighborhoods and development towns in the frontier areas, is a *Halutz* [a Zionist pioneer] project, and its contribution to Israel is large and is not less than that of the agricultural settlement [movement]. Let my friends in the movement [*Keshet*] pardon me: I am not capable, even for a minute, to become a "*Halutz*," a "settler" or a "Zionist" nor [can I] base my demands on [the ground] that the settlers in neighborhoods and development towns were brought there by the Authorities as a result of security and nationalistic considerations.[71]

In their complicity with Zionism on the issue of Palestinian rights to lands, the Mizrahi post-Zionists reject any radical dimension of Mizrahi identity and resistance as well. The introduction to the book *Mizrahim in Israel*, largely written from a post-colonialist perspective, uses Homi Bhabha's[72] notion of "hybridity" to describe the condition of Mizrahim.[73] The editors of *Mizrahim in Israel* write in the introduction of the book:

> Throughout the book, we argue that there is no one distinct and clear Mizrahi identity, and that there are many identities which at the same time are portrayed out of complex relations of inclusion and exclusion. Contrary to the Palestinians, for example, who have developed an alternative to the Zionist narrative, most Mizrahim seek to adopt the hegemonic Zionist position, despite the fact that at the same time they are its victims. The same applies to the dominant groups and institutions [of the state]: they do not entirely exclude the Mizrahim, but try to include them into the collective while permanently denoting their "otherness."

"Hybridity" added a new dimension to postcolonialism: it supplied a theoretical tool for de-radicalizing the potential militant protest of Mizrahim by blurring the boundaries of Mizrahi identity. "Hybridity" contradicts the very essence of the radical "New Mizrahim" intellectual trend, namely their emphasis on the distinct identity of Mizrahim based on their shared class and cultural oppression. This distinct identity implies a collective militant struggle against the Zionist Ashkenazi regime, as exemplified in the Black Panthers' heritage.

Consistent with the "hybridity" perspective, the editors of *Mizrahim in Israel* reject attributing any special significance to the Black Panther uprising and discourse. They argue such a position expresses an ideologically driven narrative that obscures the real history of Mizrahim—namely, that their continuous protest began as early as their immigration to Israel, and continued consecutively in different arenas of Israeli society, such as education, housing, and governmental budgets to Mizrahi Moshavim.

Strong criticism of how postcolonial "hybridity" negatively affects Mizrahim militancy continues to be voiced by a handful of radical Mizrahi intellectuals and academics, like Zvi Ben Dor of New York University and Moshe Behar of Manchester University. These individuals cherish the anti-Zionist, socialist, radical heritage of the Israeli Black Panther movement. Political scientist Moshe (Shiko) Behar notes, "the very status of a collective practical/concrete Mizrahim activity—one that deviates from the polite liberal or socio-democratic collective activity, such as that of Wadi Salib and the Black Panthers—lost its centrality within what has become the Mizrahi discourse." He concludes, "Maybe it is worth rereading the writings of a materialist economist like Karl Marx who emphasized the socio-political praxis, and not suffice with reading social-democrats, whether economists or otherwise."[74]

The leading post-Zionists' lack of solidarity with Palestinian citizens results from their reticence to confront the core nature of Israel as a settler colonial state and society. They have determined that "part of the ideas developed in the local academic research were nourished by the political thinking of Matzpen," especially by Matzpen's "emphasizing not only the connection of Zionism to Imperialism but also the nature of Zionism itself as a colonialist movement."[75] However, they did not pursue or continue the Matzpen tradition. They did not identify the connection between Zionism as a settler-colonial project, the capitalist nature of the Jewish state, and the state's role as the outpost of the imperialist hegemony in the region. They chose to reject the anti-colonial perspective that characterized Matzpen's worldview and instead adopted identity politics, multiculturalism, and postcolonialism. This has allowed them to maintain a critical stance toward the Jewish state, while at the same time they leave the fundamentals on which the Jewish state was built unchallenged. In this context, the central feature of the state is the marginalization and persecution of its Palestinian citizens—but that has been removed from the post-Zionist intellectual and political discourse. The national identity of the Palestinian citizens and their call for de-Zionization of the state of Israel have been ignored as well.

Zionist Left members decry that "post-Zionism" aspires to damage the just image of the Zionist project. But this aspiration cannot be found in post-Zionist writings. Rather, the Zionist Left's accusations against post-Zionists indicate their own closing of ranks against the potential embodied in *any* deviation from the hegemonic state narratives they created and sustained. In this context, a critique of the Zionist colonial project that brought about the 1948 Nakba is essential; it targets the very identity of the state and those committed to it. Yet post-Zionists have been cautious to address the pre-state Zionist colonization period and the Nakba. Doing so would expose their futile challenge to the prevailing national and class inequalities in Israel.

However, the true test of post-Zionism as a critical approach is in its ability to create an alternative to Zionist Left conceptions of the root cause of the Israeli-Palestinian "conflict," and after that, to propose peace initiatives capable of solving the conflict. What are the principles of the peace plans initiated by Zionist Left governments and leaders? Are they based on the recognition of the national rights of the Palestinian people? To what extent have postmodernist theories equipped their proponents to offer a real alternative vision for Israel/Palestine? I address these issues in the next, and final, chapter of the book.

CHAPTER 9

The Zionist Left and "Peace"

The Israeli establishment continues to pursue a strategy of preserving a Jewish majority in Historic Palestine; mass expulsion remains a possibility. This idea still looms in the strategic thinking of political and military elites, who seldom discuss the idea openly. Strategists are waiting for an "opportune moment," such as an extreme emergency or a major war in the Middle East, which would allow for a reprising of the 1948 ethnic cleansing.[1] In the meantime, Israel carries on with its policies of dispossession, which produce a slow but systematic ethnic cleansing. At the same time, Israel can profess that it seeks a peaceful solution to the "conflict," as the state's various peace proposals and initiatives allow for ethnic cleansing under the guise of the perpetual settlement project. By early 2011, settlements were being developed and expanded unabashedly. Policies and laws that try to systematically dispossess Israel's Palestinian citizens of their rights also amount to a gradual ethnic cleansing—albeit at a different pace. These ongoing policies lay bare the falseness of the US-Israeli peace initiatives.

The Oslo Accords

What are commonly referred to as Israel's "peace initiatives," which attempt to reach a "historic compromise with the Palestinian people," have all retained the basic principles and goals of the 1993 Oslo Accords.[2] The US and Labor-led Israel planned the Oslo Accords (1993 and 1995)[3] when they realized that the PLO leadership, ensconced in Tunisia, was prepared to accept Israel's terms of surrender. For this reason, Noam Chomsky characterized the Accords as a "sell out."[4] In the PLO, the Israelis now had the full collaborationist leadership it needed to confine the Palestinians onto their own South African Bantustan—a nominal "state" without genuine sovereignty.[5] As long as the slightest Palestinian opposition to Israel's unacceptable demands existed, the plan could not be implemented. For this reason, an independent Palestinian state had to be created, but only as an illusion. The Oslo Accords provided that illusion. The Palestinian leadership, the Zionist Left, and progressives around the world pinned their hopes to Oslo's success. For "the time being," however, an "interim limited self-governing authority" was granted to the Palestinians on part of the 1967[6] occupied territories, while Israeli maintained control over the remainder—without restrictions on further colonization. The Oslo Accords thus facilitated the construction of settlements and reinforced Israel's control over the territories. This fragmented the West Bank, and prevented the establishment there of any viable Palestinian state.

The Oslo Accords needed legitimacy from the "Palestinian people." It could not just be a plan dictated by the United States and Israel. So it was designed not only to restore the exiled leadership of the PLO and its chairman Yasser Arafat to the '67 occupied territories, but also to provide for elections that would grant a semblance of democracy to the fake entity ruled by Israel—the Palestinian National Authority. Israel won recognition from the Palestinians, which it had long aspired to, thanks to the Oslo Accords. And in return, Israel did not have to offer an end to the occupation, or even recognize the reality of the occupation, not to mention discontinue the settlements. Zionist Left intellectuals saw the Oslo Accords' section on "mutual recognition" as a recognition of the Jewish state and of Zionism, Israel's primary goals ever since its establishment. Sociologist Baruch Kimmerling explains why such recognition was necessary:

> Israel's longing for PLO recognition of Israel as a Jewish Zionist state is the result of Israel's colonial society's inability to deal with its relationship with the local [Palestinian] society and with the entire Arab region, as have other colonial or immigrant societies. [That is,] by annihilation of the local population and by putting an end to their existence as an organized society, or by the immigrants' gradual assimilation within the indigenous society. This inability led to its very right to exist (as a Jewish state) being held perpetually in doubt. Hence, Israel's longing to be accepted in the region and to become a *fait accompli* there without having to relinquish its Zionist character. If this aspiration is fulfilled, this will be the Zionist Movement's greatest victory as a movement of immigrant colonizers.

> The recognition by the PLO and the obtaining of an agreement . . . with that or-
> ganization are the preconditions for the realization of this chance.[7]

Dovish Israeli author A. B. Yehoshua spoke for a wide swath of the Zionist
Left when he characterized Palestinian recognition of Israel as, in fact, accepting
the Zionist colonial project: "I have an immense sense of relief [because of the
agreement with the Palestinians]. In this conflict Arafat represents the first
Palestinian shepherd who was confronted by the first Bilu[8] who came to cultivate the land of Israel. And my joy is at the compromise and the acceptance."[9]

Over time, the explicit recognition of the Jewish identity of the state of Israel—and not just its right to sovereignty—became even more critical. Israel
insisted this condition be met before it would consider negotiations for a peaceful solution. The "implied" recognition of Israel as a Jewish state, as presented
in the 1993 Oslo Agreement, was not enough. Israel demanded the Palestinians
explicitly declare its right to exist as a Jewish state. This would force the Palestinians to waive the right of return for Palestinian refugees. Even the fully collaborative leadership of Abu Mazen cannot publicly accept that.

The US-Israeli Oslo plan, and subsequent US-orchestrated "peace initiatives" that followed Oslo's collapse in 2000, had a crucial economic dimension
as well—the US-neoliberal project planned for Palestine and the Middle East
at large. In addition to its hopes to control access to the region's oil resources,
the United States has pursued a policy over the last two decades of integrating
its bases of support in the region within a single, neoliberal economic zone tied
to the United States through a series of bilateral trade agreements. Spanning
from Bahrain and Jordan to Egypt and Saudi Arabia, these free trade agreements have been signed or are being negotiated throughout the region, and each
contains a clause that commits the country in question to normalize relations
with Israel, forbidding any boycott of trade. "What this means," says Marxist
political economist Adam Hanieh, "is that Israel's historic destruction of Palestinian national rights must be accepted and blessed by all states in the region."[10]
This is but the economic equivalent of Israel's political demand for recognition
of the Jewish state.

Accordingly, the fragmentation of the West Bank had the economic function
of formalizing "a truncated network of Palestinian-controlled cantons and associated industrial zones, dependent upon the Israeli occupation, and through
which a pool of cheap Palestinian labor will be exploited by Israeli, Palestinian
and other regional capitalist groups."[11] The misleading slogan of the "two-state
solution" fits well into this plan.

Establishing a "Palestinian state" is seen as a condition for achieving stabilization in the Middle East, through which Israel hopes to end the national resistance and bring about a "historic compromise." However, the situation was not considered "ripe" for a Palestinian state since full Palestinian surrender was not yet achieved. Hence, Israeli governments, both Right and Labor, used the prolonged "peace process" during the 1990s as a pretext for arguing that the talks with the Palestinians are·indeed leading to a peace settlement in the near future. The peace process permitted "moderate" Arab states to cooperate with the US-Israeli political and economic project as well. This produced a de facto end to the boycott of Israel, while strengthening the cooperation of these "moderate" states with Israel in the US-led "war against terror" in the Middle East.

The Israeli business elite enthusiastically embraced the vision of a new Middle East and the "development" plans assigned to the Palestinians. The Israeli business elite has supported all peace plans since the Oslo Accords in 1993. These plans were in fact initiated by Zionist Left parties—Labor and Meretz—which, ironically, have acted as the "home parties" of Israel's capitalists and upper middle classes.[12]

The Oslo process was doomed to fail. It eventually collapsed after the staged peace summit orchestrated by US President Bill Clinton at Camp David in July 2000. At the summit, Arafat had no alternative but to reject Israeli Prime Minister Ehud Barak's "generous offer," giving way to the second Intifada. Nevertheless, the writing on the wall for Oslo's failure could be seen as early as the mid-1990s. While negotiations continued, the frantic construction of Jewish settlements and bypass roads[13] continued unabated. Contact between the Gaza Strip and the West Bank was almost completely cut off. The blockade of Gaza from Israel and the outside world escalated until the Palestinians were on the verge of sheer suffocation. In the Oslo years, Israel deepened its military and economic control over the occupied territories and rendered meaningless even the misleading formal language of the Oslo Accords.

The Collapse of the Oslo Accords—Camp David 2000

Baruch Kimmerling elaborates on the systematic policies of the Labor Party, which in fact prepared the ground for the collapse of the Camp David Summit and the end of the Oslo process.[14] He reviews Prime Minister Barak's disregard for the Palestinian leadership that had been begging for concessions to ease the pressure they faced from their people. The Israeli Intelligence Services warned that the Palestinian Authority's control was weakening, and Hamas and the Islamic Jihad were becoming strengthened. But Barak insisted that there would be no release of prisoners "with blood on their hands" or any territorial "concessions" until a *final status* agreement had been reached. "Hence," writes Kimmerling, "though the central negotiations conducted at Camp David were preceded by innumerable talks at all levels, these were unproductive. Arafat was opposed a priori to Barak's approach—a freeze on the third, more extensive redeployment and other previous Israeli commitments [stipulated in the Oslo Accords], and [instead] transitioning straight to talks on the conditions for a final comprehensive settlement—and still had nothing to display to an increasingly restive Palestinian populace as fruit of the Oslo accords. Yet because all the cards were in Israel's hands, Arafat had no alternative but to agree to take part in Camp David."[15]

Arafat could not accept the plan, described as a final settlement, presented to him at Camp David. Under this plan, the seven Israeli settlement blocs, comprising around 80 percent of the Jewish settler population, would be annexed to Israel. A viaduct would be built to link the Gaza Strip and West Bank. The possibility of Israel holding a long-term lease on an additional 10 percent of the West Bank along the Jordan Valley, "for security reasons," had also been discussed. It would later be argued that keeping the river under Israeli control was important for Jordan, which was anxious about Palestinian irredentism and the possible unification of the two banks. The right of return of refugees was rejected, and Israel declined to acknowledge any moral or legal responsibility for the creation of the problem. The municipal boundaries of Jerusalem would be expanded—"apparently to include the annexation of Abu Dis, Azariya and a few other villages—so there would, nominally, be something to share. The intention was to leave most of the current area of the city under Israeli sovereignty; the additional territory would be sold to the Palestinians as their 'Jerusalem' and Abu Dis as the capital of the future Palestinian state."[16]

Tanya Reinhart, the late renowned linguist and insightful political analyst, emphasized that the crucial turning point at Camp David was Barak's demand for a signed "final agreement" accompanied by a Palestinian declaration of the end of the conflict. Had the Palestinians signed such a declaration, they would have lost all legal standing for future claims based on UN resolutions.[17] Kimmerling comments, "The Palestinians called the portions allotted to them Bantustans; but the original enclaves created by the Afrikaners for South African blacks were far better endowed than those of Barak's 'generous offer.'" The second

Intifada was inevitable. "After seven years of futile talks that had failed to make any significant advance in the Palestinian cause—accompanied by the intensification of the Jewish colonization process in the Occupied Palestinian Territories—the question was not whether but when the anger and violence would erupt, and in what form."[18]

The Camp David "shameful document," as Reinhart called it, was largely based upon proposals put forward by Yossi Beilin, who later became the chair of Meretz, the most left-wing party within the Zionist camp.[19] Beilin, who was also a central figure in the secret talks that produced the Oslo Accords, embodied the Zionist Left's approach toward the "peace initiatives" after the summit's collapse. Ignoring the intensified oppression of Palestinians during the Oslo years, the Zionist Left continued to support Oslo. Former Prime Minister Rabin famously admitted that Oslo aimed to subcontract rule over the Palestinians to Palestinian collaborators whose repression would not face limits enforced by the Supreme Court and human rights organizations in Israel. Rabin's candor did not force the Zionist Left to retreat from, much less to reevaluate, the Oslo process.

True to form, the Zionist Left turned a deaf ear to the voices of Palestinians and others who pointed to the disaster that Israel's policies would bring about. Azmi Bishara repeatedly warned against the deceptions spread by the Zionist Left with regard to the Oslo Accords' prospects for peace. In October 2000, when the Intifada broke out, he recalled the warning about the Camp David Summit that he had sent to the Zionist Left.

> Very few joined us during those months [before the Summit] when we tried, time after time, to make it clear that no Palestinian would accept such an ultimatum [by PM Labor Barak], and that this was a dangerous policy that would lead to war . . . The Zionist Left gambled on a peace based on the existing relation of forces and did not set up principles of justice and equality. That is the reason it did not confront Israeli public opinion on the terms for a just peace, and instead of criticizing Barak's initiative, supported and aided the accusation made against the Palestinians who opposed an agreement based on an apartheid state, divided into cantons.[20]

The Zionist Left overlooked the anger and frustration of the Palestinians in the '67 occupied territories, both of which gave birth to the second Intifada. It took the same attitude when it came to the Palestinians in Israel. The latter's strengthened national consciousness and the NDA's articulation of their demands for national equal rights had no resonance among Zionist Left intellectuals. The

Zionist Left ignored protests against the Israeli governments' continuous dispossession of Palestinians within Israel and the '67 occupied territories. They uncritically accepted the liberal semblance of Labor governments during the Oslo years.

The collapse of the Camp David Summit and the breakout of the second Intifada[21] signaled a turning point in policy and discourse. In the ensuing years, the "peace negotiations" strategy of the 1990s was abandoned and replaced by "unilateralism," which no longer sought Palestinian consent. The slogan "there is no partner for peace," coined by Barak after the failure of the Camp David Summit,[22] was hailed by the majority of the Zionist Left. The second Intifada proved the Palestinians' "deep-rooted unwillingness" to accept the existence of Israel and to live in peace. The Zionist Left backed the attempts of Barak's Labor-Meretz government to crush the popular resistance in the '67 occupied territories. They also defended the suppression of militant demonstrations organized by Palestinians in Israel in solidarity with their brethren. Thirteen Palestinian citizens were killed in these confrontations with the Israeli police.

Zionist Left intellectuals supported the myth of Barak's "generous offer."[23] Radical Left writer and poet Yitzhak Laor describes the role Zionist Left intellectuals played in legitimizing the surrender plan dictated to the Palestinians at Camp David.[24] Laor singles out Hebrew University philosophy professor Menachem Brinker: "[He] announced to the Israeli Left during Barak's journey to Camp David, in an article in *Haaretz*: 'Barak came to Camp David with a far-reaching political plan. No former Israeli leader has ever offered the Palestinians a similar plan. The Left has no reason whatsoever to criticize his [Barak's] "red lines" . . . I am interested in peace on the ground, not merely on paper, and therefore I must understand that there are some objective circumstances that impose certain limits on Barak's concessions.'"[25]

"Anyone familiar with the map of Barak's proposals," emphasizes Laor, "knows what Brinker had in mind by 'certain limits'—the lying sales-talk of all who marketed a shopping list for the Palestinians that offered them '90 percent' of the West Bank: that is, 90 percent of what would be left after Israel kept its expansion around Jerusalem, its military roads and bases, its settlements." Laor notes the dehumanizing approach that Brinker, along with others on the Zionist Left, took toward the Palestinians and the fragmented nature of the territory allocated to the future Palestinian state.

Laor adds, "To those who over the years have gotten used to thinking of the Palestinians as a 'demographic threat,' calculating with fear 'how many Arabs will be living among us,' it comes quite naturally to reduce their lands to percentages, too. What is unthinkable is to envisage them as citizens of their own country, capable of traveling from place to place within it without countless roadblocks (which Barak's map granted them forever), with a natural love of their land, and of freedom of movement within it. Laor notes that Brinker even asserts that "annexing settlement clusters in which most of the current settlers in the West Bank will live, does not in his view contradict the minimal aspirations of the Palestinians and does not undermine their chances of establishing a viable Palestinian state."

Misreading Support for Oslo and Globalization to Mean Liberalization of Political Culture

Post-Zionists viewed the 1990s as the era of political liberalization, and this view was based on the fake "search for peace" under the Oslo Agreements.[26] The post-Zionist (mis)reading of the peace process was accompanied by an erroneous understanding of Jewish society as well. In accordance with their own perceptions, they interpreted the Jewish majority's support for Oslo as though it indicated a decisive transformation in Israel's political culture— namely, a genuine desire among the political establishment and society at large to reach a peace settlement based upon a willingness to make "painful" territorial concessions. The fact is, however, the wide support for the Oslo process did not indicate any real change in the hegemonic Zionist consensus, or the approach of Israeli society toward Palestinian national rights. Nor did it point to a challenge to the "Jewish-democratic" definition of the state, or a realization that these two supposed identities of the state were incompatible.

On the contrary, the exclusivist, sectarian dimensions of Israel's political culture were strengthened during the Oslo "peace years," as historian Shlomo Sand has confirmed: "Ethnization of the state super identity, which has been growing since the 1967 occupation, and strengthened more so since the first Intifada, has not weakened following Oslo . . . The political elite attempted more than ever in the past to insert values and historical consciousness considered to be more Jewish into the education system while part of the old time producers of culture [established social scientists and intellectuals] responded favorably to this."[27]

Post-Zionists' misleading assumption, that substantive ideological shifts in Israel's political culture created the readiness to accept the Oslo Accords, relied upon the idea that economic globalization's effects on world culture and ideology were weakening the nation state, emancipating people from national ideologies, and creating a turn toward "enlightened" individualism. In the Israeli case, the economic and social changes that accompanied neoliberalism had supposedly gnawed away at the Zionist supra-structure, with respect to questions of both identity and commitment to the Zionist state. In their wake, "civil society" was said to have been strengthened and ready to challenge state-backed Zionist hegemony.[28]

Turning their back on "grand" narratives, objecting to the state's hegemonic culture, and believing in the radicalizing potential of identity politics, some leading multiculturalists came to support the "free market" model of neoliberalism. Neoliberalism ostensibly granted the market total control over civil society, offsetting state discrimination in the allocation of resources and power. Accordingly, muticulturalists argued that the state should, as far as possible, not involve itself in the lives of citizens. The state's roles should be left to civil society and the powers of the free market. Multiculturalists Yossi Yonah and Yehouda Shenhav remark: "To this day we have not seen the state set out to defend the weak people who were supposed to be the main beneficiaries from social democracy." On the contrary, the state collaborates with big capital in its monetary policy and privatization process. Hence, "One may say something which also justifies the dismantling mechanisms of the market forces. For example, one may conclude that the Palestinian citizens of Israel would be happy to see the market forces responsible for allocation of state lands instead of the discriminative policy of Israel Land Authority—ILA."[29] (See chapter 3.)

Social Democrat historian Daniel Gutwein of Haifa University points to the reactionary neoliberal worldview embedded in the multiculturalism espoused by Yonah and Shenhav. "It is an ideology anchored in the neoliberal value world that has grown out of the reciprocal relations of globalization, privatization, and postmodernism. It blurs the exploitation and oppression inherent in 'free competition,' creates an ideology of the market forces, while presenting them as a liberating and democratic force and supplies an ideological basis for a policy that destroys the welfare state and increases economic gaps."[30]

Post-Zionist sociologist Uri Ram elaborates on the cultural blessing economic globalization brings to Israeli society as argued by his colleagues Yonah and Shenhav. Ram determines that Post-Zionism embodies a local instance of the "trend towards cosmopolitanism and citizenry which grew out of the fundamental changes in economic and social structure of the Globalization era." At the same time, Ram contends, a contradictory phenomenon has developed, which he terms "neo-Zionism." Post-Zionism, as a product of globalization, is

identified with the inclination toward the "decline of national identity," preparedness to reach a peace settlement, and the aspiration "to strengthen uni-
versalism, namely, to develop democracy in Israel." In contrast, "neo-Zionism"
shoots for "escalated particularism, namely the establishment of an ethnic
apartheid regime." It expresses the "combination of a religious perception and
primordial nationalism as well as opposition to any political compromise [with
the Palestinians]."[31] In the political arena, "neo-Zionism" constitutes the local
version of the ethnic chauvinist fundamentalist Right, as seen in various for-
mations throughout Europe. This tendency is embodied in parties like Mafdal
(the National Religious Party, the extreme right-wing settler party) and by substantial parts of the Likud and Shas parties. On the other hand, argues Ram,
the Labor and Meretz parties represent to a great extent the policies which ostensibly derive from "Postism," inclinations toward liberalism, political compromise, and peace.

The Nonexistent "Sharp Rift" between Left and Right

While focusing on the "sharp rift" between the Labor and Likud parties, Uri
Ram ignores their common political approach, allowing them to close ranks
around policies such as the destruction and siege of Gaza, the Apartheid wall,
and the puppet regime in the West Bank. Like the Zionist Left and the peace
camp at large, Ram considered the clash between post- and neo-Zionists as the
central fault line in modern-day Israel. This clash is seen as a reformulation in
principle of the classic historical confrontation between the ideology of Enlightenment—utilitarianism, individualism, rationalism, and pragmatism—which is
at the heart of the post-Zionist approach, and the romantic—reactionary, fanatical, religious, backward, fundamentalist, and chauvinist ideologies—which is at
the heart of neo-Zionism.[32]

The idea of a sharp rift between Left and Right in Israel is based on misleading assumptions about the "enlightenment" of the Israeli Zionist Left. It
highlights Ram's own skewed liberalism. Ram closes his eyes to, among other
things, Zionism's hypocritical secularism, which has never demanded the separation of religion and state, and to the colonial arrogance and Orientalism that
has characterized the discourse of those on the Zionist Left. He also does not
question the very peace initiatives that the Zionist Left initiated, or the most
atrocious policies that are directed toward Palestinians, which the Zionist Left
has supported. He ignores how the Zionist Left's conclusion—that there was

"no partner to peace"—paved the way for Sharon's victory in the 2001 elections. Moreover, when Sharon began advertising his "unilateral strategy" to replace the Oslo process, he became the "champion of peace" in the eyes of large parts of the Zionist Left. Since 2001, the Labor Party has supported the oppressive policies launched by the Israeli Right—most of the time participating in governments led by Kadima or Likud. Sharon, four Likud ministers, and many high-level Likud activists founded Kadima on November 21, 2005. A number of Labor leaders (including Shimon Peres and Haim Ramon) joined the new party.[33] Its establishment signified the adoption by Sharon and wide sections of Likud of what is known as the traditional "pragmatism" of the Labor Party. After 1967, this pragmatism found expression in the rhetoric of supporting a peace settlement with the Palestinians, while gradually expanding Zionist colonization, an apparent contradiction in terms. Additionally, the gradually expanding colonization has encompassed a variety of methods of "politicide," "sociocide," and actual ethnic cleansing.

The Apartheid Wall—Beginning in 2002

The plan for building the "Apartheid Wall" (officially named the "separation fence") between Israel and the West Bank was initiated by a number of Labor Party leaders and implemented by the first Kadima-Labor government (and later by Likud-Labor governments). The official reason for the wall was that it would sustain Israel's security. However, expansion plans, including annexing the majority of settlements to Israel, and fragmenting the West Bank, played a major role in determining the route of the barrier. Many on the Zionist Left have criticized the fact that the wall separates villages from nearby cultivated lands. But they have not challenged the wall's existence. A 2008 interview with Labor Party member and political philosopher Yuli Tamir, the Minister of Education in the Kadima-Labor government and founder of Peace Now, was fairly typical. Asked her opinion on the wall and on Jewish-only roads in the West Bank, Tamir replied: "There are processes which have been institutionalized, like road 443 [for Jews only].[34] And I have always supported a wall. When our citizens are killed in terror operations, I am not a vegetarian. This is not the role of the Left. It [the left] should be activist in regards to the comprehensive solution and the unnecessary attacks on innocent civilians."[35]

The 2005 Staged "Disengagement from Gaza"

In the Knesset in October 2004, Labor and Meretz provided crucial support for passing Sharon's plan to "disengage" from the Gaza Strip. They gave the international community the go-ahead to celebrate what was, in essence, a significant step in the total war against the Palestinian people.[36] The Zionist Left at large ignored information and analysis regarding the real aims of disengagement from Gaza, publicized in the run-up to the maneuver. For example, then-MK Azmi Bishara said in a debate that took place in the Knesset on October 25, 2004:

> There is no withdrawal here, but a redeployment of the Israeli army around the Gaza Strip. . . . Sharon's plan is not a unilateral withdrawal like [the Israeli army's] in Lebanon, not a replacement of one sovereignty by another, but an occupation from the outside and a siege from the sea, earth, and air. The Palestinians are supposed to live in one big detention camp and prove that they can be "OK" and behave like good children . . . within a ghetto. And when they don't "behave themselves," Israel will both re-invade [Gaza] and have again arguments for not carrying out any negotiations [with the Palestinians].

Bishara also said:

> A US-Israeli scheme to give up nothing of value, in exchange for an explicit promise from the US to allow Israel to continue controlling the majority of the West Bank. This is explicitly written into the third clause of the first section of the plan, which reads: "It is clear that various regions in the West Bank will remain part of Israel. Israel will annex the central Jewish settlement blocs, towns, security areas, and other lands which Israel has an interest in keeping." But it isn't Sharon who has changed. It's the US who has officially adopted his political strategy.[37]

Members of the Zionist Left not only ignored warnings from the Palestinians, they also refused to listen to the highest levels of Sharon's government, who were frankly admitting that disengagement was a US-Israeli scheme that sought the world's approval for continuing other parts of the "unilateral project."[38] This included the continued erection of the Apartheid wall, and the deepening of Israel's control over the remaining, fragmented parts of the West Bank beyond the wall and in the Jordan Valley.

2006—Admitted No Difference

Already by the 2006 Knesset election campaign, which began a short time after the August 2005 "disengagement" from Gaza, Zionist Left political leaders were publicly admitting that there were no "principled differences" between themselves and Kadima. Amir Peretz, the Labor Party's new chairman and the former chair of Histadrut, declared early on as part of his campaign for prime minister, "It is Kadima who adopted the Labor Party's position on political and security matters." A political commentator from Israeli television's Channel 1 asked, "So why should the public vote for you?" Peretz answered proudly, "[Because] we are the original."[39]

Meretz MK and spokesperson Zehava Galon, reputed to be the "most leftist" among the Meretz leadership, also claimed authorship of Kadima's political positions. Galon lamented how "Kadima is now plucking the fruits" of the wide impact of Meretz's "peace approach."[40] The similarity between the Zionist Left's positions and those of Kadima was also pointed out as early as January 28, 2006, in a *Haaretz* editorial. "From the moment that Olmert [who replaced Sharon as prime minister and head of Kadima] agreed to open negotiations on a political settlement with the Palestinians, and when Peretz agreed to unilateral steps if these negotiations fail, the two parties have positioned themselves on the same starting line *vis-à-vis* the Palestinians." The admission of no difference between the Zionist Left and Kadima reflected a reality in which Labor and Meretz were devoted supporters of Kadima's bloody policies (and later Likud's) against the Palestinians and Lebanon.

A Wholesale War against Hamas

Hamas's victory in the January 2006 general elections gave Amir Peretz the excuse to revive the "no partner" slogan of Barak, and to support the Olmert government's policies of oppression against the Palestinians. This included boycotting the Hamas government, ending tax payments to the Palestinian Authority (which Israel collects from Palestinian imports), starving the Gaza Strip, escalating the daily assassinations of Palestinians, strengthening the siege on the entire '67 occupied territories, and turning them into one big prison. Large numbers of the Israeli peace camp, even members of its radical wings, did not welcome the democratic victory of Hamas. They claimed that Hamas's Islamic worldview contradicted their own secular, enlightened self-image. They were unable to recognize the resistance-based popularity of Hamas among a wide strata of Palestinians, well beyond the scope of its religious membership. The Zionist Left did not bother to respond to analysts, like Azmi Bishara, who time and again emphasized that in supporting Hamas, the Palestinian people had declared their opposition to the former

Palestinian Authority policies for succumbing to Israeli dictates. Yet most of the Israeli Left refused to see the reformist and pragmatic nationalism of Hamas's election platform (albeit wrapped in a loose Islamic discourse) and ignored the democratic basis of its rule. They continued to support the open opportunity for advancing the separation of Gaza from the "pacified" West Bank, beyond the use of physical barriers. Israel's attempt to ban all Palestinian Authority contact with the Hamas government of Gaza was intended to exclude Hamas from the Palestinian national body, with whom Israel was conducting "peace talks." In effect, Abu Mazen's collaborationist regime became the only "legitimate representative of the Palestinian people," who hopefully would sign a full surrender agreement on behalf of his people, when, and if, the appropriate time came about.

2006 Kadima-Labor War on Lebanon

The last remnants of a distinct Left discourse were buried after the March 2006 Israeli elections. The Labor Party joined the Kadima coalition government. Amir Peretz was appointed minister of defense, and led the onslaught of Lebanon in July 2006, with the blessing of Meretz (except MK Zehava Galon) and most of the Zionist Left intellectuals. Famous Israeli authors and ideological leaders of Peace Now—the largest part of the Israeli peace camp[41]—declared their full support for the war as the devastation of Lebanon reached its peak. The world-renowned author Amos Oz played a central role for the political and military establishment. In a July 20, 2006, article, during a moment when the destruction of Lebanon was already well underway, Oz describes the war as one of self-defense. "This time [in contrast to the 1982 war against Lebanon], Israel is not invading Lebanon. It is defending itself from a daily harassment and bombardment of dozens of our towns and villages by attempting to smash Hezbollah wherever it lurks."[42] He also argues for the moral superiority of the Israeli army over Hezbollah, claiming, misleadingly, "Hezbollah is targeting Israeli civilians wherever they are, while Israel is targeting mostly Hezbollah."[43]

Yitzhak Laor notes,[44] "On the day Oz's article was published, there [were] already over half a million refugees in Lebanon, 300 killed, the great majority of whom were civilians, and entire regions of its land destroyed—villages, towns, bridges, schools, hospitals."[45]

Oz also helped form the broad consensus in Israel for the US-led "war against terror." He supported the campaign both in general and against Iran in particular, now a central target of Israel's political and military strategy. Oz hurried to legitimize the American "New Middle East agenda," declared after the war on Lebanon, by articulating the framework of a war for a "free world." In his acceptance speech for the Corina Prize for lifetime achievement in literature, presented in Munich on September 24, 2006, Oz declared: "The war that is taking place at present, is not any more [a war] between nations but between the fanatics of all sides and the tolerant of all sides."[46]

Legitimizing the Extreme Secular Right, Even Lieberman

The explicit identification of the Left with the US-led "war on terror" in the Middle East, and especially against Iran, became the new pretext for the "open war" declared against Hamas and any Palestinian or other resistance. This identification has encouraged the political collaboration of the Labor Party with the most extreme, secular Right. Since 2006 and until January 2011,[47] the Labor Party participated in governments that included the most racist and right-wing elements of the Israeli political spectrum, including the likes of Avigdor Lieberman, head of the Israel Beytenu Party. As a disciple of sheer power politics, Lieberman has no need for the traditional Zionist dependency on the Bible and the "divine right"—articulated by Ram's "fanatic religious neo-Zionists"—to justify a blatant policy of war in the Middle East, including against the Palestinian citizens of Israel. Lieberman calls for transferring Palestinian-populated areas in Israel to the sovereignty of the future Palestinian state. He also believes in conditioning civil rights upon service in the Israeli army or a loyalty oath to the Jewish and democratic state.[48] While Lieberman's open racism seems at odds with secular rationalism and humanism, the Zionist Left has more in common with Lieberman's worldview than it would like to admit. Azmi Bishara notes:

> He [Lieberman] is trying to change the balance between religion and the state, not to make it more liberal or democratic, but more communal and sectarian, though without distinguishing between the two. For Lieberman a Russian needs only to serve in the army to be treated as a converted Jew. This nationalistic, rather than religious dimension of conversion is close to that of the Zionist Left—for example, Yossi Beilin [chair of Meretz at the time]—and it constitutes the basis of dialogue between them, but it is not the only common ground. He also shares with the Left a concern with "the demographic issue" and the need to get rid of the Palestinians in the framework of an agreement in which they give up all their historic demands with the exception of a political entity,

which just happens to be an Israeli interest as well. Lieberman clearly wants an entity to be an agent for Israel.[49]

Labor's willingness to participate in governments with Lieberman has not only conferred legitimacy to his racist party, it has also widened the boundaries of acknowledged Zionism to include even the "fanatic" secular Right, something the latter has long aspired to. The wheel has come full circle. The disciples of the extreme Right, Jabotinsky and Ben-Gurion, have openly united to implement the destruction of the Palestinian nation. What remains of the so-called rift between them, says Meron Benvenisti, "is nothing more than an internal Zionist spat."[50]

2009 Kadima-Labor Massacre in Gaza

Ehud Barak, the minister of defense in Ehud Olmert's Kadima government, led the carnage of Gaza in December 2008–January 2009. The determined resistance of Hamas, supported by the population, had to be repressed. "In this context," writes Noam Chomsky, "destruction of Gaza and annihilation of its social and cultural institutions makes good strategic sense."[51] The barbaric attack on Gaza was planned well in advance.[52] As confirmed by *Haaretz* senior political commentator Akiva Eldar, "The enormous power was sent to Gaza not only or even mainly in order to hit the military infrastructure of Hamas. The main mission that the political level assigned to the IDF was to dismantle the civil infrastructure of the regime, [ruled] by the only organization which challenges the government of Mahmoud Abbas [Abu Mazen]."[53] Rockets fired onto southern Israeli towns was accepted by Meretz as a justifiable pretext for the attack. Says Yitzhak Laor, "for Meretz the war was just in its first stage, but not afterward." In the face of these apologetics, Laor asks, "How many children should die for 'not afterward' and for understanding that it is forbidden for a Left movement to take part in Israel's military games?" Laor concludes, "Let's admit it: all Zionist parties were intoxicated at the time of the 'war' . . . Now it seems as if they were hit by blindness. Just a hangover."[54]

Zionist Left intellectuals refrained from explicitly accepting the Goldstone Report,[55] which disclosed Israel's war crimes committed during the Gaza massacre. Many even criticized the report for being politically biased against Israel. They did not speak up and demand an Israeli investigation of the army, which a number of liberals suggested as an alternative to the "unbalanced" Goldstone Report.[56] Nor did they react to the attempt to distinguish the responsibility of Israeli political leadership from that of the military, as Professor Zeev Sternhell advocates. Sternhell explicitly argues that there was no reason to investigate the army because the army received orders from the political leadership as to what "means" they should use in Gaza. However, Sternhell does not condemn the decision that engineered the onslaught of Gaza. He also refrains from criticizing the political leadership for what it set out to achieve in this "operation": namely, to destroy the civilian infrastructure and to devastate Gaza, including the mass killing of the civilian population. Instead, he indirectly credits the political leadership for empowering the army and giving them a means to wage war while preventing injuries and deaths to Israeli soldiers.

> It is well known that after the 2006 assault on Lebanon, Israel realized that Israeli society would not be ready anymore to withstand a war which demands [Israeli] lives. Israel wants military victories, but refuses to pay the human price it involves. [Therefore,] a sober decision was taken, as a result of a cold political consideration, to administer the punishing voyage into Gaza without [Israeli] losses. There is no Israeli, especially among those who themselves had been soldiers [who does not consider the] life of youngsters in uniform . . . [as] dear to him. But the practical meaning of this decision was that the heavy price would be paid by the entire Palestinian population without discrimination. Therefore, there is no need for an Israeli investigation committee. The case is clear like the sun at noon time. [Namely,] that since Hamas operates from within a crowded population in one of the most densely populated regions in the world, any attempt to reach them [Hamas] without hurting civilians—is impossible. A decision to defend the lives of [Palestinian] citizens would require an entirely different pattern of action: pointed incursions deep into the enemy's areas which could be very expensive in terms of our soldiers. Thus, in order to launch a war with zero losses to our forces, the political and military leadership decided to employ massive fire, without the capability of differentiating between a fighter who was preparing a rocket for firing and a child playing in the yard.

Indeed, all decision-makers in Israel knew in advance that a heavy disaster was imminent in Gaza, says Sternhell. "The army committed precisely the directives it received from their moral leaders, commanders and the government. They [the army] did not seek intentionally to kill civilians. They only bombed, eliminated and leveled everything which seemed necessary for observation, maneuver and advance, since every building could be a combat position for Hamas . . . All this demonstrates how cheap was the cost of Palestinian life, but the price was not determined on the ground. It is inscribed in the parameters that had been determined in the first place by the Israeli leadership."[57]

Sternhell's lengthy attempt to clear the army of blame finally leads to a restrained, controlled condemnation of the carnage. Yet even this is somewhat neutralized after he introduces the same criticism the Goldstone Report received, for "being unbalanced and failing to confront the crimes committed by Hamas." Sternhell's emphasis on practical implications of the means employed further limits the significance of his condemnation of "Operation Cast Lead." He largely focuses on the damage to Israel's image and not on the immorality of the Gaza massacre. Sternhell's condemnation is far from the disgust and rage one might expect from a Social Democrat committed to basic human rights.

> This is a severe warning [the Goldstone Report] because it expresses the approach of the international community towards Israel. In a final analysis, Operation Cast Lead has contributed an additional layer to the wall of de-legitimation which gradually encloses the state of the Jews. Even if no Israeli reaches [the International Court in] the Hague in the near future, the moral *stain* would not be wiped away and its implications still lie ahead of us.

The Disappearance of the Zionist Left

The "reasonable" rhetoric that has prevailed among liberal intellectuals like Sternhell, and the "pragmatic" perspective that has characterized the Zionist Left, are now shared by Likud and even the extreme secular Right. The latter have declared their support in principle for the establishment of a Palestinian Bantustan—in the form of "the two-state solution." A "Palestinian state" has come to mean little more than the fragmented and encircled Palestinian enclaves of the West Bank and the devastated and enclosed Gaza Strip. It is a cynical remnant of the original two-state solution endorsed by progressives like Noam Chomsky, who called for a full independent Palestinian state in the '67 occupied territories, in line with the 1988 PLO demand for the establishment of a Palestinian state.[58] More than any other political force in Israel, it is the Zionist Left that is responsible for equating this fake "solution" with Chomsky's genuine quest for a just peace, as expressed in his two-state formula.

It is no wonder, then, that the Zionist Left—once a force that represented a distinct political, social, and economic worldview—has vanished from the political map. In the 2008 elections, the Labor Party won only thirteen seats in the Knesset (reduced to only eight MKs after Barak quit Labor in January 2011) with Meretz taking a pathetic three. Together, they made up about 13 percent of the 120 MKs. This was half the number of seats Labor won in the 1998 elections (26), and less than a third of the votes won then by Meretz (10). Toward the end of November 2008, when polls were predicting the greatly diminished powers of both Labor and Meretz, Yossi Beilin announced his resignation from his post as Meretz chair. Beilin, who had been among the most active and formative in shaping Israel's various peace plans, claimed he had accomplished his and Meretz's political goal regarding the "partition of Eretz Israel." He declared this goal has now been adopted by the majority of Israeli society.

What a pathetic victory for the historic Zionist Labor movement! Its ideological triumph has been so complete that its distinct political framework was made obsolete.[59] The majority of Israeli society has by now adopted the duplicitous discourse of the Left: calling for peace while supporting a devastating war against the Palestinians that blocks said peace. Since the Zionist Left had, by the end of the 2000s, disappeared as a distinctive force, did the post-Zionists fare any better? In a word: no.

Post-Zionists' Support of Zionist Left Peace Initiatives

Uri Ram argued that a liberal post-Zionist culture prevailed in Israel throughout the 1990s. However, it proved to be shaky and vulnerable, since it was dependent on the Oslo peace process. "From its onset," Ram writes, "liberal 'post-Zionist' [culture] and the peace process were perceived as connected and as reciprocally conditioning each other, such that one could not be sustained without the other. Therefore one should not be surprised at all when the collapse of one brings about the downfall of the other. No wonder that with the rise of the level of bloodshed, the political level of neo-Zionism rises as well."[60]

Avoiding why the "bloodshed" was increasing prevented the post-Zionists from reexamining their assumptions regarding the "liberal culture" of the Oslo years. Unable to condemn the Labor Party government for the failure of Oslo and the brutal repression that followed, the post-Zionists instead concluded that the bloody confrontations with the Palestinians precipitated the decline of democratic values in Israel, not vice versa. The undemocratic Zionist values embraced by Israel's "enlightened" Zionist Left—and accepted by whole sections of Western liberals—allowed for false hopes in the "peace process," as well as for its eventual collapse, producing the second Intifada.

Sharing the Zionist Left's disappointment with the Oslo framework after Camp David 2000, a number of post-Zionists began emphasizing their commitment to the Zionist Left consensus.

Some of those who were attacked for their "post-Zionism" hurried to refute the accusations by explicitly declaring their commitment to Zionism. These soul-searching declarations read like acts of repentance. Professor Yehouda Shenhav's 2005 confessional interview with Erik Gelsner is a perfect example.[61] In the introduction, Gelsner notes the significant shift in Shenhav's political positions:

> The relation of Prof. Shenhav to the issue of Jewish nationality is surprising and in my opinion, reflects a move which might be seen as very small, but is rather dramatic in the world of the radical Left, and may be called, "an implicit soul searching." This is so especially considering that the radical Left, to which Shenhav is one of its most conspicuous spoke-persons in the last decade and a half, laid down one of the biggest internal challenges which Zionism has ever confronted. *Theory and Criticism*, the journal edited by Adi Ophir since 1991 and later, by Yehouda Shenhav since 2000, emphasized the centrality of the sexual and ethnic identity as an alternative to national identity . . . and was very critical of the Jewish national project—"Zionism."

In the interview, Shenhav's commitment to Zionism is clear cut, albeit somewhat defensive:

> Shenhav: I don't come from the position in which there was no justification for Jewish nationality, and I do not think that Zionism is *a priori* colonialist. At the same time, I think that there is a contradiction between ethnocentric nationalism and justice. Even more so, when you look at the historic Labor movement you realize that it was the biggest oppressor of Mizrahim, Arabs and women . . . therefore they [the Labor movement] are the harshest critics of identity politics.
>   Gelsner: And nevertheless you say that the national paradigm is not disqualified in principle?
>   Shenhav: Look, I am not a nationalist person. I would be happy with post-Nationalism, but there is justification for Jewish nationalism when in any case we are not moving towards a post-national era. I think that global and national processes have been strengthened rather than have replaced each other. *Brit Shalom* was an option—an option which was a missed opportunity—but it was a Zionist option. I could identify with such Zionism.[62] I don't belong to the camp which says that the state of Israel is not legitimate. I wish there would be here a bi-national solution. This is my interest as a Jew and an Israeli. I am also concerned about the future of this place. I am not a detached intellectual. But I know that a bi-national solution is not a simple thing.

Gelsner notes: "When I ask Shenhav if back in 1995 he would also have said that it is legitimate to argue for a Jewish nationality, he says he is 'not sure.'"

> Shenhav: Last August [2004], in a meeting with Palestinians, a sentence escaped my lips: "I am an Israeli patriot." A friend of mine commented to me: "Have you noted what you have just said?" This took place in a meeting with Palestinians where we were exchanging ideas, in which for the first time I felt

that I was speaking not as a sociologist, but also as a Jew. It feels difficult to admit it. But whether I chose [to live in] this place or I had no other alternative, then to defend Bishara's positions [who challenged the Jewish state and called for "a state of all its citizens"], he does it better than I do. In 1995 I would not have said to you "I am an Israeli patriot." Maybe I have matured. I know that to leave this place is not a realistic option. I am attached to my family, friends, ideas, to the struggle here. The question is what space of action do I have as a Jew, without forsaking both my positions and Judaism.

What we have in hand is sheer opportunism. Shenhav defends his retreat from his earlier challenge to Zionism by referring to his Jewish identity, and even to his personal condition and needs. In turn, the fight for democratization of the state is left to the Palestinians. Indeed, Azmi Bishara "can better defend *his own* positions [emphasis added]" because they are absolutely contradictory to those of Shenhav. The Israeli establishment persecuted Bishara precisely because he refused to be "an Israeli patriot" like Shenhav. "How can it be," asks Bishara, "that we—the original inhabitants of the land—are compelled to prove our loyalty to Israel? They want us all the time to explain and justify ourselves. But they should remember: I am a Palestinian-Arab democrat and not an Israeli patriot."[63]

The unbearable ease with which Shenhav returns to the bosom of Zionism is expressed in his appeal to his personal life. His "maturity"? His "living here"? What do these things have to do with being an "Israeli patriot," if not pure cynicism? He uses his personal life to excuse his retreat from commitment to universalistic values.

The fact that Zionism so permeates the political and intellectual culture of Israel explains how even its harshest critics can succumb to it. The late sociologist Baruch Kimmerling—one of the most courageous scholars of Zionism, who labeled it a colonialist movement—distanced himself from the post- and anti-Zionist camp.

> But I am a Zionist. I am a Zionist due to the fact that I live here and am part of the Hebrew culture, even if I am in opposition to the existing [present] regime and criticize it bitterly. I object to the definitions and practices of Zionism. They achieved monstrous forms, alongside islands of humanism and wonderful creativity. Of course, there is a political and cultural struggle about the question of what is Zionism and who is a Zionist. In the meanwhile, I am on the losing side of this struggle. Therefore I am defined as anti-Zionist. Let it be.[64]

After the Palestinians rejected Barak's "generous offer" in 2000, a series of peace initiatives emerged.[65] These initiatives supposedly adhered to the principle of a two-state solution that the PLO endorsed. But Azmi Bishara knew better. In April 2008, Azmi Bishara criticized the two-state solution that had characterized all peace initiatives in the past.[66] He rightly argued that the nonviability of the ever-reduced land mass proposed as the basis of the future Palestinian state) is but a part of the comprehensive deficiency of the peace plans: the non-recognition of the national rights of the Palestinian people: "Israel and the Bush administration have worked hard to fit the Palestinian demand for statehood into a package that clips, trims and essentially eliminates all Palestinian national rights." But it is these Palestinian national rights that hold the key to a lasting peace, Bishara explains. "All peace initiatives reject the notion of the unity of the Palestinian people and thus reduce the Palestinian-Israeli conflict to a territorial dispute with the residents of the 1967 occupied territories alone." The cause of the refugee situation is systematically neglected, thus ignoring the position of Palestinian leaders who are not part of the negotiations. Namely, this is "the very root and heart of the problem and thus carries considerable qualitative and moral weight, since it pertains to the actual suffering of millions of people . . . The proposed political settlements offer them no more than the 'chance to change their status from "refugee" to foreign subjects or aliens.'"

The fate of the Palestinian citizens in the Jewish state is also ignored, says Bishara: "A solution which is not associated with a true transformation of the nature of the exclusivist state of Israel will also intensify its drive to Judaize the state and become ever-more overbearing and arrogant in its relations with its Palestinian-Arab citizens, who will be forced to choose between total allegiance to Israel, including mandatory conscription and restrictions on their civil rights, or exile. For those who insist on expressing their national identity inside Israel, the state will inform them that that identity has found sufficient expression in the Palestinian entity next door."

The failure to recognize the national rights of the Palestinian people diminishes the relevance of their history of dispossession. The Zionist Left refrains from identifying the root cause of the conflict—that is, Zionist colonialism, which culminated in the 1948 ethnic cleansing. Many "post-Zionists" have adopted a stance which does recognize Israel's responsibility to the 1948 Nakba but did not incorporate it into their preferred political settlement. Hence, contrary to the living collective memory and daily experience of the Palestinian people, post-Zionists and critical social scientists do not unequivocally demand the reparation for the consequences of the Nakba before outlining the dimensions for a "just" solution, or for that matter, for the democratization of Israel as well. As a result, post-Zionists end up accepting the Zionist project and its embodiment in the Jewish state.

For example, Baruch Kimmerling acquired the fait accompli attitude of the Zionist Left. He disregarded the fact that Palestinian citizens, in trying to understand the structural inequality of the state of Israel, have increasingly focused on the Nakba and the history of Zionist colonization and dispossession. In a 2006 interview with *Haaretz*'s Dalia Karpel,[67] Kimmerling argues that the wrongs of the past should be excluded from consideration when looking for solutions to Palestinian inequality and peace settlement plans in general.

> We have built here a society on the ruins of another society. Maybe the mistake was [there] from the beginning. The forefathers of Zionism were not aware of the complexities of the solution they suggested. They grew up in the later stage of the colonial era, when it was still only natural that the European person may settle in any place outside the old continent, for his own benefit and also as one who brings the annunciation of progress to the natives. And they also grew up in the beginning of the era of nationalism—the combination of these two factors gave birth to Zionism and its consequences for the people of the region, of course mainly for the Palestinians. Does this justify the dismantling of the state [of Israel]? I don't think so. We have built here a splendid society and culture, for better or for worse. You don't erase a wrong by creating another one. History is not a time tunnel in which you can drive backwards. There is also no point for the two sides to nostalgically embrace the past. It is vital to try and find solutions for the future. The debate over who is guilty for the situation leads nowhere but to the growth of reciprocal hatred.

It is frustrating to see how, despite his honesty, courage, and clarity of thought, Kimmerling uses the same argument to justify Zionism that he and others had used to criticize the establishment sociologists. Kimmerling clings to the subjective consciousness of Zionist settlers who did not identify themselves as colonialists, and who did not understand the "complexity" of the situation. He softens his moral estimation of Zionist colonialism to the extent that he uses a forgiving tone toward the "unaware" forefathers who adopted the ideological and moral justification of colonialism that prevailed at the time.

This tolerant attitude toward Zionism is inevitably connected to support of the Jewish state. In an article published in 2005,[68] Kimmerling remarks, "[since] Israel was founded as a Jewish state, I do not believe that this identity should be stripped from it, just as Italy is in principle an Italian country."[69] On the other hand, he avoids recognizing the contradiction between a Jewish state and full equal rights for its Palestinian citizens. "However, it should be borne in mind that a collective has been created here that also includes *non-Jewish citizens* [emphasis added], who would be difficult to term a 'minority' and who have the right to full participation in citizenship. Therefore, Israel cannot help but be a 'state of all its citizens' as well [as Jewish]."

Kimmerling, like other critical social scientists and post-Zionists, joins the Zionist Left in refraining from noting how the "Jewish state" necessarily denies full citizenship and national rights to Palestinians in Israel. The Zionist Left does not make the connection between insisting on recognition of the Jewish state (as part of a peace settlement) and rejecting the national rights of Palestinians in the '67 occupied territories, the Diaspora, and in Israel itself.

In their refusal to completely separate themselves from Zionism and the Jewish state, many post-Zionists supported the various peace initiatives dictated to a Palestinian leadership that had lost any legitimacy in the eyes of their people. For example, Avi Shlaim of Oxford University, one of the first four New Historians, expressed his belief that the Clinton/Barak parameters, submitted at negotiations at Taba[70] four months after the breakout of the second Intifada, represented a solid basis for reaching a peace settlement. "[A]t Taba the two teams made considerable progress . . . and came closer to an overall agreement than at any other time in the history of this conflict."[71]

It is amazing to hear Shlaim uncritically repeat the words of the Taba talk participants without attending to the circumstances that gave birth to the talks in the first place. Nor did he criticize Barak for using Taba to boost his election campaign, instead of using the talks for the pursuit of a just peace.[72] Shlaim thus joined those on the Zionist Left who continued to assert that, against all evidence, Barak's proposal in Taba could lead to a peace settlement. Like the Zionist Left, Shlaim blamed the failure of this peace mirage on transitions of power. "By this time Clinton and Barak were on their way out and Sharon was on his way in."

The readiness of a New Historian like Shlaim to accept such a strikingly unjust solution is astonishing. As Tanya Reinhart summarized, Israel was offering at Taba "essentially the same as what it has been offering before and after Oslo: preservation of the Israeli occupation within some form of Palestinian autonomy of self-rule. Everything that regards land, water (not even discussed in Taba), control of the borders, and many other aspects will remain under total Israeli control, but the Palestinians will be allowed symbolic tokens of 'sovereignty,' including even the permission to call their enclaves a 'state,' and Abu Dis its 'capital.'"[73]

Geneva Initiative as an Illustration

Perhaps the best example of the willingness of post-Zionists to adopt any "peace" plan was the 2003 Geneva Initiative, which followed Camp David and Taba. The Geneva Initiative was the name given to the agreements between a group from the Zionist Left (headed by Yossi Beilin, then chair of Meretz) and a number of Palestinian officials, mostly from the PA, headed by Yasser Abed Rabbo (then minister of information).[74] The initiative was supported by a wide spectrum of Zionist Left public figures, from Meretz MKs to authors such as Amos Oz, David Grossman, and A. B. Yehoshua. They all helped to publicize its details and mobilize public opinion for adopting what they considered to be the most just and practical peace solution.[75]

The Geneva Initiative, in a nutshell, incorporates everything the Zionist Left stands for, and what critical scholars and post-Zionists consider a fair solution to the Israeli-Palestinian "conflict."[76]

Historian Ilan Pappé[77] points to the similarity between the Geneva Initiative and Israel's proposal at Camp David in 2000:

> Three years after the breakout of the second Intifada we are witness again to the renewal of peace efforts [in the form of the Geneva Initiative] ... The same formula is activated again. An Israeli initiative designed primarily for Jewish public opinion in Israel and in need of American support, as a disguise for an honest mediator ...
>
> And now we have the Geneva bubble. This is an impressive production, both as a document and as an Hollywood ceremony, with all the peace stunts which accompanied it. ... All its principles appear in the introduction to the Israeli version which was written by [the renowned Israeli author] David Grossman: Palestinian recognition of the state of Israel as the state of the Jewish People, a Palestinian struggle against terror, an Israeli capital in Jerusalem, annexation of the big settlement blocks and East Jerusalem in exchange for a demilitarized Palestinian state without an army. Seventy five percent of the Jews who now live beyond the Green Line, will remain within the area of the state of Israel ...
>
> The conspicuous characteristic of this introduction and of the entire document is that the right of return is presented as an impediment to peace which has to be removed, while the Zionist nature of the state—namely of the political entity which officially rules over 80 percent of the area together with the big settlement blocs and Greater Jerusalem—is not an impediment to peace. To the contrary. According to this logic, what is lacking [for achieving peace] is a Palestinian recognition of expanded Israel. Namely, a state built on most of the area from which they were ethnically cleansed in 1948, and from additional areas which were taken from them in 1967. What is the generous offer that the Israeli peace seekers insisted that their scared partners accept on the eve of signing the Geneva

document? A mini-state on 15 percent of Palestine with a capital near Jerusalem and without an army? A careful examination of the authorities and powers suggested for such a mini-state reveals contempt towards the very concept of statehood as recognized by the international reality or political science textbooks.

Of course even this mini-state is conditioned on the PA's repression of "terror and incitement," which in practice means abolishing any resistance to the collaborative Palestinian leadership. Pappé adds:

> But what is even more important, is that the vision of the Geneva Initiative leaves the refugees in their exile and camps . . . It suggests that the refugees choose whether they want to return to the 15 percent [of Historic Palestine] or remain in the camps. It stands to reason that they will continue to wait for the international community to implement its commitment to an unconditional return as stipulated in [UN] Resolution 194. Millions of Palestinians will remain refugees within [the framework] of this "peace," crowding along the borders of Israel, and 1.5 million will continue to be second-class citizens under Israeli sovereignty in the remaining 85 percent [of the state of Israel]. There is no recognition [in the Geneva Initiative] of the root cause of the conflict—the ethnic cleansing of 1948; there is no process of reconciliation which will demand from Israel [to recognize] the responsibility for what it committed in 1948. It is therefore impossible that the Jewish state be accepted by the Palestinians or the Arab world.

Pappé reports on the atmosphere in which the talks took place and points to the patronizing, condescending attitude of the Zionist Left, who used intimidation and scare tactics in order to persuade Palestinians that they had no choice but to make substantial concessions. "Those who watched Israeli television recently could peep backstage behind the curtains of the signing of the Geneva agreement. The clip which we saw in November [2003] presented a group of renowned Israelis—writers and activists of Peace Now—shouting at a group of somewhat scared Palestinians, most of whom [were] lesser well-known officials of the Palestinian Authority. The Israelis scolded the Palestinians . . . claiming they are on the verge of missing an opportunity. The Palestinians were told that this is their last chance, and that what was submitted to them is a very generous offer that may not return in the future." Pappé adds, "This scene repeats the atmosphere that prevailed in previous negotiations which took place between Left Israelis and Palestinians in Oslo in 1993 and at Camp David in 2000."

Many post-Zionists support the Geneva Initiative.[78] As mentioned, their support reveals their inability to translate post-Zionist, relatively critical discourse, regarding the Nakba and the policies of the state of Israel, into any alternative to the Zionist Left position toward "peace."

The self-defined post-Zionist Yoav Peled, despite his knowledge of the sharp criticism of the "peace plans" initiated by Yossi Beilin and the Zionist Left (who supported governments that implemented the ever-escalating waves of settlement construction), accepted the Geneva Initiative and other earlier peace initiatives after Oslo.[79] He determined these initiatives proposed a viable two-state solution that was acceptable to the Israeli establishment and public because they "would have involved the removal of only 80,000 settlers." Peled fails to mention that the remaining settlements in the West Bank are but the narrow tracts of Israeli sovereignty that plunge deep into the West Bank, cantonizing it, and thus enabling Israel's continued control of the Palestinian Bantustan state-to-be.

As Virginia Tilley[80] rightly emphasizes in discussing support for the Geneva Initiative, "I find it surprising that so many smart and responsible people have considered Geneva a major step forward when its lack of substance casts it as no more than a well-intended chimera. Its only significant contribution was seriously to dent Israel's claim that the Palestinians offer 'no partner for peace'— a good gain, but circumscribed by a lack of broader support for the Accord that is unsurprising, given its fundamental flaws."

It may not be that surprising, however, in light of Peled's commitment to the "Jewish state." In his article critiquing the one-state solution Virginia Tilley advocated, Peled argues that the Jewish state is a condition for any peace settlement based on the two-state solution, as outlined in the Geneva Initiative. Two irreducible tenets are fundamental to the "Jewish national home": free immigration of Jews, and Jewish control over land. Without a Jewish state, these "ethnic privileges" would evaporate, and the Jewish "national home" along with them.

> But adherents of the one-state solution should have the courage to face the fact that without Jewish domination of whatever portion of Palestine/Israel, there will be no Jewish national home. If the Palestinians had their way, the first thing they would do would be to abolish the Law of Return, or else balance it off with a law of return of their own. The next thing would be to demand, at least, their proportional share of the land: territory that used to be entirely their own and is now mostly defined, legally, as national Jewish land. Immigration and land were, historically, at the heart of the Jewish-Palestinian conflict and, as we saw, even the most liberal Zionists have considered Jewish control of these two resources vital for the existence of a Jewish national home. These people would hardly be persuaded by Tilley's argument that a Jewish national home could exist safely within a secular democratic state with a Palestinian majority.[81]

Thus, it is not "Jewish identity" or "national life" that are essential to the Jewish state, but rather sheer Jewish domination. This is the rationale behind

Peled's adherence to Israel's control over immigration and land—that is, supporting the Law of Return and rejection of the Right of Return of Palestinian refugees. "Since otherwise," asks Tilley, "in what way would the elimination of the Law of Return or its reform, in itself, dissolve Jewish-national life for a Jewish-Israeli population?"[82]

In this conception of the Jewish homeland, there is no place for Palestinian citizens' political positions. By 2006, the Palestinian intellectual elite and political leadership's challenge of the Jewish state, and their demands for national collective rights, had been widely publicized. Their strengthened national affinity with the rest of the Palestinian people and the entire Arab nation was also known. Still, these were not considered relevant to the peace solution the critical scholars supported.

The peace solutions that Israeli post-Zionist intellectuals support have no basis of legitimacy among the Palestinian people. Any solution that excludes the Palestinian refugees in the Diaspora is automatically out of the question, says Azmi Bishara.[83] Nor are the solutions acceptable to the masses throughout the Arab East, who are well aware of the unholy alliance between US imperialism, Zionism, and the oppressive Arab regimes. Their basic solidarity with the Palestinians remains. "The brutality that Israel has unleashed to drive the Palestinian people from resistance and to compel them to bow to Israeli conditions has fed popular rancor and fueled the tendency to hurl accusations of treachery at Arab parties lending themselves to the settlement process," Bishara notes. "Israel has rejected what broad segments of the Palestinian and Arab people regard as legitimate solutions. It has, thereby, opted for permanent conflict, regardless of whatever other arrangements it pursues outside the framework of a just and lasting peace. The conflict will continue, even if it scores the type of settlement it has in mind."

Post-Zionists, like the Zionist Left, have ignored the growing rage among Palestinians against the "peace" solutions they support. Adhering to the notion of a "Jewish state"—which, in practice, means Jewish domination over all of Palestine—ties them to the Israeli establishment and whatever future disaster awaits Palestine, Israel, and the entire region. Both share responsibility for helping to build the wide consensus in Israel in favor of peace plans that will deliver neither peace nor justice to the Palestinians.

Indeed, this amounts to the most serious betrayal of the intellectuals.

Epilogue

They that sow the wind shall inherit the whirlwind.

—*Hosea 8:7*

This book has explored the Zionist Left's discourse regarding the Jewish state. I have focused on how Zionist Left intellectuals have granted ideological and "scientific" legitimacy to both the legal system and government policies that have made possible Zionist colonialism in the Apartheid settler state of Israel.

My emphasis has largely been on Israel "proper," despite recognizing that Israel's rule has spread to the rest of Historic Palestine, wiping out the Green Line and creating a unitary colonial regime between the Mediterranean Sea and the Jordan River. Zionist Left discourse on Israel's "internal" regime necessarily includes positions and attitudes toward Israel's continued rule over the 1967 occupied territories and the citizenship status of Palestinians in Israel, and how these positions and attitudes function in the context of a peace settlement.

The resolution of the Israeli-Palestinian conflict and the fate of the Palestinian citizens of Israel are of central importance to US imperial interests in the Middle East—namely, sustaining Israel's role as chief enforcer of US strategies and safeguarding Israel's military hegemony in the region. The division of the Arab world by British and French imperialists after the defeat of the Ottoman Empire in World War I; the erasure of Historic Palestine through the partition between Israel and Jordan; and US-intensified efforts to abolish Arab nationalism since 1967 have all failed to do away with the solidarity of the Arab masses with the Palestinian people and their cause. In the Arab masses' eyes, the continuing Palestinian Nakba embodies the oppression and exploitation by US imperialism, Zionism, and Arab authoritarian regimes.

In recent years, Palestinian citizens of Israel have reinforced their Arab national identity along with their ever-strengthened Palestinian nationalism. Embodied by a determined challenge of the Jewish Zionist state and a growing understanding of the state's role in the region, the Palestinians threaten more than just the Israeli Apartheid regime. They threaten the stability of US rule in the region by increasing popular solidarity with mass resistance forces in Palestine and the Arab world. The Israeli and US political and military establishment's awareness—that they must eliminate this danger—is emphasized in a front page article by *Haaretz* senior political analyst Aluf Ben:

> The main effort of Netanyahu's government aims to repress the political aspirations of the Arabs in Israel. The [Israeli] establishment invests more energies in [attaining] this goal than those invested in the political peace process or in thwarting the Iranian threat. This multifront strategy is implemented through legislation initiatives, introducing changes in the education system, symbolic activity and through diplomacy. [The] aim is to reinforce the Jewish identity of Israel while demands are made upon the Arab minority to give up its struggle for a more equal democracy.
>
> Aggravation of the internal tension is usually identified with Avigdor Lieberman who has headed the campaign aimed at the oppression of the Arab community. Behind him [however] hides the Likud Prime Minister Benyamin Netanyahu. He is the initiator and director of this policy even if he himself hardly talks about it or incites [against the Palestinians].[1]

Like most of the Zionist Left, Ben ignores the Labor Party's role in designing the ideology and policies that have paved the way for the recent intensification of the state of Israel's Apartheid nature. Moreover, until January 2011, Labor has been a senior partner in the Netanyahu/Lieberman government, and supported the strengthened oppression of the Palestinian citizenry, which Ben depicts as the government's main goal—namely, to crush the Palestinian community.

"The Unmasking Laws"[2]

"Anti-terror" legislation has enabled the recently intensified persecution of Palestinian political leaders and community-based NGOs. From the onset, the state of Israel under Labor governments delimited its legal system within the framework of a declared "state of emergency," which still exists today. Tens of emergency laws and regulations, most of which were legalized by the British Mandate, have been in use since the beginning, while amendments to these laws have become an integral part of the Israeli legal system.[3] Of course the state's incorporation of emergency measures into daily use violates peremptory norms of international law, including the imposition of collective punishment and arbitrary deprivations of liberty. However, beneath the pretext of security (affirmed by the perpetual "state of emergency"), these laws were activated to root out the emergence of any determined national identity or movement that might arise from within the Palestinian citizenry.

What we are witness to at present, then, is how "anti-terror" laws are being applied to almost the entire spectrum of Palestinian life. Israel's strategy—of branding the Palestinian struggle for freedom and equal rights as terrorism—has reached a stage in which any contact with a Palestinian or Arab outside Israel can be depicted as a connection with "a foreign agent"; hence, Palestinian citizens can be charged with spying.

Zionist Left political and intellectual elites have never launched a systematic campaign against the "anti-terror laws" or the prolonged "state of emergency." Their inaction helps to perpetuate these laws. Thus, in the case of Azmi Bishara, the most significant initiator of the Palestinian struggle for democratization of Israel, not one member of the Zionist Left party or intellectuals, and hardly a handful of post-Zionists, defended him against the Shabak's accusation of spying for Hezbollah.

The deepening of the Israeli regime's Apartheid nature finds a rather cynical expression in the law that reformed how "state lands" are managed in Israel. This land, which was confiscated from Palestinians for "public use," is now being privatized, and can be sold to the highest bidder. However, in order to block Palestinians from purchasing land in the free market, the government decided—via Amendment 7 to the new law—to increase the number of the JNF representatives in the ILA's governing council to supervise land transactions. Via this amendment, the government also reserved the right to increase its own representation on the council. It thus grants the ILA the right to set limits on the sale of a plot of land for building a house in communal localities.

The increased drive to Judaise the land is further evidenced in a residency bill that would give communal localities the power to turn down interested residential candidates if they do not "concur with the settlement's fundamental view as defined in its regulations"and who lack "social suitability to the spirit of the communal locality."⁴ The new bill would not change the current situation, as these localities have never accepted Palestinians as members. Still, it seemed necessary in order to prevent a future decision by the Supreme Court not to allow Palestinians into communal localities.

The Zionist Left believes the new bill is in contradiction to the Supreme Court's Katzir ruling, which they misleadingly interpreted as a measure to grant Palestinians the right to purchase a plot of land in a communal locality and to be accepted as members of the Jewish community. However, as demonstrated in chapter 3, the language of this ruling is rather equivocal: it does not explicitly define the ruling as a precedent for future cases, and repeatedly expresses Israel's justified commitment to Zionist values. And indeed the ruling has not served as a solid base for challenging the new bills regarding the rights of Palestinians to buy land.⁵ At its winter session (October 2010–April 2011), the Knesset has been discussing a number of bills, submitted by MKs of Israel Beytenu orLikud. These bills aim to erase the national identity and self-organization of Palestinian citizens, and crush the Palestinian opposition to their second-class citizenship. The "Nakba bill" requires the state to fine local authorities and other state-funded bodies for holding events marking the Nakba Day.⁶ Another bill would prohibit Palestinian NGOs from being funded by Arab organizations abroad, and others would target people who initiate, promote, or publish material that might serve as grounds for either imposing a boycott against Israel or suing senior civil or military figures for committing war crimes.

A Demand for Declared Recognition of the Jewish State

The demand for Palestinians to explicitly recognize Israel as a Jewish state is a demand for Palestinians to legitimate the central premise of Zionism and its embodiment in Israel's Apartheid regime. PM Benyamin Netanyahu has announced time and again that "advancement" in the peace talks is conditioned on a declaration by Abu Mazen. Namely, Mazen must recognize Israel as the "Jewish state," or as "the state of the Jewish nation."

At the same time, the prolonged legal attack against the shaky status of Palestinian citizenship has reached a new stage. An amendment to the Citizenship law, proposed by Israel Beytenu, Lieberman's party, was approved by the Israeli cabinet on October 10, 2010 (when Labor was still a member of the government coalition). The bill requires all non-Jewish, newly naturalized citizens to add to the original "State of Israel" loyalty oath the words "as a Jewish and democratic state." A bill that demands the same oath from non-Jewish Israeli citizens appears possible.[7]

"In essence, the loyalty oath law is not a revolutionary law," says post-Zionist Hanan Hever. "It does not contradict the Declaration of Independence but only ratifies it. Nor does it contradict the fixed position of all Zionist parties . . . Also the attempt made by Defense Minister Barak to add [to the original oath's wording a provision of loyalty to] 'the Declaration of Independence' [instead of "the Jewish state"] does not indicate a real difference between him and Lieberman and for sure—not between him and Netanyahu."

The incessant demands for Israel to be recognized as a Jewish state are but a step forward in the long process that empties Palestinian citizenship of its political essence. For example, Section 7A added to the Basic Law in 1984 bars any political party and person that does not recognize Israel as a Jewish and democratic state from participating in parliamentary elections.

Conditioning Palestinian citizenship on "loyalty" to the state has always been a part of Zionist Left thought. It found explicit expression in the words of sociologist Sammy Smooha in the joint sessions of progressive Jews and moderate Palestinian intellectuals hosted by the Democracy Institute. (See chapter 3.)

Smooha and jurist David Kretzmer defined "loyalty" in terms of recognition of the Jewish state, and Smooha insisted that individuals fulfill "responsibilities" like services to the state—military or otherwise—to confirm their loyalty. The Palestinian participants' refusal to define Israel as a Jewish state brought about the failure of this project, which aimed to issue a document regarding Israeli-Palestinian relations in Israel.

Members of the Zionist Left have expressed their unease with a law that conditions the very citizenship of Palestinians on their declared recognition of the Jewish state. During the second half of 2010, the Zionist Left widely participated in discussions on the new bill in the Israeli media. Most, however, tended to perceive the recent bills as though they were a new phenomenon created by the extreme Right. In doing so, they avoided making a connection to the Apartheid nature of Israel. The blunt language of the recent bills and discourse is what provoked these voices on the Zionist Left to say something, albeit without challenging the Jewish state and its destructive implications for its Palestinian citizens.

The following is a summary of three articles written by three representatives of different streams of the peace camp whose past discourse was mentioned in various chapters of this book: Shlomo Avineri, Mordechai Kremnitzer, and Uri

Avnery. Their somewhat feeble rejection to the loyalty bills and their arguments reflect their commitment to the Jewish state, which these laws aim to fortify.

Political Scientist Shlomo Avineri

Shlomo Avineri is perhaps the only prominent vocal member of the Zionist Left who unequivocally justifies the law requiring all newly naturalized citizens to take an oath of loyalty to the Jewish state. In a *Haaretz* article,[8] Avineri whitewashes this new law with the same arguments he used to defend the Jewish state and the Law of Return. Accordingly, the new law is just an "immigration law," which is no different from immigration laws in other democratic states, such as the US and Norway, that demand oaths of allegiance from immigrants. As in the past, Avineri repeats misleading information in order to justify Israel's Apartheid citizenship laws. In the cases he cites, the oaths do not require allegiance to a specific ethnic/religious group and its dominant ideology. Rather, the pledge is made to universal values of democracy and human rights, and to the country as a whole—not to a particular, dominant population group. However, although Avineri supports the oath loyalty law, he would prefer formulations that are "less vulnerable to criticism." An oath "to recognize the legitimacy of the state of Israel" would suffice, since the nature of the state is well known to everyone.[9]

Two months later, Avineri responded in *Haaretz* to PM Netanyahu's demand that the Palestinian leadership declare its recognition of the Jewish state in the framework of the peace negotiations.[10] Again he mentions that he could do without this explicit recognition, but in the same breath, he presents his expectations of the Palestinian negotiators. However, these expectations are even more demanding than "recognition" alone. They serve to counter Abu Mazen's refusal to publicly accept Israel as a Jewish state as a condition for the peace talks. Avineri claims that the current rejection represents the traditional Palestinian position, which is the "root of the dispute"—namely, "their unwillingness to recognize the Jews as a nation and hence their right for self determination in a state of their own." By Avineri's logic, his own suggestion "to recognize the legitimacy of the state of Israel" appears insufficient. He demands the Palestinian negotiators renounce any historical connection to the part of Palestine that would constitute the state of Israel in a future two-state solution. In other words, Avineri rejects the concept of Palestine as a geographic/symbolic area, regardless of the boundaries of the two states. He also demands the Palestinians renounce their self-definition as a unified people who reside in the entire area of Historic Palestine, failing to even mention the refugees from the 1948 Nakba.

"Palestinian leaders should be asked whether it is clear to them that the territory of Israel proper is not part of Palestine, and should not be presented as such in the Palestinian narrative and in Palestinian schools, just as a majority of Israel's Jewish citizens distinguish between "the State of Israel" and "the Land of Israel" . . . . It should be clear to us, and to them, that Acre, Jaffa and Be'er Sheva are not part of Palestine."

Unsurprisingly, Avineri expects Palestinian citizens of Israel to relinquish their national identity in order to help resolve the conflict. "Their leaders prefer to relate to themselves as '*Palestinian* citizens of Israel,' and that, of course, is their right . . . But [if the Palestinians maintain that] when their independent state is established, they would continue to view the territory of the State of Israel as 'occupied territory' that belongs to the Palestinian homeland, it will obviously not facilitate the process of mutual reconciliation."

Other Zionist Left intellectuals reject the Loyalty Oath law proposal more fiercely than Shlomo Avineri, albeit not in unequivocal language. They argue that the law is superfluous, or insignificant, since the Jewish state is already a recognized fact, and does not need the declared legitimacy of the Palestinians.

Jurist Mordechai Kremnitzer

Liberal Israeli Mordechai Kremnitzer was the Israeli co-chair of the aforementioned series of dialogue meetings, which failed because the Palestinians refused to declare their recognition of the Jewish state.

In an October 11, 2010, article in *Haaretz* entitled "To Where Has Our Common Sense Disappeared?" Kremnitzer opposed the new law that would condition Israeli citizenship upon an oath of allegiance to the Jewish state.[11] Like others on the Zionist Left, he prefers the current law, which only requires an oath of allegiance to "the state of Israel." His reasons for opposing the new law relate to the "international implications," as its purpose is "to put in doubt Arab citizen loyalty to the state, many of whom refuse to sign such a declaration."

Kremnitzer certainly understands why Palestinians would object to this stipulation. His Palestinian partners at the dialogue meetings told him that such a demand entails a renunciation of their national identity and their right to equal citizenship. But Kremnitzer ignores the Palestinian claim that the erasure of their national identity is structural to the Jewish state. Instead he suggests that their refusal to sign a declaration of loyalty is because: "The state has accustomed them to see the expression 'Jewish state' as a code for justifying the deprivation and systematic discrimination of the Arab minority and because the Palestinian demand for National self-determination in an independent Palestinian state is not clear yet." In other words, there is no real contradiction between a Jewish state and democracy. It is the state's discriminatory policies that confer this incorrect impression.

What is most important for Kremnitzer is the fact that Israel "as the democratic nation state of the Jewish people is confirmed in its basic laws, the Declaration of Independence and in the hearts of the majority of the [Jewish] citizens." So who needs this "peculiar" law that challenges the "obvious?" Moreover, even the debate about the law is superficial, since it may create the false impression that many Israelis disagree with the "Jewishness" of the state. All that is needed is self-confidence. The potential damage of this law is great, so one should ask: "To where has [our] common sense disappeared?"

Once again we are witness to the unbearable ease with which progressive Zionists ignore Palestinian discourse and thus proudly support the Jewish state, knowing full well its implications. Uri Avnery is not an exception to this tendency.

Peace Leader Uri Avnery

Uri Avnery's contribution to the ongoing debate about the demand for Palestinian recognition of the Jewish state is of the utmost importance for understanding his shared commitment to Zionism with other streams of the Zionist Left. As a founder of Gush Shalom, the Israeli Peace Block, he is recognized as a champion for those who support peace via a two-state solution. Even radical international progressives like Steven Friedman and Virginia Tilley, who strongly criticize his positions, describe him as one who has "fought, written, published and campaigned for Palestinian rights for some sixty years. He has stood on the political barricades and faced down bulldozers to defend Palestinians from Israeli military abuse."[12]

This is precisely what makes Avnery's participation in the debate so important. It discloses the moral and political danger inherent in the commitment to the Jewish state while ignoring Palestinian national aspirations. A determined activist like Avnery ends with the support of the Palestinian Authority, which collaborates with the United States and Israel in oppressing the Palestinian people.

In his October 16, 2010, article,[13] Avnery joins other Zionist Left intellectuals and publicists who call the new demands for recognizing the Jewish state superfluous. Moreover, the demands indicate a serious psychological problem, "a collective loss of self-confidence." Hence, Avnery poses the following question: "What is the source of this obsession, this demand from near and far, strangers and non-strangers, to declare that Israel is the 'Nation-State of the Jewish People?' . . . . What is the reason of this obsessive need for confirmation and for respect of the entire world? A collective mental disturbance? A matter for political psychologists, or perhaps for political psychiatrists?"

Apparently the existing laws, which maintain the Jewish identity of the state of Israel, are sufficient for Avnery. To explain how the new demand is redundant, this determined fighter for peace describes Israel as follows: "The State of Israel has existed for the last 62 years. It is a regional military power, a state with nuclear capabilities, with an economy that arouses envy in a world steeped in crisis; it has a dynamic cultural, scientific and social life." Avnery continues to glorify the pre-state Yishuv and then says: "And here we are now, twelve times larger. We have a state that most of the world's peoples can only envy. And we are begging to be recognized: I cannot abstain from comparing this pathetic need to our mood when I was young."

In his effort to justify Zionism, Avnery intentionally denies that the "Jewish state" is a central premise of Zionism, as emphasized in the "Declaration of Independence," which was signed on May 14, 1948, by the temporary People's Council headed by the Labor Party chair David Ben-Gurion.

> Why "a Jewish state"? For Ben-Gurion, this was not an ideological definition. He just quoted the resolution of the UN General Assembly, which partitioned the country between an "Arab state" and a "Jewish state." The framers of the resolution did not have any ideological character in mind. They simply took note of the fact that there were in the country two rival populations—the Jewish and the Arab—and decided pragmatically to divide the country between them.[14]

Ignoring the wide consensus around the Jewish identity of the state of Israel, Avnery mocks the new demand for recognition as a demand for recognizing "a state of Bla-Bla-Bla."

To strengthen this conclusion, Avnery describes the demand as "a trick" played by the Right "to sabotage the peace negotiations that haven't yet started."

Avnery continues to mislead his supporters by portraying the current framework of the US-designed peace negotiations as seriously intending to resolve the conflict. It is the Right that prevents the Zionist Left peace vision from coming true, since "these negotiations, God forbid, would lead to a peace agreement that would compel us to evacuate the settlements and return the West Bank, the Gaza Strip, and East Jerusalem to the Palestinians."

Betrayal of the Israeli Left: Zionist and Post-Zionist

Refusing to depict Zionism as a colonial enterprise and the Jewish state as a settler Apartheid state resulted in the Zionist Left and Post-Zionists' betrayal of the national rights of the Palestinian people on both sides of the Green Line. Inevitably it resulted in them turning their backs on the Palestinian resistance against their oppressors—the United States, Israel, and the PA.

Supporting a Collaborative PA: Abandoning Palestinian Citizens

Avnery's commitment to the present model of a two-state solution betrays his declared support of the national rights of Palestinians living on either side of the Green Line and in the Diaspora.

In the Oslo Accords, which Avnery enthusiastically supported, Palestinian citizens were abandoned to the "benevolence" of the Jewish state. The Zionist Left has rightly understood the stipulation for mutual recognition mentioned in the accords (that the PLO recognized Israel and that Israel recognized the PLO [as representative for the Palestinian people]) implies the recognition of Israel as a Jewish state.

This understanding has enabled the alliance between the PA and the Israeli peace camp, which was founded in the wake of the Oslo Accords, to continue. However, the PA does not currently represent the resistance forces in the Palestinian national movement and in the struggle within Israel. At the end of 2010, there was an increase in public declarations made by members of the Palestinian government in the West Bank. These declarations compromisingly supported not only the Jewish state for a peace solution, but also the Jewish people's historical right to the land.[15] Several leaders and Knesset members representing the Palestinian community in Israel raced to Ramallah to meet with Abu Mazen and to communicate their indignation. Unlike Avnery and the Israeli peace camp, the Palestinians in Israel understand the disastrous implications such a declaration has to a future peace settlement. They rightly interpret Netanyahu's latest demand as a cynical move to bypass his "own" Palestinian citizens and persuade Abu Mazen to negotiate away their rights.

Moreover, as Nazareth-based journalist Jonathan Cook indicates, this demand reveals the Israeli political and "security" establishment's aspirations to suppress any campaign by Israel's Palestinian citizens to democratize the Jewish Apartheid state. Thus with Palestinian backing, Israel will label resistant forces as "traitors" and expel them to the fragmented future Bantustan state. In the meantime, they will have received permission to abolish any remnant of Palestinian citizenship rights through loyalty oaths and via the dismantling of Palestinian parties in the Knesset (unless Palestinians sign up as Zionists).[16]

In the 1967 occupied territories, there is already full cooperation between Israel and the PA, headed by Abu Mazen and Salam Fayyad and controlled by US envoy General Dayton. Together they have been laying the infrastructure for a totalitarian regime that would ensure the interests of the United States and Israel. Avnery's continued support of the West Bank leadership is in fact support for an authority that has renounced the Palestinian right to an independent democratic state.

In an article from November 4, 2010,[17] Avnery glorifies Salam Fayyad, the prime minister of the Palestinian government responsible for the emerging horror in the West Bank. "It is impossible not to like Fayyad. He radiates decency, seriousness and a sense of responsibility. He invites trust. None of the filth of corruption has stuck to him . . . In the confrontation between Fatah and Hamas, he does not belong to either of the two rival blocs . . . Fayyad believes, so it seems, that the Palestinians' only chance to achieve their national goals is by non-violent means, in close cooperation with the US." Avnery explains this as a version of Zionist labor "pragmatism." "This is reminiscent of the classic Zionist strategy under David Ben-Gurion. In Zionist parlance, this was called 'creating facts on the ground.' He [Fayyad] plans to build the Palestinian national institutions and create a robust economic base, and by the end of 2011, to declare the State of Palestine."

Avnery is thrilled at the idea of "statehood" taking form as Palestinian security forces, trained by General Keith Dayton, the US security coordinator for the Palestinians since 2005. "Anyone who has seen them knows that this is for all practical purposes a regular army. On Land Day demonstration, the Palestinian soldiers, with their helmets and khaki uniforms, were deployed on the hill, while the Israeli soldiers, similarly attired, were deployed below. That was in Area C [60% of the West Bank], which according to the Oslo Accords is under Israeli military control. Both armies used the same American jeeps, just differently colored."

What a cynical scene! A staged gesture by the occupier, to allow a military unit of the occupied to parade in an area fully under Israeli control—on the very day the Palestinian people commemorate the unabashed and ongoing robbery

of Palestinian land, in both Israel proper and the West Bank. And a famous Israeli peace struggler watches with admiration?!

Avnery's hair-raising, misleading portrayal of his allies in the PA is somewhat clarified in a well-documented study by Aisling Byrne of the Conflicts
Forum in Beirut.[18] The study highlights the contradictory positions of even the
most radical wing of the Israeli peace camp. While Avnery and his supporters
fight determinedly against Israeli oppression in the 1967 occupied territories,
they wholeheartedly support Abu Mazen and Fayyad, who brutally oppress any
opposition to their collaboration with the US and Israel.[19]

Below are a few paragraphs from Byrne's essay (references are excluded).

Dayton's military aims

"Dayton is a political actor who essentially is overseeing and facilitating a
process of political cleansing in the West Bank, the consequences of which for
the Palestinian national project, for political reconciliation between Fatah and
Hamas, and for political engagement and prospects for peace are damaging, if
not disastrous . . . Dayton has been clear about his aim: to reduce the 'IDF
footprint' in the West Bank by developing Palestinian capabilities and 'proven
abilities'; that is, capacity-building and training of the Palestinian security
forces ('paramilitaries,' as the *Wall Street Journal* describes them); turning
them, as he explained, into the 'new men of Palestine.'"

A totalitarian and repressive regime led by Abu Mazen and Fayyad

"Dayton's 'capacity-building' initiatives are facilitating the creation of an auto-
cratic and totalitarian 'state' led by Mahmoud Abbas and Salam Fayyad: political debate is almost non-existent, criticism not allowed, and the extent of
collusion between the Abu Mazen/Salam Fayyad government and their security forces with Israel is extensive . . .

A recent report in the British newspaper *Mail on Sunday* exposed 'the horrific torture of hundreds of people by Palestinian security forces in the West
Bank [which] is being funded by British taxpayers. The report documents how
not only are PA forces carrying out torture but that the authority [also] ignores
judges' orders to release political detainees.'"

Israel's admiration of the Palestinian Authority collaboration

"This process of creating 'new Palestinians' has complimented the political
metamorphosis of the Palestinian Authority. A high-ranking Israeli defense

officer explained to leading Israeli journalist, Nahum Barnea [of *Yediot Ahronot*], in early October 2009: 'the Palestinian Authority changed right in front of our eyes . . . The Fayyad government was formed [and] it was clear that they wanted to give Hamas a fight. We began to meet with the heads of the [Palestinian] security organizations . . . At the top of our agenda we put law and order in the cities and the war on Hamas . . . We were surprised by the intensity of their willingness to cooperate."[20]

Methods of crushing resistance

"The Israeli officer explained how this has been done, systematically and collaboratively: 'We took the 200 wanted men in Judea and Samaria and marked 15 who were the explosives experts. We assassinated most of them and arrested the others. What ensured our success was the cooperation between the IDF and the [Palestinian] GSS. A key turning point was the intensification of American involvement . . . We learned the lessons that the Americans learned from the fighting in Iraq. You take one place, Jenin for example, you crush terror there, you put a strong police force there and move on. We started with Jenin. At first, it failed. Fayyad said, let's try again. We tried again, and it caught. We needed a lot of patience . . . The greatest achievement was that the moderates defeated the extremists.'"

Uri Avnery represents the misleading trust that the Zionist Left had preached in order to reach a "peace settlement" with the collaborative PA. Like the Zionist Left, he also ignores the Palestinian resistance in the '67 occupied territories. This disregard for progressive political forces also characterizes those who are considered the most radical in Israel's political geography—post-Zionist intellectuals. Chapters 6, 7, and 8 dealt with the post-Zionists' failed attempt to create an alternative to the Zionist Left perspective, an alternative that would have challenged the Jewish state and defined Israel as a colonial settler state. As a result of this failure, Yehouda Shenhav, the champion of the enlightenment promised by post-Zionists, betrayed the national aspirations of the Palestinians.

Keeping the Settlements in an "Open Space" Resolution

Yehouda Shenhav's book *In the Trap of The Green Line*[21] presents a specific case of the "betrayal of liberal intellectuals." It proves the danger inherent in the ideologically inflected theories of identity politics that underlie Shenhav's work as well as the work of his colleagues among Israeli post-Zionists—

namely, disregarding the authentic, national demands of Palestinians on both sides of the Green Line and in the Diaspora. In translating the theories of multiculturalism and postcolonialism to the issues of the Israeli-Palestinian conflict's origin and resolution, Shenhav reveals how limited these theories are for understanding the colonial essence of Zionism and the state of Israel. Moreover, the theories' underlying identity politics lead him to abandon Palestinian national aspirations and the resistance movement. He also turns his back on the Palestinian citizens' struggle for the democratization of the state of Israel. In straying from nationalism, Shenhav misleadingly describes Israelis and Palestinians as two people who deserve equal national rights, not as a colonial power and the colonized subjects fighting for liberation. This enables him to present a deceptive and even cynical peace settlement plan of a single "open space" throughout the entirety of Historic Palestine. Accordingly, the settlements in the West Bank would remain among a multitude of Jewish and Palestinian cantons—religious, civic, and national—that would live peacefully alongside each other.

Exposing the assumptions that lead to this totally unacceptable solution is crucial because Shenhav represents, among liberal intellectuals in Israel and abroad, a radical Left that is presumed to share universal values of justice and equality.

Ignoring Zionism as the Source of the Israeli-Palestinian Conflict

Shenhav claims that the "liberal Left" is responsible for freezing the political process. Specifically, the Left took unacceptable positions on Israel's post–Oslo Accords peace initiatives. The "1967 paradigm" behind these initiatives understands the 1967 occupation to be the moral turning point for what was previously a just Israel. For the liberal Left, the 1967 war is the source of the Israeli-Palestinian conflict—doing away with the consequences of the war is the key to resolving the conflict. This would entail dismantling the settlements and enforcing an Israeli withdrawal to the Green Line, thus creating a basis for a two-state solution. However, argues Shenhav, this solution is futile because it does not address the four central issues underlying the conflict: "the '48 refugees, the '48 Palestinians [Palestinian citizens of Israel who survived the Nakba], the settlement project," and finally what he calls the "Third Israel" (largely the Mizrahi settlers). Hence, he argues, the "'67 Paradigm" should be replaced by the "'48 Paradigm." It was the 1948 war that gave birth to all the problems that can't be solved within the framework of the 1967 Paradigm. 1948 is point zero, the foundational event that contains within it the true basis for the conflict.

In stating that the 1948 war (and not 1967) is the source of the conflict, Shenhav ignores the colonial nature of the Zionist project and the settler state. Almost from its inception, the state was involved in colonial practices of dispossessing the indigenous Palestinian population. It aspired to be an exclusivist Jewish state over all of Historic Palestine and to affect a mass expulsion of the Palestinians, which was indeed implemented in 1948.

Tom Segev asks Shenhav:[22] "The Israeli-Palestinian conflict is an inseparable part of the Zionist enterprise [so] why determine 1948 as the point zero for the conflict? . . . [and not for example] the Balfour declaration or the 1936 Great Arab Rebellion?" Despite Shenhav's evasive and fuzzy language, his answer discloses his motivation—justifying Zionism and the Jewish Zionist state:

> I have intentionally chosen 1948 because I think that the State of Israel should not be smashed. I have chosen 1948 precisely because I want every historic analysis to include the achievements of the State of Israel. If we go back to the Balfour Declaration, we return to a very difficult situation from the point of view of the Jews. . . . At the very place I chose as point zero I stop considering the bifurcations and accept what happened until then as natural. From this perspective, the place you choose [to start with] is the one in which you establish your political position. I accept as a presupposition the existence of Israel, its characteristics, as a necessary part of the analysis, because I don't want to destroy it [Israel].

The "Ashkenazi State" and the "Ashkenazi Left"— Blurring Palestinian Nationhood

Shenhav's attack against the "Liberal Left" wrongly assumes that the Left genuinely sanctifies the Green Line, calling for the dismantlement of the settlements and separation from the 1967 occupied West Bank. These assumptions are made despite Labor's significant role in implementing policies that erased the Green Line and institutionalized a single, unified Israeli regime throughout Historic Palestine. In accordance with his identity politics, Shenhav asserts that it is the Zionist Left of Ashkenazi origin and the Orientalist worldview that determine the Left's support for the two-state solution, which would retain the current European majority in Israel. Hence, the allegedly similar victimization of Mizrahim and Palestinians (discussed in chapter 8) creates their similar interests for a joint political resolution—the erasure of the Green Line.

Shenhav embraces the objection to the Green Line, disconnecting the de-marcation from its political and ideological context. Thus the quest for the "era-sure of the Green Line" can be seen as a common denominator for a variety of different and even contradictory ideological and political forces. These groups include not only large sections of the "democratic" settlers and "democratic" Right in Israel, but also of the Palestinian people, such as the 1948 refugees; a radical political group of 1948 Palestinians, including parts of the National Democratic Assembly (NDA), "who do not accept the Green Line"; and Pales-tinian intellectuals "who have advanced this agenda in the last few years."

Shenhav assumes that the Mizrahi settlers, "the Third Israel," are motivated to embrace Shenhav's vision for a comprehensive political settlement. The Mizrahi settlers consist of lower socioeconomic strata of Israeli Jews who went to live in settlements in an attempt to improve their living conditions. However, as Shenhav insists, Mizrahi settlers' positions are based on more than socioeco-nomic considerations. They share with most Mizrahim within the Green Line an ethnic-Arab identity, which could mobilize their support for a political reso-lution that "opens the space." As proof, Shenhav recalls the joy felt by many Mizrahim when, following the 1967 war, a continuous space between the Mediterranean and the Jordan River was created, thus ending the separation from the Palestinians that was enforced by the Green Line. "The '67 war granted independence, status and possibilities for progress for an entire generation of Jews from Arab countries who celebrated the opening of the space. It permitted a renewed definition of the Mizrahi identity in Israel, not as an antithesis to the Ashkenazi identity, but as an option for integrating into the space, even though in this case the circumstances are those of an oppressive integration."[23]

The Arab identity attributed to the Mizrahim in Israel is emphasized by Shenhav in his recent book even more than in his academic writings. He de-scribes how a group of Mizrahi intellectuals who defined themselves as "Arab Jews" shared in the celebration of the open space that followed the 1967 war. Shenhav quotes the Jewish Israeli author Shimon Balas, who is of Iraqi origin and wrote immediately at the end of the war: "A new wind is blowing in the land, the Eastern wind with one stroke, we have been ejected from our small, provincial and tangled world and have been confronted with our existential re-ality in the region—past, present, and future."[24] Shenhav's family and his family's friends developed connections with Arab singers and musicians soon after 1967, and celebrated "the space" that had been opened: "Although they accepted the cosmology of the Green Line, they expanded its margins." And here comes a list of names of the Arab musicians with whom they "sang and played music in parties, cafés and private homes and imagined their past in the Arab countries."[25]

All this joy, while many Palestinians were expelled—becoming refugees for the second time—many were killed, and a lethal blow was dealt to the Palestinian national movement. Again, one would expect a progressive sociologist such as Shenhav to sharply criticize both those Mizrahi and Palestinian musicians who partied together in these "wine and roses" gatherings. But identity politics does not allow for solidarity with the struggle for liberation of other "identity groups." Self-proclaimed "Arab Jews" are not an exception to this rule.

Shenhav, along with other Mizrahi intellectuals who are proponents of identity ideology, label Mizrahim as "Arab Jews."[26] However, as Ein-Gil and Machover correctly point out, this label is erroneous:[27] "Of course, we are not questioning the right of any individual to self-identify as an Arab Jew if s/he feels inclined to do so. But there is no justification for thrusting this label upon the mass of Mizrahim, who do not choose to identify themselves as 'Arab,' and who would at best regard this label as alien to their self-identity." Hence, they argue, "the felt cultural affinity of individuals has never had any relevance to an Arab ethnic/national identity. On the contrary, even Mizrahim who took part in violent uprising against their discrimination, except for the Black Panthers in 1971, have not connected their opposition to solidarity with the oppressed Palestinians in Israel. Since 1977 the Mizrahim have for the most part supported the Right en masse, be it the secular Likud or the Mizrahi Shas movement, which has gradually become an extremely racist party."

The Solution

As mentioned, Shenhav opposes a solution that would include dismantling most of the settlements. He contends that the Zionist Left plan to uproot settlements as part of a two-state solution is not only unrealistic because of the settlers' objection to it, it is also immoral: "Is an [Israeli] government allowed to renounce its responsibility towards a hundred and twenty thousand of its citizens [namely, the settlers]? Is it permitted to uproot their life project and its meaning . . . I am not sure it is moral to evacuate generations of people who live there. I don't think that you need to correct one injustice by another injustice."[28]

Tom Segev asks Shenhav: "Where is the Palestinian who would agree to a peace agreement which does not include the dismantling of the settlements? A significant part of the Palestinian resistance concentrates on the issue of their stolen land." But Shenhav does not bother with the stance of the Palestinian majority or their national right to the land. "If there would be a reciprocal demand that permits a land swap [Lieberman's plan!] I cannot see any special reason not to leave the settlements in their place."

Justice, according to Shenhav, is achieved by denying both the colonialists and the colonized the ability to implement their presumed equal rights in the form of a sovereign state.

The preferred model for Shenhav is "a consociational democracy, of partnership which assumes that the national and religious rights of the two peoples would be expressed by means of a partition of the 'space' into small national spaces and into religious and civic communities in the form of cantons."[29] These sovereign or municipal communities, scattered throughout Palestine, would be granted autonomy on the basis of their different identities: religious, civic, and also national—should the inhabitants demand it. The 1948 Palestinians are thus invited to create a separate canton alongside the variety of others throughout Palestine. The same goes for Zionists. They may find their expression in permitting large communities to retain their uni-national character if demanded.

Against Anticolonial Resistance

Replacing Palestinian nationhood and Zionist colonialism with identity politics results not only in a lack of solidarity with the Palestinian cause, as articulated and defined by Palestinians themselves. Shenhav's book also demonstrates a case in which a post-Zionist scholar, working within the framework of identity politics, ends in twisting the democratic positions of Palestinian citizens and inventing nonexistent traitors among the Palestinians in 1967 territories who presumably agree to his plan. Again, one would expect a highly respected, extremely progressive intellectual to call for removing the yoke of Zionist colonialism from the backs of Palestinians and support the Palestinian genuine national struggle for liberation. However, one cannot find such a call in the agendas of post-Zionist Shenhav or the Zionist Left's Avnery. Inevitably, the collaborationist forces among the Palestinians are the allies of those who refuse to explicitly disconnect from Zionism—whether locating its turning point in the 1948 war or the 1967 occupation. Both the Zionist Left and post-Zionists are deaf to the majority of Palestinian voices who challenge the colonial settler state that oppresses the Palestinians in both Israel and the West Bank.

The emerging unified struggle of Palestinians against the Israeli Apartheid regime in all of Historic Palestine is systematically ignored by even the most dedicated activists in the Israeli peace camp. The case of the BDS (Boycott, Divestment, and Sanctions) movement highlights the enormous gap between the Palestinians' definition of the movement's goals and that of their supporters—largely among Israelis but also others who struggle against the 1967 occupation.[30]

The BDS derives its principles from the BDS and PACBI (Palestinian Campaign for the Academic and Cultural Boycott of Israel) Calls,[31] which together represent the most authoritative and widely supported strategic statements that have emerged from Palestine in decades. All political factions; labor, student, and women organizations; and refugee groups across the Arab world have supported and endorsed these calls. In a statement by Omar Barghouti, a founder and driving force of the BDS (together with Lisa Taraki of Bir-Zeit University), the importance of the 2005 BDS Call is emphasized:[32]

> [It takes a] comprehensive approach to the Israeli colonial and apartheid system as a whole, and its subjugation of the Palestinian people, whether as second-class citizens inside Israel, subjects under its military occupation, or dispossessed refugees . . . However despite the clarity with which the Palestinian BDS movement has enunciated the goals of the Palestinian struggle, some Israeli and other advocates of boycott have attempted to limit the goals of the BDS movement by restricting it to a call to end the Israeli occupation over the '67 Occupation territories.
>
> "This 'interpretation' of BDS," claims Omar Barghouti, is most dangerous as it attempts to appropriate the right to redefine the terms of the struggle in Palestine and to impose an ideologically suspect political agenda that lets Israel off the hook on the charges of apartheid and practicing the most pernicious form of racism and discrimination in all the territory under its control.

Not only is the commitment to Zionism and the Jewish state responsible for the treacherous positions held by the Zionist Left, their support for the collaborative PA with Israeli "security" forces, as orchestrated by the United States, and their disregard for the struggle against Israel-US and the PA. Their positions are part of a wider worldview that legitimizes any effort to abolish Palestinian national resistance nor that of Arabs against their dictatorial regimes. The lack of a radical anti-imperialist perspective, let alone an approach of anti-capitalist globalization, is in line with their support of US imperial interests in the region and Israel's role as their enforcer. The Zionist Left wholeheartedly backs the US war against "Islamic terror," which enables Israel to escalate its military involvement against "refusing" states and resistance movements in the Middle East. The current warmongering by the Israeli security and political establishments against Iran (and Syria and Lebanon) has gained the support of a wide strata of Israeli society. The Zionist Left shares this perspective of a continuous threat to the "security" of the state and has largely internalized it. Hence, no Left movement will be there to resist the disastrous war when it comes.

In the meantime, members of the Zionist Left and post-Zionists continue with their futile debate on a two-state or one-state solution, misleading progressives in Israel and abroad to believe that the conflict can be resolved within the "box" of "Historic Palestine." Matzpen, however, has argued since the 1960s that a resolution will only be possible after a thorough democratic transformation of the entire region, which would lead to a socialist Middle East. Hence, the domination of US imperialism and the Zionist colonial state of Israel must be eliminated.[33] Rejecting this comprehensive view has made the Zionist Left and post-Zionism the main obstacles to the development of a radical movement in Israel that would be part and parcel of the resisting forces among Palestinians and throughout the Arab world. This is the only way to liberate Palestinians, Arabs, and Israelis, as well.

Notes

Introduction

1. In general, the Zionist Left refers to the Labor and Meretz parties, as well as their supporters, including the wider circles of progressive/liberal intellectuals and publicists. It also refers to the peace camp at large, which calls for a peace solution with the Palestinians based on compromise. At its center is Peace Now, established in 1977 with the goal of supporting the peace settlement with Egypt. Up until 2000, it was the largest movement within the Israeli peace camp and was headed by Zionist Left Labor intellectuals and academics like professors Uli Tamir, Menachem Brinker, and Avishai Margalit, and authors like Amos Oz, A. B. Yehoshua, and David Grossman. Since the collapse of the Oslo process in 2000, when Labor PM Ehud Barak's coined slogan "there is no partner to peace" was adopted by the majority of the Zionist Left (see chapter 9), Peace Now has disappeared from demonstrating against the 1967 occupation and the war crimes committed in the West Bank and Gaza. It has focused its activity on daily monitoring of Jewish settlement construction in the West Bank and confiscation of lands, and publishing reports about them.

   Alongside this movement, which organized mass demonstrations only on specific occasions, mostly on par with the general policy of Labor and Meretz, was Gush Shalom, the Israeli Peace Block (headed by Uri Avnery). Founded in 1993, Gush Shalom first focused on supporting the Oslo agreement in cooperation with Arafat and the PLO leaders who returned from Tunis. Later it led, dedicatedly and determinedly, the protest movement against the 1967 occupation and Israel's policies in the 1967 territories, including those adopted by Labor governments. All along it retained its allegiance to Arafat and, after 2000, to the Palestinian Authority—the official leadership of the Palestinians. Gush Shalom also lost its relatively large following after the collapse of the Camp David Summit in 2000.

2. The Zionist Labor movement refers to the historic movement that began with a central stream of the General Workers Organization (Achdut Haavoda), and the anti-socialist

"Hapoel Hatzair," which in 1921 founded the Histadrut (an acronym for the General Federation of the Workers in Eretz Israel). The two parties united in 1930 and established Mapai, an acronym for Mifleget Poalei Eretz Yisrael—literally, "the Land of Israel Workers' Party"—which led the Histadrut and the Yishuv, and molded the Zionist Labor movement in accordance with its own image.

The resignation of the Kibbutz movement Hakibbutz Hameuchad and the urban Faction B (both identified with the original Achdut Haavoda) in 1944, and the establishment of a new political body, which adopted the name "Achdut Haavoda-Poalai Tzion," did not change the balance of forces in the Labor movement, and the general course of development was largely determined by Mapai.

Nor did the Zionist Marxist parties change the balance of power in the Labor movement.

Hashomer Hatzair was a Marxist-Zionist party that called for the socialism and colonization of Palestine by Kibbutzim, and was considered to be the nucleus of the future socialist society. Its members saw themselves as having an organic link with the Stalin-led Soviet Union. It was active in a number of organizations, such as an urban party known as the Socialist League, but their main power was in the framework of their Kibbutzim (Hakibutz Haartzi-Hashomer Hatzair). Mapam (an acronym for the Unified Workers Party), founded in 1948, was a Zionist socialist party that included the Hashomer Hatzair Party and the Le Achdut Haavoda-Poalai Tzion movement. It was identified with the Soviet Union and the World Communist movement, but rejected the Soviet Union's negative approach to Zionism. In 1954, the members of Achdut Haavoda resigned from the party because of its orientation toward the Soviet Union. The remaining Hashomer Hatzair participated in Israeli general elections as an independent party, starting with the third Knesset (1955) until the sixth Knesset (1965), and was partner to governments led by Mapai. Before the elections of the seventh Knesset (1969), it created a joint faction with the Labor Party, named Ma'arach, but retained its distinct framework as a party.

The Ma'arach faction existed until 1984. Mapam then resigned from the unified faction when Mapai established a coalition government with the Right. In 1992 Mapam joined Ratz (the civil rights movement) and formed the Meretz list in the Knesset. Since 1997, Mapam has not existed as a distinct party.

A Kibbutz is a form of cooperative settlement in which all members are equal partners in labor and its fruit, with no private property. The Moshav only partially adopted the collectivist principles of the Kibbutzim, like collective buying and selling, and a commitment to help members in difficult times, both in funding and labor. Hence, the Kibbutzim were perceived as embodying the most enshrined values shared by the Yishuv society and held the most prestige.

3. A leading critic of Zionist Left intellectuals is the radical poet, novelist, and thinker Yitzhak Laor. He is also the editor of *Mitaam, The Periodical for Literature and Critical Thinking,* and a regular cultural and political commentator in the daily *Haaretz.* See his collection of essays, *Narratives with No Natives: Essays in Israeli Literature* (Tel Aviv: Hakibbutz Hameuchad Publishing, 1995), and *The Myths of Liberal Zionism* (New York: Verso, 2010). Also see, for example, his criticism of Amos Oz in "A Story of Love and Darkness: Propaganda, Narcissism, and the West," *Mitaam* 7 (September 2006): 67–91, and "One Day They'll Make a Film About It," *Mitaam* 18 (June 2009): 137–150.

4. For the Jewish people as a national community "imagined" by Zionism, see Shlomo Sand,

Historians, Time and Imagination (Tel Aviv: Am Oved Publishers Ltd., 2004), and Shlomo Sand, *The Invention of the Jewish People* (London: Verso, 2009). Also see Boas Evron, *A National Accounting* (Or Yehuda, Israel: Dvir Publishing, 1988).

5. For a systematic analysis of the colonial nature of Zionism and of Israel as a settler colonial state, see A. Said (Jabra Nicola) and M. Machover, "Palestinian Struggle and Middle-East Revolution." This article originated as a position paper adopted by Matzpen. It was first published under a different title, "The Struggle in Palestine Must Lead to Arab Revolution," and without the one-paragraph preamble, in *The Black Dwarf* 14, no. 19 (June 14, 1969). A Hebrew version under the present title was published in *Matzpen* in August 1969 and in Moshé Machover, *Israelis and Palestinians: Conflict and Resolution*, Barry Amiel and Norman Melburn Trust Annual Lecture, November 30, 2006. It was reprinted in *International Socialist Review* 65 (May–June 2009): 32–34. Also see Gabriel Piterbeg, *The Returns of Zionism: Myths, Politics and Scholarship in Israel* (London, New York: Verso, 2008).

6. For elaboration on the Apartheid nature of Zionist ideology, and Israeli laws and their use of apparently universal language, see Saree Makdisi, "A Racism Outside of Language: Israel's Apartheid," *EATURES*, Issue 473 (November 3, 2010), http://pambazuka .org/en/category/features/62928. Also see Machover, *Israelis and Palestinians*, and Moshé Machover, "Is It Apartheid?" Jewish Voice for Peace, November 10, 2004, www.jewishvoiceforpeace.org.

7. Baruch Kimmerling, *Immigrants, Settlers, Natives: The Israeli State and Society Between Cultural Pluralism and Cultural Wars* (Tel Aviv: Am Oved Publishers, 2004), 21.

8. Published in the *Official Gazette 5*, no. 1 (May 14, 1948).

9. The Palestine Mandate, or Mandate for Palestine, was a League of Nations Mandate drafted by the principal allied and associated powers as part of dividing the Ottoman Empire between the winning superpowers of World War I. It was formally approved by the League of Nations in 1922. By the power granted under the mandate, Great Britain ruled Palestine (the area that spans between the Mediterranean Sea and the Jordan River) between 1920 and 1948, a period referred to as the "British Mandate."

10. *Halacha*, Hebrew for "law," represents the body of Jewish law supplementing the scriptural law and forming the legal part of the Talmud. It is the religious body of law regulating all aspects of life, including religious ritual, familial and personal status, civil relations, criminal law, and relations with non-Jews.

11. For the development of this definition as a criterion for citizenship, as it was tailored to discriminate against Palestinians and not just non-Jews, see Yfat Weiss, "The Monster and Its Creator: Or How the Law of Return Made Israel a Multi-Ethnic State," *Theory and Criticism* 19 (Fall 2001): 45, 71.

12. Aharon Barak, "The Zionist-Halachic-Heritage, a Democratic Aspect," *Kivunim Hadashim* 7 (September 2002): 22–35.

13. See *Neiman v. Chairman of the Central Election Committee* (1988) 42.P, D IV 189. The context in which this was said is significant. In 1984 the Knesset enacted the legislation (Section 7A added to the Basic Law: The Knesset) barring any political party and person that does not recognize Israel as a Jewish and democratic state from participating in parliamentary elections. The five Supreme Court judges did not challenge the law. In *The Legal Status of the Arabs in Israel*, David Kretzmer notes that there was general agreement among the judges regarding the interpretation of the law. Namely, that "it allows for disqualification of a list

that rejects the ideological underpinnings of Israel as the state of the Jewish people, even if there is no subversive element involved and no perceivable danger to state security." Yet the Supreme Court rejected a submitted appeal to disqualify the Progressive List for Peace (PLP) from running in elections to the Knesset. The majority took the view that the clear, convincing, and unambiguous evidence required to disqualify a list was lacking. For details of the law and its development, see David Kretzmer, *The Legal Status of the Arabs in Israel* (Boulder, Colorado: Westview Press, 1990), 30, and "The Case of MK Azmi Bishara: Revealing the True Nature of Israel's Democracy" in *Between the Lines*, Tikva Honig-Parnass and Toufic Haddad, ed. (Chicago: Haymarket Books, 2007): 133–151.·

14. Azmi Bishara, "Jewishness Versus Democracy," *Al Aharam Weekly,* October 27–November 3, 2004.

15. Kretzmer, *Legal Status,* 36. On how to avoid the creation of an openly Apartheid-like legal structure through special laws against Palestinian citizens, see Noam Chomsky, "South Africa, Israel-Palestine, and the Contours of the Contemporary Global Order," interview with Christopher J. Lee, *Safundi,* March 9, 2004.

16. See Sawsan Zaher, "On Institutional Discrimination in the Implementation of Israeli Supreme Court Decisions," *Adalah's Newsletter* 63 (August 2009).

17. The Green Line is the armistice border of 1949, separating Israel and what was then TransJordan, which ruled the West Bank. It was the de facto border until 1967.

18. Makdisi, "A Racism Outside of Language."

19. Kretzmer, *Legal Status,* 36.

20. Bishara, "Jewishness Versus Democracy."

21. The Basic Laws of Israel deal with the formation and role of the principal state's institutions, and the relations between the state's authorities. However, while these laws were originally meant to be draft chapters of a future Israeli constitution, they are already used on a daily basis by the courts as a formal constitution. As of today, the Basic Laws do not cover all constitutional issues, and there is no deadline set to complete the process of merging them into one comprehensive constitution. There is no clear rule determining the precedence of Basic Laws over regular legislation, and in many cases this issue is left to the interpretation of the jurisdictional system.

22. "Basic Law: Human Dignity and Liberty" and "Basic Law: Freedom of Occupation" were enacted on the final day of the 12th Knesset, March 17, 1992. The first law declares that basic human rights in Israel are based on the recognition of the value of man, the sanctity of his life, and the fact that he is free. It defines human freedom as the right to leave and enter the country, privacy (including speech, writings, and notes), intimacy, and protection from unlawful searches of one's person or property. The second law lays down the right of "every citizen or inhabitant to engage in any occupation, profession, or trade."

23. Kimmerling, *Immigrants, Settlers, Natives.*

24. For large parts of the discussions that took place in those meetings, see Uzi Benziman, ed., *Whose Land Is It? A Quest for a Jewish-Arab Compact in Israel* (Jerusalem: Israel Democracy Institute, 2006).

25. Ibid., 36.

26. Ibid., 225.

27. The document issued by the Follow-Up Committee was authored by a group of well-known Palestinian intellectuals and activists, and chaired by Shawqi Khattib (the head of

the committee). The Position Paper named the "Haifa Declaration" was written by figures identified with various parties, including the NDA and Hadash (the front headed by the Communist Party) but not with the Islamic movement. Professor Nadim Rouhana, director of Mada al-Carmel—the Arab Center for Applied Social Research—spearheaded the initiative. The two other Position Papers are "Ten Points" of the Mossawa Center, and the "Democratic Constitution" of the Adalah Legal Center for Arab Minority Rights in Israel.

28. For the full text of "Haifa Declaration," see *Haaretz*, May 15, 2007.

29. Among the approved laws by the Knesset are:

1. The Basic Law: The Knesset (Amendment 38), (Candidate Who Visited a Hostile State Illegally) 2008: Denying the right to be elected to any individual who visited certain Arab and Muslim states defined as enemy states, including Syria, Lebanon, Iraq, Iran, and others—without permission from the Minister of Interior, during the seven years that preceded the date of submitting the list of candidates. According to the new amendment, these visits are defined as "support for armed struggle against the State of Israel."

2. Extension of the validity of the Citizenship and Entry into Israel Law (Temporary Order) 2003: Banning family unification for another year. The law, first enacted in July 2003, denies Palestinian citizens of Israel the right to acquire residency or citizenship status in Israel for their Palestinian spouses from the '67 occupied territory solely on the basis of nationality. New amendments to the law, which took effect in 2007, expand the law to also exclude spouses from "enemy states," defined as Syria, Lebanon, Iraq, and Iran, and extend the ban to "anyone living in an area in which operations that constitute a threat to the State of Israel are being carried out," according to the security services.

3. Citizenship Law (Amendment No. 9), (Authority for Revoking Citizenship) 2008. The law revokes citizenship due to a breach of trust or disloyalty to the state. "Breach of trust" is defined very broadly and even includes the act of residing in one of nine Arab and Muslim states or Gaza, which are listed by the law. The law allows for the revocation of citizenship for breach of trust without requiring a criminal conviction for this action.

For an analysis hypothesizing that this wave of anti-Palestinian laws was a reaction to the strengthening of national consciousness among Palestinian citizens, see Azmi Bishara, "Loyalty to Racism," *Al Ahram Weekly* 952 (June 18–24, 2009).

30. Yoav Stern, "PMO to Balad: We Will Thwart Anti-Israel Activity Even If Legal," *Haaretz*, March 16, 2007.

31. The Likud Party was founded in 1973 as an alliance of several right-wing and bourgeois liberal parties, at the center of which was Herut (founded by Menachem Begin in 1948 as the political successor of the pre-state Revisionist Movement Party). Likud adhered to Revisionist Zionist ideology developed by Ze'ev Jabotinsky, who advocated a "revision" of the "pragmatic Zionism" of the Zionist Labor movement headed by David Ben-Gurion. In 1935, Jabotinsky and his followers seceded to form the World Zionist Organization in order to establish the Zionist Revisionist Alliance. Revisionists set up a paramilitary group (the Irgun), their own labor union (the National Labor Federation), and their own health services. Their labor and health services were intended to counteract the hegemony

of Labor Zionism over community services and address the refusal of the Histadrut to make its services available to Revisionist Party members.

32. In *Immigrants, Settlers, Natives,* Baruch Kimmerling determines that Israel was characterized by a transition from hegemony in the Gramscian sense, to "multiculturalism," which began in the 1970s. The end of Zionist Labor movement dominance (which he defines as "Ashkenazi, secular, old-timer socialists and nationalists or Zionists") started with the rise and empowerment of those groups that, during the period of Zionist Labor hegemony, were located on the margins of Israeli society. This opinion contradicts the answer to the question he raises at the end of his book, *The End of Ashkenazi Hegemony* (Jerusalem: Keter Publishing House, 2001), 106, in which Kimmerling asks, "Have they been liquidated as a social strata?" He answers, "Their rule ended; they did not."

    The Ben-Gurion University sociologist Yossi Yonah, who maintains that the Zionist Left hegemony did not collapse, notes that Kimmerling himself writes that Israel's secular middle class, the historical standard-bearer of hegemony, still rules the country's economy, media, and academic community. See Yossi Yonah, "The News of Its Death Was Premature," *Haaretz Books Supplement,* November 7, 2001.

33. By 2009 the Labor Party, headed by Ehud Barak, participated in the extreme right government led by Sharon (with Barak himself as minister of defense). The extreme Right portrayed this wide stratum in the political center as "Zionist Left elites" because it supported the very limited perspective of the two-state solution. Accordingly, Minister Moshe Yaalon, the vice prime minister and minister for strategic affairs, attacked Peace Now as a virus that constitutes a strategic threat to Israel. See *Haaretz,* August 20, 2009, 1.

34. Broadly speaking, the Mizrahim—the term is Hebrew for "Orientals"—are Jews belonging to, or originating from, communities that have lived for several centuries in Muslim countries. The Ashkenazim—the term is Medieval Hebrew for Germans—are Jews belonging to, or originating from, Yiddish-speaking communities that lived in Central and Eastern Europe.

35. Honig-Parnass and Haddad, *Between the Lines,* 195–203.

36. This thesis was elaborated in Zeev Sternhell, *Nation Building or a New Society? The Zionist Labor Movement (1914–1940) and the Origins of Israel* (Tel Aviv: Am Oved Publishers, 1995); Shlomo Sand, *Historians, Time and Imagination* (Tel Aviv: Am Oved Publishers, 2004); Gabriel Piterberg, "Erasures," *New Zionist Left Review* 10, (July/August 2001): 31–47; and Ilan Pappe, "From an 'Empty Land' to the 'Promised Land,'" *Mitaam* 1 (January 2005): 79–86.

37. Ideologues of the socialist version adopted by the movement. Katznelson was the admired political leader before Ben-Gurion; A.D. Gordon, the moral leader of the Labor movement and founder of the ethical philosophy known as "laboring religion" (*dat haavoda*).

38. Sternhell, *Nation Building,* 50.

39. Ibid., 31.

40. Ibid., 34.

41. See the illuminating article by Adam Hanieh, "From State-Led Growth to Globalization: The Evolution of Israeli Capitalism," *Journal of Palestine Studies* 32, no. 4 (Summer 2003), in which he analyzes the Histadrut's central role in developing the economy of the state, "preparing" it for the neoliberalism of the mid-1990s, which was initiated by a Labor Party–led government. The Histadrut industrial enterprises ultimately formed the core

of the four great conglomerates that for decades dominated the Israeli economy and served as the nucleus of Israel's capitalist class.

42. The source of the public capital on which the power base of the labor movement was built—the collective agricultural settlements known as Kibbutzim and Moshavim, and all Histadrut financial and industrial enterprises—was private, supplied by the middle class in Diaspora. Hence the movement's leadership was cautious not to endanger its funding sources. The two sides had profited from this arrangement, as noted by Sternhell: "The bourgeoisie gained a vague socialism which did not endanger its power, which never raised the flag of nationalization since it itself owned vast properties, which did not interfere in the bourgeoisie economic activity and in fact established its [bourgeoisie] position due to the [Labor movement's] strong responsibility to the entire national economy. In return the Labor movement gained the bourgeoisie's cooperation in what was at the center of its being: funding the agricultural colonization—conquering the land. The colonization constituted a common denominator of the employee strata organized in the Histadrut on the one hand and the middle and upper middle class on the other: both were united around the national goals." Sternhell, *Nation Building*, 47.

43. The Jewish National Fund (JNF) is an institution affiliated with the World Zionist Organization (WZO), which was a central organ of Zionist colonialism. It purchased land for settlement from absentee lords and removed their tenants (the land's real owners). Land bought by the JNF could not be sold back to Palestinians. Palestinians were also not allowed to be employed for work on JNF land. In Zionist discourse, the JNF has been perceived as a trustee for the Jewish people on behalf of the land in Israel.

44. On segregation policies, including the necessity to exclude land and labor from the competitive market mechanisms, see Gershon Shafir, "Land, Labor and Population in the Zionist Colonization: General and Unique Perspectives," in *Israeli Society: Critical Perspectives*, ed. Uri Ram (Tel Aviv: Breirot Publishers, 1993): 104–120. The article is based on the author's study, *Land, Labor and the Origins of the Israeli Palestinian Conflict, 1882–1914* (Cambridge: Cambridge University Press, 1989); also see Baruch Kimmerling, *Zionism and Territory: The Socio-Territorial Dimensions of the Zionist Politics* (Berkeley: University of California, Berkeley International and Area Studies, 1983); and a summary of Kimmerling's positions in *Immigrants, Settlers, Natives*. Also see Zachary Lockman, *Comrades and Enemies: Arab and Jewish Workers in Palestine 1906–1948* (Berkeley: University of California Press, 1996).

45. The Hagana ("Defense"), founded in 1921, was the largest paramilitary organization (in comparison to the extreme right-wing organizations that did not accept the authority of the IZO and the Jewish Agency). Membership was comprised of adults and a great majority of youth, militarily trained while continuing with their regular civil lives. The Palmach, founded in 1941, is a Hebrew acronym for *Plugot Mahatz* (storm troopers), and constituted the organized military units of the Yishuv. Youths were fully mobilized for two years (living in Kibbutzim) and afterward they were partly activated in the reserve system. The Palmach served as the elite units of the Zionist army during the 1948 war, under the command of Yigal Alon. But because it was under the auspices of the Zionist Left side of the Zionist Labor movement, Ben-Gurion quickly dissolved it toward the end of the 1948 war.

46. Machover, "Is It Apartheid?"

47. On the variety of colonial projects that were developed by the European powers between the sixteenth and twentieth centuries, including the "pure settlement colony," see Shafir, "Land, Labor."

48. Quoted from *Haaretz*, February 4, 1994, in Norman G. Finkelstein, *Image and Reality of the Israel-Palestine Conflict*, (London, New York: Verso, 1995), 20, 177. For other references confirming that ethnic cleansing had been looming in Zionist thought for decades before 1948, see Nur Masalha, *Expulsion of the Palestinians: The Concept of "Transfer" in Zionist Political Thought, 1882–1948* (London: Pluto Press, 1992); Nur Masalha, *Imperial Israel and the Palestinians, A Politics of Expansion* (London: Pluto Press, 2000); Gavriel Piterberg, *Mitaam* 1; and Ilan Pappé, *Mitaam* 1, and *The Ethnic Cleansing of Palestine* (Oxford, England: One World Publications, 2006).

 Benny Morris in the *Guardian*, January 2004, points to information supplied by recently released official documents that prove transfer had been looming in the Zionist thinking for decades before it was committed in 1948. See also Benny Morris, *1948 and After* (Oxford: Clarendon Press, 2004): 159–211, and its Hebrew version, *Tikun ta'ut: yehudim ve- 'aravim be-Eretz Isra'el* (Tel Aviv: Am Oved Publishers, 2000).

49. Confirmed by Yosef Gorni, the historian and ideologue of the Zionist Labor movement, in *Zionism and the Arabs, 1882–1948: A Study of Ideology* (Oxford: Oxford University Press, 1987), 303–04.

50. Ibid., 262.

51. The proposed Arab state had 725,000 Arabs and 10,000 Jews. Jerusalem was designated an international zone, and had 105,000 Arabs and 100,000 Jews. The Jewish state was allotted 56 percent of the territory of Palestine and most of the arable land, but Arabs held ownership rights to approximately 90 percent of this land. See BADIL Occasional Bulletin No. 17, May 2004. A copy of this report can be found at: www.badil.org/Publications/Bulletins/Bulletin-17.htm.

 The UN partition resolution of 1947 defines the envisaged Jewish and Arab states on the basis of the composition of their population, not on the basis of any notion of historical connection or rights. The resolution makes no reference to Jews (or Arabs for that matter) who do not reside in the country, nor does it base its legitimacy on the idea that anyone who is not already a citizen/resident can have claims to citizenship or to any other political rights in the new states. The resolution does not accord any status to the Balfour Declaration (in fact, it does not even mention it), or to the League of Nations Mandate (except to say that it is terminated). Hence, rightly concludes Ran Greensten, "The old/new Israeli government call to recognize Israel as the nation-state of the Jewish people has no basis in international law, then, since the founding document of the state (UN GA 181) makes no mention of that." Alef List Serve, September 2, 2009, alef@list.haifa.ac.il.

52. *Final Report of the United Nations Survey Mission for the Middle East (Part I)*. UN Doc. A/AC.25/6 cites a figure of 750,000 refugees. The total number of refugees rises to around 900,000 if the number of persons who lost their livelihood but not their homes is added. This includes approximately one hundred "border" villages where the 1949 armistice lines separated villagers from their lands. For a register of villages depopulated during this period, see Salman Abu Sitta, *The Palestinian Nakba 1948, Register, The Register of Depopulated Localities in Palestine* (London: Palestinian Return Centre, 2001). By 1946, the estimated population of Palestine was 1,952,920, including 583,327 Jews. See Salman

Abu Sitta, *Atlas of Palestine 1948* (London: Palestine Land Society, 2005), 11. Also see "Survey of Palestinian Refugees and Internally Displaced Persons 2008," Badil Resource Center for Refugee and Residency Rights, 2009, ch. 1.

53. According to demographic projections by Janet Abu Lughod, between 890,000 and 904,000 Palestinians would have been living in the territory that became the state of Israel if no displacement had taken place. "The Demographic Transformation of Palestine," *The Transformation of Palestine*, edited by Ibrahim Abu-Lughod (Evanston: Northwestern University Press, 1971), 159. This was roughly equal to the size of the Jewish population at the end of 1948. Israel Central Bureau of Statistics, *Statistical Abstract of Israel*, No. 52 (2001), Table 2.1, "The Population by Religion and Population Group," 2–9.

54. For the variety of invented efforts to block the return of the expelled, see Gabriel Piterberg, "Erasures," 31–47; and Pappé, *The Ethnic Cleansing*.

55. See Avi Shlaim, *Collusion Across the Jordan: King Abdullah, the Zionist Movement and the Partition of Palestine* (Oxford: Clarendon Press, 1988); Avi Shlaim, *The Iron Wall: Israel and the Arab World* (New York, London: W. W. Norton & Company, 2000); Ilan Pappé, *Britain and the Arab-Israeli Conflict, 1948–51* (London: Macmillan, 1988); and Ilan Pappé, *The Making of the Israeli-Arab Conflict* (London: I. B. Tauris, 1992).

56. Yigal Alon was considered to be the embodiment of "Beautiful Israel," as portrayed by the values and image of the Zionist Labor movement. He later became one of the most respected ministers in various Labor governments.

57. Anita Shapira, *Yigal Alon, The Spring of His Life: A Biography*, (Tel Aviv: Hasifria Hachadasha, Hakibbutz Hameuchad Publishing House, 2004), 375–376.

58. For a detailed analysis of the Alon Plan in the context of Zionism and US Imperialism, see Gilbert Achcar, "Zionism and Peace: from the Alon Plan to the Washington Accords," *New Politics*, vol. 5, no. 3 (Summer 1995): 95–115. Achcar cites Yigal Alon, *Israël: la lutte pour l'espoir*, Stock, Paris, 1977.

59. Alina Korn has thoroughly studied that period in her publications: "Crime and Law Enforcement in the Israeli Arab Population Under the Military Government, 1948–1966," in *Israel—The First Decade of Independence*, ed. S. Ilan Troen and Noah Lucas (Albany: State University of New York Press 1995): 659–679; "Crime and Legal Control: The Israeli Arab Population During the Military Government Period (1948–1966)," *British Journal of Criminology* 40, no. 4 (2000): 570–589; Sabri Jiryis, *The Arabs in Israel* (New York: Monthly Review Press, 1976); and Ian Lustick, *Arabs in the Jewish State* (Austin, Texas: University of Texas State Press, 1980). For a personal experience of a Palestinian political activist from Lydda, see Fawzi El-Asmar, *To Be an Arab in Israel* (Beirut: The Institute for Palestine Studies, 1978).

60. It should be remembered that Israel was admitted to the UN (as per UNGA resolution #273, May 11, 1949) on a conditional basis, dependent on its compliance with UNGA Resolution 181 and Resolution 194 of December 11, 1948, which stipulates the right of return for the Palestinian refugees and equality for the Palestinian minority.

61. For the building of Labor hegemony in the first years of the state, see Kimmerling, *Immigrants, Settlers, Natives*.

62. For a Marxist approach, see Ein-Gil and Moshé Machover, "Zionism and Oriental Jews: A Dialectic of Exploitation and Co-optation," *Race and Class* 50, no. 3 (2008): 62–76. For the attempts made by Mizrahim to revolt against their oppression, see chapter 6 in

this book and Sami Shalom Chetrit, *The Mizrahi Struggle in Israel, 1948–2003* (Tel Aviv: Am Oved Publishers, 2004).

63. Kimmerling, *Immigrants, Settlers, Natives*, 151.

64. On the state's role in the capitalist class formation, see Adam Hanieh, "From State-Led Growth to Globalization: The Evolution of Israeli Capitalism," *Journal of Palestinian Studies* 128, vol. XXXII, no. 4 (Summer 2003); and Hanieh, "Class, Economy, and the Second Intifada," *Monthly Review* vol. 54, no. 5 (October 2002): 29–42. For class formation in Israel see Emmanuel Farajoun, "Class Divisions in Israeli Society," in *Forbidden Agendas* (London: Al Saqi Books, 1984): 56–69; and Farajoun, "Palestinian Workers in Israel: A Reserve Army of Labor," in *Forbidden Agendas*: 77–123.

    For the emergence of ethnic division of labor between Ashkenazim and Mizrahim in the process of Israel's industrialization, see Shlomo Swirski, *Israel: The Oriental Majority* (London: Zed Books, 1989), and *Not Backward but Made Backward: Mizrahim and Ashkenazim in Israel* (Haifa: *Machbarot le Mechkar ve Bikoret*, 1981).

65. Shlomo Swirski and Dvora Berenstein, "Who Worked in What and for What Rewards? The Economic Development of Israel and the Emergent Ethnic Labor Division," *Machbarot le Mechkar ve Bikoret* 4 (May 1980).

66. See note 63.

67. Since the mid-1970s, military-related industries were the fastest growing area of Israel's economy. By the early 1980s, they employed about one quarter of the country's labor force.

68. Aziz Haidar, *On the Margins, The Arab Population in the Israeli Economy* (London: St. Martin's Press, 1995).

69. The capitalist elite were raised and sustained under the wings of the state until they were permitted to seek expansion and independence through the economic neoliberal policies introduced by Labor government in 1985. See Hanieh, "From State-Led Growth," in note 64.

70. Baruch Kimmerling, "Merchants of Fear," *Haaretz*, June 24, 1994.

Chapter 1: The Physical and Symbolic Erasure of the Palestinian Presence from the Land, Past and Present

1. On the central characteristic of Israel being a "settler society," involved daily in settling the land, and one whose borders are yet to be fixed, see Baruch Kimmerling, "Neither Democratic nor Jewish," *Haaretz*, December 27, 1996.

2. Pappé, *The Ethnic Cleansing*.

3. For a sharp criticism of Zionist authors erasing the Palestinian Nakba from Israeli Jewish collective memory, see Yitzhak Laor, *Narratives with No Natives: Essays in Israeli Literature* (Tel Aviv: Hakibbutz Hameuchad Publishing House, 1995).

4. Ibid., 156.

5. Amnon Raz-Krakotzkin, "Exile Within Sovereignty, On 'Denial of Exile' in Israeli Culture," *Theory and Criticism* (Autumn 1992): 28–55, and continued in *Theory and Criticism* (Autumn 1994): 113–132.

6. Joel Beinin, "No More Tears: Benny Morris and the Road Back from Liberal Zionism," *Middle East Report* 230 (Spring 2004).

7. Baruch Kimmerling, "Merchants of Fear," *Haaretz*, June 24, 1994. Also see Laor, *Narratives*.

8. See note 2 in introduction.

9. Yossi Amitai, *Fraternity of Nations Under Test* (Tel Aviv: Tchrikover Publishing, 1998), 43.

10. Beinin, "No More Tears."

11. Amos Oz, *Under This Blazing Light* (Jerusalem: Keter Publishing House, 1999), 75.

12. Ibid., 96. These ideas, which were written in 1968, were not removed from this ninth edition of Oz's collection, published before the collapse of the Oslo peace process in July 2000. For a refute of this narrative, see Gilbert Achcar, *The Arabs and the Holocaust, The Arab-Israeli War of Narratives* (London, San Francisco: Saqi Books, 2010).

13. Ibid., 76.

14. Zeev Sternhell, "Zionism or Colonialism?" *Haaretz*, June 28, 2002. See the debate between Sternhell and Gabriel Piterberg on the colonial nature of Zionism and the state of Israel in *New Zionist Left Review* 62 (March–April 2010): Sternhell's critical essay, "In Defense of Liberal Zionism," on Piterberg's book *The Returns of Zionism, Myths, Politics and Scholarship in Israel* (London, New York: Verso, 2008) and Piterberg's response, "Settlers and Their States: A Reply to Zeev Sternhell."

15. For the new historian refutation of the established Zionist narrative, see chapter 7. Also see Pappé, *The Ethnic Cleansing*.

16. Shlomo Avineri, "Wickedness and Stupidity," *Haaretz*, May 31, 2009.

17. See Matzpen founder Moshé Machover's speech to the Barry Amiel and Norman Melburn Trust Annual Lecture, "Israelis and Palestinians: Conflict and Resolution," November 30, 2006, reprinted in *International Socialist Review* 65 (May–June 2009): 32–45.

18. Zeev Sternhell, "The Logic in Counting Corpses," *Haaretz*, April 2, 2004.

19. Sternhell, "Zionism or Colonialism."

20. Zeev Sternhell, *Nation Building or a New Society?* (Tel Aviv: Am Oved Publishers, 1995), 419.

21. Yuval Azolai, "Dalia Golomb: My Father Erected the Hagana, Not the Occupation," *Haaretz*, May 27, 2009.

22. Amos Oz, *But These Are Two Different Wars* (Jerusalem: Keter Publishing House, 2002), 134.

23. Ibid., and Oz, *Under This Blazing Light*.

24. This happened after the collapse of the Arafat-Barak-Clinton Summit at Camp David, which put an end to the Oslo peace process. Zionist Left intellectuals joined the entire Zionist Left in attributing the collapse to Arafat's "rejectionist" stance, and subsequently condemned the breakout of the second Intifada.

25. Uri Avnery, "80 Theses for a New Peace Camp," *Haaretz*, May 16, 2001.

26. Uri Avnery, "A Jeremiad: A Letter to Dov Yermiya," CounterPunch.org, April 25, 2010, www.counterpunch.org/avnery08042009.html.

27. The sabra is used to designate stereotypical Israelis. It refers to a plant that grows naturally in Palestine (*al saber* in Arabic; *Tzabar* in Hebrew) and was a local symbol even before Zionism adopted it. Zionists began to use the symbol in the 1930s as a general name for "the sons of the land," especially in reference to the youth. It expressed a distinction between the "ghetto-like" and "new" Jews, as the latter were associated with the saber fruit, which "has thorns (male toughness) on its outside, but is sweet on the inside"—that is, a delicate and sensitive soul.

28. A line from a popular Palmach song, "The Day Will Come," sung during the 1948 war. It describes the flourishing future state that Palmach would establish.

29. For Gutwein's sharp criticism of the identity politics inherent in some post-Zionist writings (discussed in chapter 8), see Daniel Gutwein, "Identity vs. Class: Multiculturalism as a Neo-Liberal Ideology," *Theory and Criticism* 19 (Fall 2001): 241–259.

30. Daniel Gutwein, "To Split Labor," *Haaretz*, March 25, 2009.

31. From 2001 on, the Labor Party has supported the oppressive policies launched by the Israeli Right—most of the time participating in governments led by Kadima or Likud. Kadima was founded on November 21, 2005, by Ariel Sharon, who left Likud with four ministers and many high-level party activists. A number of Labor leaders (including Shimon Peres and Haim Ramon) joined the new party. For the reshuffling of the political map, which reflected the wide consensus among the majority of Israeli society, see chapter 9 and Tikva Honig-Parnass, "One People, One Leader, One Emperor: Redrawing the Boundaries of the Legitimate Zionist Collective" in *Between the Lines*, 274–280.

32. Daniel Gutwein, "To Split Labor."

33. Noam Chomsky, "Why We Can't See the Trees or the Forest: The Torture Memos and Historical Amnesia." See www.informationclearinghouse.info/article22659.htm.

34. See Adalah official position regarding the commission's report, issued on September 4, 2003.

35. For more on the Geneva Initiative, see chapter 9.

36. Mazal Mualem, "A Strengthening Player Has Joined the Publicity Campaign [for the Geneva Initiative]," *Haaretz*, October 15, 2003.

Chapter 2: "Jewish Majority" Spells Racism

1. This is a reference from the meetings between Israeli and Palestinian intellectuals reported in the introduction. Benziman, *Whose Land Is It?*, 27.

2. Hassan Jabarin, "On the Connection Between Recognition of National Identities and Civil Equality in Jurisdiction," *Adalah Electronic Monthly* 32 (January 2007).

3. Piterberg, "Erasures"; Pappé, *The Ethnic Cleansing*.

4. Benziman, *Whose Land Is It?*, 31.

5. The New Citizenship and Entry into Israel Law was enacted on July 31, 2003, by the Knesset as the Amendment to Nationality and Entry into Israel Law (Temporary Order) 1950.

6. For criticism of the Supreme Court decision, see Adalah, May 14, 2006, at http://adalah-english.c.topica.com/maaeNF1abqy3nbftE4jc/.

7. Hassan Jabarin, *Haaretz*, May 18, 2005.

8. Azmi Bishara, "Separation Spells Racism," *Al-Ahram Weekly*, July 1–7, 2004.

9. Ariella Azoulay and Adi Ophir, *This Regime Which Is Not One: Occupation and Democracy Between the Sea and the River (1967-)* (Tel Aviv: Resling, 2008).

10. Oren Yiftachel, "Judaize & Divide: Shaping Spaces in Israeli 'Ethnocracy,'" *News From Within* VI no. 11 (December 1999). Also see Yiftachel, *Ethnocracy: Land and Identity Politics in Israel/Palestine* (Philadelphia: University of Pennsylvania, 2006).

11. See Oren Yftachel, *News from Within*, vol. XV, no. 11 (December 1999).

12. Ibid.

13. Dani Rabinowitz, *Haaretz*, December 21, 2005.

14. Ron Shani, "Together, but Definitely Separated," *Haaretz*, June 7, 2009.

15. Noam Chomsky, "A Turning Point?," Znet, June 7, 2009, www.zmag.org/znet/viewArticle/ 21649.

16. Sara Roy, "The Peril of Forgetting Gaza," *The Harvard Crimson*, online edition, June 2, 2009, www.thecrimson.com/article.aspx?ref=528434.

17. For the reasons behind the staged "disengagement" from the Gaza Strip, see Tikva Honig-Parnass, "The Misleading Disengagement from Gaza: Unilateralism Replaces Peace Process," 265–274, and Toufic Haddad, "Gaza: Birthing a Bantustan," 280–290, in *Between the Lines*.

18. Ran HaCohen, "Ethnic Cleansing: Past, Present and Future," Antiwar.com, December 30, 2004, www.antiwar.com/hacohen/?articleid=672.

19. Meron Benvenisti, *Guardian*, April 26, 2004.

20. 2.46 million Palestinians in the West Bank, 1.55 million Palestinians in the Gaza Strip, 1.5 million Palestinians who are citizens of the state of Israel, and another 0.32 million people characterized as "other non-Jews."

21. Azoulay and Ophir, *This Regime*.

22. On the "secular" Zionist Left's racist approach toward orthodox Jewry, see chapter 4.

23. Quoted by senior political analyst Avirama Golan, *Haaretz*, December 1, 2005.

24. Shahar Ilan and Amiram Bareket, "To Win Hitler, an Interview with Avraham Burg," *Haaretz*, June 8, 2007.

25. David Grossman, *Sleeping on a Wire* (Tel Aviv: Hakibbutz Hameuchd Publishing House, 2002), 97.

26. Asa Kasher, "The Democratic State of the Jews" an interview with Yossi David, in *The State of Israel: Between Judaism and Democracy*, Yossi David, ed. (Jerusalem: The Israel Democracy Institute, 2000): 111–133. See also, in the same book, Menachem Brinker, "A Democratic State: Form and Content—an Interview," 77–93.

27. Ibid., 119.

28. See note 1 in introduction.

29. "The state of Israel explicitly declares that we are a tool in the service of the Zionist movement, for implementing its aims." Sammy Smooha in David, *The State of Israel*: 319–324.

30. Brinker in David, *The State of Israel*, 85.

31. Ibid.

32. By 2010, the rate of Jewish majority has been reduced to 80 percent.

33. Brinker in David, *The State of Israel*, 78; See also Kasher, "The Democratic State of the Jews," 111–33; and A. B. Yehoshua, "The Israeli State," 45–53.

34. None of the Zionist Left intellectuals who support the Law of Return have raised the logical question: Why not replace the existing law with an immigration law suited for specific persecuted individuals?

35. Avishai Margalit and Moshe Halbertal, "Liberalism and the Right to Culture," in *Multiculturalism in a Democratic and Jewish State*, Menachem Mautner, Avi Sagi, and Ronen Shamir, eds. (Tel Aviv: Ramot Publishing House, Tel Aviv University, 1998): 93–107.

36. Ibid., 104.

37. Ibid.

38. Grossman, *Sleeping on a Wire*, 87, 88.

39. Ibid., 98.

40. Ibid., 102.

41. The ninth edition of his interview with Grossman was published in 2002, most certainly without the opposition of Michael.

42. Sami Michael, *Haaretz*, September 24, 2004.

43. See chapter 1 for the interview with Amos Oz conducted by Ari Shavit, published in *Haaretz Weekly* on March 1, 2002. Also see Oz, "Two Different Wars," 134.

44. Aluf Ben, *Haaretz*, February 2, 2005.

45. In a number of articles published between 2002 and 2004 (in the *Guardian* in February and October 2002, and another on January 14, 2004, in addition to a long interview in *Haaretz* with Ari Shavit, January 9, 2004), Morris says that there was no choice but to commit the expulsion in 1948. See chapter 7 on Benny Morris and New Historians.

46. Benny Morris, *Haaretz*, January 9, 2004.

47. Adi Ophir, "An Answer to Benny Morris," published on many progressive internet sites, including CounterPunch.org, after being rejected by *Haaretz* in January 2004.

48. Tanya Reinhardt, *Israel/Palestine* (New York: Seven Stories Press, 2002), 203. Quoting *Haaretz*, March 23, 2001.

49. Uzi Arad, in an interview with Herb Keinon in the *Jerusalem Post*, conducted just before the 2004 Herzliyah Conference, December 3, 2004.

50. Ibid.

51. Meron Benvenisti, *Haaretz*, December 30, 2005.

Chapter 3: Equal Rights

1. Benziman, *Whose Land Is It?*, 25.

2. "Courageous, But Belated," *Haaretz*, June 28, 2009. Reflecting on a lecture by former Supreme Court President Aharon Barak on behalf of the New Israel Fund's Jurists for Human Rights.

3. Kretzmer, quoted in Benziman, *Whose Land Is It?*, 26.

4. Ibid.

5. Ibid.

6. Palestinian citizens have been deprived of this right by the 1984 law (which has not been implemented yet) that disqualifies those who do not recognize Israel as a Jewish state from running for the Knesset.

7. Hassan Jabarin, "Israeliness: On Looking Towards the Future of the Arabs According to Jewish-Zionist Time, in a Space Without a Palestinian Time," *Mishpat ve Memshal* 6 (2000); Azmi Bishara, "Loyalty to Racism," *Al Ahram* no. 95218 (June 24, 2009).

8. Bishara, "Loyalty to Racism."

9. Ibid.

10. Uzi Benziman, *Haaretz*, August 16, 2002. He cites Dani Rabinowitz and Khawla Abu Baker, *The Stand-Tall Generation: The Palestinian Citizens of Israel Today* (Jerusalem: Keter Publishing House, 2002).

11. Sammy Smooha, The Jewish-Arab Relations Index 2007, Haifa Conference for Social Responsibility. See http://soc.haifa.ac.il/~s.smooha/download/Index_2007_Highlights _Eng.pdf.

12. Hassan Jabarin, "On the Connection Between Recognition of National Identities and

Civil Equality in Jurisdiction," *Adalah Electronic Monthly* 32 (January 2007). Much of the discussion in this section draws from this article.

13. Saree Makdisi, "A Racism Outside of Language: Israel's Apartheid," *EATURES* 473 (March 11, 2010).

14. Moreover, as discussed in chapter 8, post-Zionist scholars struggled for a share of Mizrahim in the privatized state lands leased by collective settlements—including Kibbutzim—in the center of Israel, without acknowledging the fact that most belonged to Palestinians and were confiscated, not to mention the fact that they did not fight for Palestinians to share rights to enjoy the suggested relocation of these state lands.

15. Ilan Pappé, "The Green Lungs and the Blue Box," *Mitaam* 4 (December 2005): 89–103.

16. The Israel Land Administration (ILA) was established in 1960 as a government body with the task of administering all land in Israel, including JNF land. 2.5 million dunams of land are currently owned by the JNF—around 13 percent of the total land in Israel and around 19 percent of ILA land. Most of this land (close to two million dunams) were transferred to the JNF by the state between 1949 and 1953, and before the 1960 law was legalized—as part of the mass robbery of land that was taking place at the time.

    The Jewish Agency for Israel and the JNF have explicit mandates (approved by the Basic Law, which grants state status to "National Institutions") to settle and develop the country for Jews alone. The Jewish Agency for Israel's role is to "encourage Jewish immigration and aid in the successful absorption of immigrants; Jewish-Zionist education in world wide Jewish communities and strengthening Israeli society, especially in preference regions: Galilee, Negev and Jerusalem."

    The JNF was in charge of purchasing land in the pre-state period, and was considered the trustee of the nation's land in the homeland on behalf of the Jewish nation. It continued to play this role after the foundation of the state, while expanding to other areas as well, including those related to the Zionist project of the systematic de-Arabization of the landscape—names, geography, and most of all the history of the villages that had been wiped out.

17. Ilan Pappé, "From an 'Empty Land' to the 'Promised Land'" *Mitaam* 1 (January 2005): 78–87.

18. Azmi Bishara, "Israel, Palestine and the Question of Citizenship," a talk at St. Anthony's College, Oxford University, February 6, 2004. Transcribed by BTL supporter from which this quotation is taken. For revised version, see www.sant.ox.ac.uk/events/lecturesarchive/Bishara.pdf.

19. Oren Yiftachel, "Judaize & Divide," 13–19; Oren Yiftachel, "Lands, Planning and Inequality: A Position Paper," Adva, Information on Equality and Social Justice in Israel, November 2000; and Oren Yiftachel, *Ethnocracy*.

20. Except for the erection of seven townships in Negev in the early 1960s, which the Bedouins were forced to join so that their land could be confiscated.

21. Pappé, "From an Empty Land."

22. Supreme Court, Bagatz 6698/95 25 (1), March 8, 2000.

23. Editorial, "Dvar Hama'arechet," *Machbarot Adallah* 3 (Winter 2000): 2.

24. Quoted in Ruth Gavizon, "Zionism in Israel? In the Footsteps of the Qa'dan Verdict," *Mishpat Ve Memshal* 6 (2001): footnote 2, 25.

25. Meron Benvenisti, "A Debate Within the Family," *Haaretz*, July 18, 2002.

26. Israel Supreme Court, *Bagatz* 6698, 2000.

27. Jabarin, "On the Connection Between"; Jamil Dakwar, "To What Extent Is This an Achievement?" *Haaretz*, March 5, 2000. See also the editorial in *Machbarot Adallah* 2 (Winter 2000).

28. Dakwar, "To What Extent."

29. The cities of Acre, Jaffa, Ramle, and Lydd, in which Palestinian survivors of the Nakaba live in slum neighborhoods, neglected or dispossessed by the authorities, alongside a majority Jewish population who enjoy preferred municipal and state services.

30. Dakwar, "To What Extent."

31. Especially Bedouin villages in Negev, half of which are deemed "unrecognized"—that is, illegal, by the Israeli government, so as to force this community to abandon its land. Unrecognized villages are ineligible for any civil, educational, infrastructural, or medical services, or municipal services such as connection to the electrical grid, water, or trash pick-up.

32. Dakwar, "To What Extent."

33. Jabarin, "On the Connection Between." Land Day began as a general strike in 1976 to protest Israel's policy of confiscating Arab land, and ended with the deaths of six Palestinians from Sakhnin and Arrabeh, shot by the Israeli police.

34. For analysis of the law, see Adalah's *Newsletter* 63 (August 2009).

35. Smooha in Benziman, *Whose Land Is It?*, 184.

36. Kretzmer quoted in Benziman, *Whose Land Is It?*, 26.

37. Smooha in Benziman, *Whose Land Is It?*, 183.

38. Ibid., 201.

39. Ibid., 199.

40. Ibid., 184.

41. Khaled Abu-Usba in Benziman, *Whose Land Is It?*, 190.

42. Azmi Bishara, "Loyalty to Racism," *Al Ahram Weekly* 952 (June 18–24, 2009), http://weekly.ahram.org.eg/2009/952/focus.htm.

Chapter 4: A Theocratic Jewish State

1. See note 11 in the introduction.

2. For the Jewish people as a national community "imagined" by Zionism, see Shlomo Sand, *The Invention of the Jewish People* (London: Verso, 2009).

     In his book, Sand argues that the Jewish people are only a Jewish religion/cultural group and that the exile also never happened. Hence, there was no "return." Sand rejects most of the stories of national identity formation in the Bible, including the exodus from Egypt. He argues that the story of the Jewish nation—the transformation of the Jewish people, from a group with a shared cultural identity and religious faith into a vanquished "people," was a relatively recent invention, hatched in the nineteenth century by Zionist scholars and advanced by the Israeli academic establishment in order to supply an excuse for the creation of the State of Israel. It was, argues Sand, an intellectual conspiracy of sorts. It is all fiction and myth that served as an excuse for the establishment of the State of Israel.

3. Yoav Peled, "Inter-Jewish Challenges to Israeli Identity," *Palestine-Israel Journal*, vol. 8, no. 4 and vol. 9, no. 1, Special Issue on National Identity (2002), 18.

4. See note 11 in introduction.

5. Azmi Bishara, "Thoughts on the Tension Between Religion and Politics in the Middle Eastern Context," *Theory and Criticism* (Jerusalem: The Van Leer Jerusalem Institute, 1991): 105–143.
6. Baruch Kimmerling, "Neither Democratic nor Jewish," *Haaretz*, December 27, 1996.
7. Ibid.
8. See introduction for a discussion of the Jewish Agency for Israel, the executive arm of the World Zionist Organization (WZO), which acted as the government of the Yishuv.
9. The two laws relating to the monopoly on jurisdiction of the religious establishment in family affairs are: Hok Shiput Batai Din Rabaniim (Nisuim ve gerushim), 1953, and Hok Hadayanim, 1955. Two other laws influenced by Jewish Halacha are the Work Hours and Days of Rest Law, and the Freedom of Occupation Law.
10. Baruch Kimmerling, "Religion, Nationalism and Democracy in Israel," *Zmanim* 13, no. 50–51 (Winter 1994): 116–132.
11. Baruch Kimmerling, "The Strangling Connection of Zionism and Religion," *Haaretz*, April 29, 1990.
12. Kimmerling, "Religion, Nationalism and Democracy."
13. Menachem Brinker, "A Democratic State: Form and Content" in David, *The State of Israel*, 84.
14. Ibid., 81.
15. See Anita Shapira, Agreement on the Boundaries of Non-Agreement, in David, *The State of Israel*, 17–33; also see A. B. Yehoshua in David, *The State of Israel*.
16. Ibid., Yehoshua, 45.
17. A. B. Yehoshua, "Israel for Israelis," *Haaretz* supplement, June 10, 2009.
18. Shlomo Avineri, "Nevertheless, the State of the Jews," a response to A.B. Yehoshua in *Haaretz*, June 14, 2009. The overlapping between Jewish religion and Jewish nationality was determined in the case of Oswald Rufeisen, who converted to Catholicism during World War II and immigrated to Israel in 1958. He demanded the automatic right of citizenship granted by the Law of Return, on the grounds that he was a Jew by nationality and Catholic by religion. The Israeli government refused to recognize him as a Jew and the Supreme Court upheld this refusal, arguing that Rufeisen could not be considered a Jew because he converted to Catholicism. See Akiva Orr, *The UnJewish State* (London: Ithaca Press, 1983), 63–99. Binyamin Theodore Herzl, considered the "father of the Nation," envisioned the state of the Jews in "Eretz Israel" as the solution to the "Jewish problem." In 1897 he organized the first Zionist conference in Basel, during which the foundation for the WZO was laid. Herzl chaired the WZO until his death in 1904.
19. Brinker, "A Democratic State," in David, *The State of Israel*: 77–93. Also see Asa Kasher, "The Democratic State of the Jews," and A. B. Yehoshua, "An Israeli State," in David, *The State of Israel*.
20. Amos Oz, *But These Are Two Different Wars* (Jerusalem: Keter Publishing House, 2002), 7.
21. For a thorough attack on "Negation of Exile" as a key concept of Zionism, see Amnon Raz-Krakotzkin, "Exile Within Sovereignty: Toward a Critique of the 'Negation of Exile' in Israeli Culture," *Theory and Criticism* 4 (Autumn 1993). For a Zionist response and analysis, see Anita Shapira, "Where Has the Negation of Diaspora Gone?" *Alpayim* 25 (2003): 9–55.
22. The distinction made between the ghetto-like Jew and the new Jew was decisively expressed in the pre-state period by replacing the concept "Jew" with that of "Hebrew," a synonym for "Zionist."

23. See note 27 for chapter 1.
24. Oz Almog, *The Sabra: A Profile* (Tel Aviv: Am Oved Publishers, 1997): 127–37.
25. Ibid.
26. Anita Shapira, *Land and Power* (Tel Aviv: Am Oved Publishers, 2002).
27. Oz, *But These Are Two*, 7.
28. Ibid., 10.
29. Ari Shavit, "Under the Tuscan Sun: An Interview with Amos Elon," *Haaretz*, December 23, 2004.
30. Ibid.
31. Noam Chomsky, "Rabin and Peres Were Not Quiet About All of This: An Answer to Dan Epstein," August 20, 2004. See http://list.haifa.ac.il/mailman/listinfo/al.
32. Amnon Raz-Krakotzkin, "Rabin's Legacy: On Secularism, Nationalism and Orientalism," in *Contested Memory: Myth, Nation and Democracy*, Lev Grinberg, ed. (Be'er Sheva, Israel: Humphrey Institutes for Social Research, Ben-Gurion University, 2000): 89–109.
33. Ibid.
34. Ibid., 95.
35. As mentioned, in his tenure, thirteen Palestinian citizens were killed by the police during demonstrations that followed the breakout of the second Intifada.
36. Shlomo Ben Ami in *Contested Memory*, "Rabin's Assassination: Between Memory and Forgetfulness." A Panel Discussion on the Implications of the Assassination on Israeli Democracy, A Day Seminar, Ben-Gurion University in Negev, September 4, 1998: 153–57.
37. Jamal Zahalka in *Contested Memory*: 159–64.
38. Meron Rapoport, interview with David Ochana regarding Ochana's book, *The Rage of the Intellectuals*, in *Haaretz*, Weekend Supplement, January 28, 2005.
39. See note 22 for chapter 1.
40. Prime Minister Ariel Sharon's general plan for the Middle East was to establish a new order in Lebanon and Jordan, to destroy PLO institutions and leadership in Lebanon, and to annex the West Bank to Israel by expanding settlements. All this continued under the shadow of a permanent threat of expelling the Palestinians from the West Bank and Gaza Strip. For reports on demonstrations, leaflets, and publications organized and issued by the Committee Against the War of Lebanon, see www.israeli-left-archive.org.
41. Oz, "On Life and Death," 101.
42. Ibid., 110.
43. Ibid., 111.
44. Ibid., 108.
45. Ibid., 102.
46. Ibid., 189. The main idea in these pages is that it may be necessary to be content with lesser aspirations, to give up the entire land for the benefit of the external and internal peace, and to give up holy Jerusalem for Jerusalem of Musrara and the Katamons (poor neighborhoods populated largely by Mizrahim).
47. Uri Misgav, "Then and Now in Eretz Israel," *Yediot Ahronot*, Weekend Supplement, July 10, 2009.
48. Amos Harel and Yonatan Lis, "A Criminal Investigation Against the Jewish Agency for Building in Ofra," *Haaretz*, July 19, 2009. The article deals with a police investigation in the wake of a June 2008 petition by the Palestinian heirs of the original landowners (with the help of Israeli civil rights organizations "B'tzelem" and "Yesh Din") against nine struc-

tures built by Ofra in the settlement's southern neighborhood.

49. As mentioned, during demonstrations, thirteen Palestinian citizens were killed by the police.

50. For "what Barak offered in Camp David 2000," see Tanya Reinhart, *Israel/Palestine* (New York: Seven Stories Press, 2002), 30–33. Also see chapter 9 in this book, which deals with various proposed peace solutions.

51. This strategy led to the end of peace negotiations in the framework of the Oslo Accords and, later, to a complete freeze by the Kadima-Labor and Likud governments.

52. The Kinneret Covenent was prepared by the Forum for National Responsibility, under the auspices of the Yitzhak Rabin Center for Israel Studies. Discussions took place in the Tiberius Hotel, along the shores of Lake Kinneret (the Sea of Galilee).

53. See note 1 in the introduction.

54. Other Zionist Left public figures were writers Sami Michael, Eli Amir, Haim Be'er, and Dalia Ravikovitz; actors Haim Topol and Gila Almagor; Dov Lautmanm, the former chair of the Israeli Association of Industrialists; and Shimon Shamir, professor emeritus of Middle Eastern Studies at Tel Aviv University. Shamir was a former ambassador to Egypt and Jordan (1988–1990) and first ambassador to Jordan (1995–1997).

55. Others on the right were Emuna Alon, a settler journalist representing the most extreme strain of the settler movement, and several rabbis, including "moderate settler" Yoel Ben Noon. Additional right-wing participants included former Air Force chief Herzl Bodinger.

56. Ellis Shuman interview in *Haaretz*, January 11, 2002.

57. Ibid.

Chapter 5: The Assertion of the Democratic Nature of the State

1. See Matzpen pamphlets and articles from the 1960s through the 1990s at the Matzpen website: www.matzpen.org.

2. See note 17 in chapter 1. Machover rightly comments, "Significantly, Israel never officially defined its own international borders. The Green Line became its de facto border until 1967."

3. Azmi Bishara, "A Short History of Apartheid," in *Al Ahram Weekly*, no. 672 (January 8–14, 2004).

4. Idith Zertal's introduction to the issue of the historical quartely *Zmanim*, which she edits, published by Aranne School of History at Tel Aviv University, in conjunction with Zmora-Bitan Publishers, in the Democracy edition, vol. 13, no. 50–51 (Winter 1994).

5. Azoulay and Ophir, *This Regime Which Is Not One*.

6. Ibid., 363.

7. Oren Yftachel, "One Book, One Regime: Reflections on Azoulay and Ophir," *Mitaam* 17 (March 2009), 63.

8. Meron Benvenisti, *The Sting and the Club* (Jerusalem: Keter Publishing, 1988). Also see Baruch Kimmerling, *Politicide: Sharon's War Against the Palestinians* (London: Verso, 2006).

9. Ibid.

10. Sammy Smooha, "Ethnic Democracy: Israel as Archetype," *Israel Studies*, vol. 2, no. 2 (Fall 1997): 198–241.

11. Sammy Smooha, "Ethnic Democracy: Israel as Prototype" in *The Jewish-Arab Rift: A Reader*, edited by Ruth Gavizon and Dafna Hacker (Jerusalem: The Israel Democracy

Institute, 2000), 153–200.

12. Kimmerling, "Religion, Nationalism and Democracy."

13. Bishara, "The Question of Citizenship."

14. Ibid.

15. Azmi Bishara, "A Short History of Apartheid."

16. This is the headline of a review by the military and security expert Reuven Pde Tzur, *Haaretz* Sfarim Supplement, June 3, 2009, which reflects the conclusion of an academic study, *New Approaches to Civil-Security Relations in Israel*, edited by Gabriel Sheffer, Oren Barak, and Amiram Oren (Haifa: Carmel Publishing House, 2009). The volume, which includes thirteen articles, is the product of studies and discussions undertaken by members of a three-year interdisciplinary research workshop that was organized by the three editors at the Van Leer Jerusalem Institute. The idea behind the project, which ran from 2003 to 2007, was to critically reexamine the relations between the civil and security spheres in Israel.

17. *Haaretz*, February 9, 2001.

18. Shlomo Avineri, "Hatikva Shall not Die," *Haaretz,* October 1995.

19. Shlomo Avineri, in an interview with Ariela Ringel-Hofman, *Yediot Ahronot* 1 (February 2002).

20. Nor is Israel a "consensual democracy," says Smooha, since it is not a binational state, such as Belgium or Canada, in which the state officially recognizes ethnic groups within it and grants them collective rights in addition to equal political rights. In a consensual democracy there are arrangements that ensure a relational representation, a coalition government autonomy, and veto rights to the minority in order to prevent essentially harmful decisions to it.

21. Sammy Smooha, "Ethnic Democracy," 153–201. Also see Smooha in *The Nation Before the State in the State of Israel: Between Judaism and Democracy*, Yossi David, ed. (Jerusalem: The Israel Democracy Institute, 2000), 319–325. For critical analysis of Smooha, see Azmi Bishara, "The Sovereignty Process Has Not Yet Been Completed," in David, *The Nation Before the State*, 325–329.

22. Smooha in David, *The Nation Before the State*, 320.

23. In the second half of the last decade, the persecution of many of those NGOs by Israel's security establishment (under the pretext of their connections with Hezbollah or Iran) has increased tremendously.

24. Ibid., 321.

25. Bishara in David, *The Nation Before the State*, 325.

26. Yoav Peled, "Strangers in Utopia: The Status of Palestinians in Israel," in *The Jewish-Arab Rift in Israel,* edited by Ruth Gavizon and Dafna Hacker (Jerusalem: The Israeli Institute of Democracy, 2000), 213–245. For his more recent work on the solution to the Israeli-Palestinian conflict, see chapter 9.

27. Ibid.

28. Joje Bruner and Yoav Peled, "On Autonomy, Capabilities and Democracy: Criticism of the Liberal Multi-Culturalism," 107–133, and Avishai Margalit and Moshe Habertal, "Liberalism and the Right to Culture," 97–103, in *Multiculturalism in a Democratic and Jewish State,* Menachem Mautner, Avi Sagi, and Ronen Shamir, eds. (Tel Aviv: Ramot-Tel Aviv University, 1998).

29. Republicanist theory and ideology that sparked the French Revolution concentrated on anti-monarchism and emphasized the rule of the people. In modern political science, Re-

publicanism refers to a specific ideology that is based on civic virtue and is considered contradictory to Liberalism. However, the exact meaning of Republicanism varies on the cultural and historical context and sometimes definitions conflict.

30. Peled, "Strangers in Utopia," 216.

31. Ibid., 217.

32. Ibid., 218.

33. On supremacy of collective goals in Israel's political culture, see Baruch Kimmerling, "Between the Primordial and the Civil Definitions of the Collective Identity: Eretz Israel or the State of Israel?" in *Comparative Social Dynamics*, edited by Erik Cohen et al. (Boulder, Colorado: Westview Press, 1985); Kimmerling, *Immigrants, Settlers, Natives*; Peter Medding, *The Founding of Israeli Democracy 1948–1967* (New York: Oxford University Press, 1990), chapter 4; Charles Liebman and Don Yehiya, *Civil Religion in Israel: Traditional Judaism and Political Culture in the Jewish State* (Berkeley, California: University of California Press, 1983); Dan Horowitz and Moshe Lissak, *From Yishuv to a State: Eretz Israel Jews as a Political Community in the Mandate Times* (Tel Aviv: Am Oved Publishers, 1986), chapter 8; Shapira Yonatan, *Democracy in Israel* (Masada: Ramat Gan, 1977); Shapira Yonatan, *Elite Without Disciples—Generations of Leaders in Israeli Society* (Tel Aviv: Sifriyat Poalim, 1984); Shmuel N. Eisenstadt, *Israeli Society in Its Transformations* (Jerusalem: Magnes, 1989); Dan Horowitz and Moshe Lissak, *Trouble in Utopia, The Overburden Polity of Israel* (Tel Aviv: Am Oved Publishers, 1990), chapter 6; Gershon Shafir, *Land, Labor and the Origin of the Israeli Conflict 1882–1914* (Cambridge: Cambridge University Press, 1989).

34. Peled, "Strangers in Utopia," 223.

35. Ibid., 220.

36. Uri Ram, "Society and Social Science: Establishment Sociology and Critical Sociology in Israel" in *Israeli Society: Critical Perspectives*, edited by Uri Ram (Tel Aviv: Breirot Publishers, 1993), 7–40.

37. Talcott Parsons, *The Social System* (New York: The Free Press, 1951).

38. Peled, "Strangers in Utopia," 221.

39. Shmuel N. Eisenstadet, *Israeli Society: Background, Development and Problems* (Jerusalem: Magnes, 1967). Also see a critical review in Ram, *Israeli Society: Critical Perspectives*, 7–37.

40. Peled, "Strangers in Utopia," 223.

41. Ibid.

42. Ibid.

43. Ibid., 234.

44. See chapter 9 for discussion on Peled's critical review of Virginia Tilley's book, *The One-State Solution: A Breakthrough for Peace in the Israeli-Palestinian Deadlock*, in Yoav Peled, "Zionist Realities," *New Left Review* 38 (March–April 2006).

45. Yoav Peled and Gershon Shafir, *Who Is Israeli?* (Tel Aviv: Tel Aviv University Press, 2005).

46. Oren Yftachel, "Ethnocratic Donkey with a Democratic Hump: on Three Israeli Illusions," in *The Israeli Situation*, I. Gur-Zeev, ed. (Tel-Aviv: Panim, 2002), 43–55; Oren Yftachel and A. Ghanem, "Towards a Theory of Ethnocratic Regimes: Learning from the Judaization of Israel/Palestine," in *Rethinking Ethnicity: Majority Groups and Dominant Minorities*, E. Kaufman, ed. (London: Routledge, 2004), 179–98; and Oren Yftachel, *Ethnocracy: Land and Identity Politics in Israel/Palestine* (Philadelphia: University of Pennsylvania Press, 2006).

47. Yoav Peled, "Citizenship Betrayed Israel's Emerging Immigration and Citizenship Regime," *Theoretical Inquiries in Law* 8:2 (July 2007): 333–58.

48. J. Bruner and Yoav Peled, "On Autonomy, Capabilities and Democracy: Criticism of Liberal Multi-Culturalism," in *Multiculturalism in a Democratic and Jewish State*, Menachem Mautner, Avi Sagi, Ronen Shamir, eds. (Tel Aviv: Ramot-Tel Aviv University Publishing House, 1998): 107–33.

49. W. Kymlicka, *Multicultural Citizenship* (Oxford: Clarendon Press, 1995).

50. Ibid. A conspicuous example is the defense of the indigenous tribes in Canada.

51. For the same approach regarding Palestinians in Israel, see in chapter 3 the reaction to the Supreme Court decision on Katzir. See also the Haifa Declaration, one of the four Position Papers mentioned in the introduction.

52. Bruner and Peled, "On Autonomy," 126.

53. Avishai Margalit and Moshe Halbertal, "Liberalism and the Right for Culture," in *Multiculturalism in a Democratic*: 93–107.

54. Ibid., 102.

55. See Isaiah Berlin, "Two Concepts of Liberty," in *Four Essays on Liberty* (Oxford: Oxford University Press, 1969).

56. Bruner and Peled, "On Autonomy," 126.

57. Reference is made to Levin-Epstein and Semitone, *The Arab Minority in Israel's Economy: Patterns of Ethnic Inequality* (Boulder, Colorado. Westview Press, 1993).

58. Bruner and Peled, "On Autonomy," 126.

59. Ibid., 127.

60. Margalit and Halbertal, "Liberalism and the Right," 102.

Chapter 6: Post-Zionism—a Failed Departure from Zionist Left Discourse

1. Robert Fisk, who entered the camps the morning after the massacre took place, writes in *Counterpunch* on September 19, 1982: "If the Israelis had not taken part in the killings, they had certainly sent militia into the camp. They had trained them, given them uniforms, handed them US army rations and Israeli medical equipment. Then they had watched the murderers in the camps, they had given them military assistance—the Israeli airforce had dropped all those flares to help the men who were murdering the inhabitants of Sabra and Chatila—and they had established military liason with the murderers in the camps."

2. Sand, *Historians, Time and Imagination*. Sand mentions in this context Benedict Anderson, Eric Hobsbawm, and Ernest Gellner, as well as Edward Said's *Orientalism*. Also see Ilan Pappé, "Zionism Under the Examination of Nationalist Theories and the Historiographic Methodology," in *Zionism—A Contemporary Debate: Research and Ideological Approaches*, edited by Genosar Pinchas and Avi Bareli (Sede Boker: The Center for Ben-Gurion Heritage, 1996) 223–263. While the postmodern or post-national writers were not explicitly present in the first critical writings of New Historians and critical sociologists, the second wave of post-Zionism addressed them in the basis of their analysis.

3. Among others, Ilan Pappé, "Post-Zionist Critique on Israel and the Palestinians," *Journal of Palestinian Studies* XXVI, no. 2 (Winter 1997): 29–41; Uri Ram, *The Time of the "Post,"*

Nationalism and the Politics of Knowledge in Israel (Tel Aviv: Resling Publishing, 2008); Sand, *Historians, Time and Imagination;* Laurence J. Silberstein, *Post-Zionism Debates* (New York and London: Routledge, 1999).

4. See chapter 9 for a detailed account of Oslo and the failure of other peace initiatives.

5. See the Matzpen website, www.matzpen.org, for pamphlets and articles. For a sample of their works, see *Forbidden Agendas* (London: Al Saqi Books, 1984); *The Other Israel, The Radical Case Against Zionism,* Arie Bober, ed. (New York: Anchor Books, Doubleday & Company, Inc., 1972); Haim Hanegbi, Moshé Machover, and Akiva Orr, "The Class Nature of Israeli Society," *New Left Review* 65 (1971): 3–26; Emmanuel Fargoun, "Class Divisions in Israeli Society" and "Palestinian Workers in Israel: A Reserve Army of Labor," in *Forbidden Agendas*: 56–69 and 77–123, respectively. Also see an early publication, "The Palestine Problem and the Israeli-Arab Dispute," May 1967, at http://matzpen.org/index.asp?u=120&p=doc1. The document was read to the public at a meeting held in Paris on May 18, 1967, just a short time before the breakout of the 1967 war. The meeting was sponsored by Arab and Palestinian student organizations, and was reported in *Le Monde* on May 20, 1967.

For further elaboration and developments of Matzpen's Marxist and anti-imperialist perspectives, see articles by Moshé Machover (a founder of Matzpen), such as "Israelis and Palestinians, Resolution of the Israeli-Palestinian Conflict: A Socialist Viewpoint," reprinted in *International Socialist Review* (May–June 2009), and Machover "Is it Apartheid?" Jewish Voice for Peace, www.jewishvoiceforpeace.org, November 10, 2004.

6. The four had been expelled for criticizing MAKI for its lack of internal democracy and its ban of free discussion within the party—though formally, for "factional activity," especially signing a joint letter by members of two different branches. (Joint activity of members of different branches was allowed only if mediated through the central leadership. See http://matzpen.org/index.asp?p=hatrani.) While in MAKI, however, they also criticized its slavish attitude to the USSR and its refusal to discuss MAKI's own history since its foundation in 1948. At that point they had not yet fully challenged MAKI's anti-Zionism. MAKI had supported the UN Partition Plan and the establishment of the Jewish state of Israel, and signed together with all Zionist parties the Declaration of Independence on May 14, 1948, a day before the official end of the British Mandate. See Matzpen website: www.matzpen.org.

7. See Abu-Manneh, "Israel in the U.S. Empire," *Monthly Review* 58 (March 10, 2007), in which he emphasizes Palestinian Marxist Jabra Nicola's (1912–74) foundational influence on Matzpen. Nicola's most important work is unpublished: "Theses on the Revolution in the Arab East," 1972. Ernest Mandel dedicated *Revolutionary Marxism Today* (London: New Left Books, 1979) to Nicola in glowing terms: "Pioneer Arab Marxist & Palestinian Trotskyist, the most impressive internationalist I ever met." In 2009 it was published on the Matzpen website. Also see Nicola and Machover, "Palestinian Struggle and Middle-East Revolution."

This article originated as a position paper adopted by Matzpen. It was first published under a somewhat different title ("The Struggle in Palestine Must Lead to Arab Revolution"), and without the one-paragraph preamble, in *The Black Dwarf* 14, no. 19 (June 14, 1969). A Hebrew version under the present title was published by Matzpen in August 1969.

8. Machover, "Conflict and Resolution."

9. Nicola, "Theses on the Revolution."
10. Hanieh, "From State-Led Growth."
11. Hanieh, "Palestine in the Middle East."
12. Ein-Gil and Machover, "Zionism Oriental Jews." For a presentation of Matzpen's approach and its debate with the culture's identity and ideologies, see chapter 8.
13. Amnon Raz-Krakotzkin, quoted in Neri Livne, "The Ascendance and Fall of Post-Zionism," *Haaretz*, September 21, 2001.
14. Yehouda Shenhav, quoted in Livne, "The Ascendance."
15. See chapter 1 for discussion of Zionist Left's differentiation between 1967 and 1948, and its role in symbolically erasing the collective memory of the Zionist colonization's dispossessive policies that led to the 1948 Nakba, which allowed the Zionist Left to retain their own humanist image.
16. Shenhav, in Livne, "The Ascendance."
17. Shlomo Avineri, "The Lie of Post-Zionism," *Haaretz*, July 6, 2007.
18. Erik Gelsner, "After Post-Nationality, After Post-Modernism," *Eretz Acheret* 27 (March–April 2005): 48–55, a conversation with four Left intellectuals, dedicated to the subject "The Israeli Left: Alive or Dead?"
19. Baruch Kimmerling in an interview with Dalia Karpel, "All in All I Had an Happy Life," *Haaretz*, October 26, 2006.
20. The term "New Historians" was coined by Benny Morris in "The New Historiography: Israel Confronts Its Past," *Tikkun* (November–December 1988). Also see Ilan Pappé, "Post-Zionist Critique on Israel and the Palestinians," part 1, in *Journal of Palestinian Studies* XXXVI, no. 2 (Winter 1997): 29–41, for how the Israeli new history was born from the "new history" in Europe. Pappé explores the difference between the two, which leads him to prefer the term "revisionist" over "new."

     The term "critical sociologists," in comparison with the "established sociologists," was coined first by Uri Ram in "The Colonization Perspective in Israeli Sociology: Internal and External Comparisons," *Journal of Historical Sociology* 6, 3 (1993): 327–50.
21. For example, Simha Flapan, a leader of the extreme Zionist Left Mapam and who is recognized as the first new historian, states: "I have never believed that Zionism inherently obviates the rights of the Palestinians, and I do not believe so today." Simha Flapan, *The Birth of Israel: Myths and Realities* (New York: Pantheon, 1987), 11.

Chapter 7: Revisionist Social Sciences: Pre-State Colonization and the1948 War

1. For a discussion of the JNF's role in the "Judaization of the land" before 1948, and since the establishment of the state, including the '67 occupied territories, see chapter 3.
2. Baruch Kimmerling, "Merchants of Fear," *Haaretz*, June 24, 1994.
3. Simha Flapan, *The Birth of Israel: Myths and Realities* (New York: Pantheon Books, 1987); Benny Morris, *The Birth of the Palestinian Refugee Problem, 1947–1949* (Cambridge: Cambridge University Press, 1988); Ilan Pappé, *Britain and the Arab-Israeli Conflict, 1948–1951* (New York: Macmillan, 1988); Avi Shlaim, *Collusion Across the Jordan, King Abdullah, the Zionist Movement, and the Partition of Palestine* (New York: Columbia Uni-

versity Press, 1988).

4. See Pappé, *The Ethnic Cleansing*; Morris, *1948 and After*; Benny Morris, *The Birth of the Palestinian Refugee Problem Revisited* (Cambridge: Cambridge University Press, 2004); Avi Shlaim, "The Debate About 1948," *International Journal of Middle East Studies* 27, no. 3 (August 1995); Shlaim, *War and Peace in the Middle East, A Concise History* (New York: Penguin Books, 1995); Shlaim, *The Iron Wall: Israel and the Arab World* (New York: W.W. Norton & Company, 2001).

5. For Palestinian historians before the 1980s, see Walid Khalidi, "Plan Dalet: The Zionist Master Plan for the Conquest of Palestine, 1948," in *Middle Eastern Forum* (November 1961), reproduced with a new commentary in *Journal of Palestinian Studies* 18, no. 1 (Autumn 1988): 4–70; Erskin Childers and John Kinchi, "A Debate on 1948," *The Spectator* (May–August 1961).

6. Kimmerling, "Merchants of Fear."

7. Simha Flapan, for years a member of the Hashomer Hatzair kibbutz-Gan Shmuel, was national secretary of the Zionist Left Mapam Party and the director of its Arab Affairs department from 1959 to the mid-1970s. He also edited *New Outlook*, a monthly that promoted Arab-Jewish rapprochement.

8. Flapan's book was largely based on the research of Yoram Nimrod (who credits him). See the entry about him in the Hebrew Wikipedia.

9. Shlaim, *Collusion Across the Jordan* concentrated on the contacts between the Zionist movement and King Abdullah, the ruler of Palestinians in Transjordan. Also see *Britain and the Arab-Israeli Conflict, 1948–51* by Ilan Pappé, 1988, Macmillan in association with St. Antony's College, Oxford edition (London: I. B. Touris, 1992) to shed more light on the issue by studying the active interference of Britain in this scheme. On the same subject, also see Pappé, *The Making of the Israeli-Palestinian Conflict* (London: I. B. Touris, 1992).

10. "Estimates vary," says Shlaim, "but the best estimates suggest that on 15 May 1948 Israel fielded 35,000 troops whereas the Arabs fielded 20–25,000." See Avi Shlaim on the new history of 1948 and the Palestinian Nakba in MIFTAH, May 6, 2006. Ilan Pappé determines that with an estimated 50,000 well-trained and well-equipped military forces, the cleansing began against what proved to be a passive Palestinian population and a militarily inactive and ineffective Arab defense force. See Pappé, *The Ethnic Cleansing*.

11. On June 21, 1948, the ship "Nora" arrived in Haifa, bringing the first delivery of Czech arms.

12. Pappé, "Post-Zionist Critique," 29–41.

13. Ibid. Also see Pappé, *The Ethnic Cleansing*.

14. A. Israeli (A. Orr and M. Machover), *Peace, Peace, and No Peace: Israel-Arab States 1948–1961* (Jerusalem: Bokhan, 1961).

15. In the second (1999) Hebrew edition, the following disclaimer was included: "At the end of 1962 we participated in the founding of the Israeli Socialist Organization (Matzpen). In the framework of this organization we developed together with our comrades, a principled critique of Zionism that was far more extensive than the one we had formulated in the book. We no longer see the 1948 war as an Israeli liberation struggle against British imperialism, as the book suggests, but as a continuation of the colonizing enterprise of Zionism. Our position on the Soviet Union also became, after 1962, much more critical than the one reflected in the book, but the roots and basic direction of our critical position on Israeli policies and Zionism are clearly discernible in this volume."

16. Anita Shapira, *Land and Power*. The Hebrew name of the book expresses well the Zionist myth: *Herev Hayona* means "the sword of the dove."

17. Beinin, "No More Tears."

18. Walid Khalidi, "Plan Dalet: The Zionist Master Plan for the Conquest of Palestine, 1948," in *Middle Eastern Forum* (November 1961), reproduced with a new commentary in *Journal of Palestinian Studies* 18, no. 1 (Autumn 1988): 4–70; and Erskin Childers and John Kinchi, "A Debate on 1948," in *The Spectator* (May–August 1961).

19. For discussion on the difference between the Israeli and Palestinian narratives and his own position that accepts that there was a master plan to expel the Palestinians, see Pappé, *The Making of the Israeli-Arab Conflict*, and Pappé, *The Ethnic Cleansing*.

20. Plenty of literature before and after Morris's 1987 book deals with the question of whether there was a master plan to expel the Palestinians. In addition to Khalidi, and Childers and Kinchi, see *The Transformation of Palestine*, Ibrahim Abu Lughod, ed. (Louisville, KY: Evanston Publishing: 1971); *Blaming the Victims*, Christopher Hitchens and Edward Said, eds. (London, New York: Verso, 1988); Masalha, *Expulsion of the Palestinians*; Sharif Kanane, *The Expulsion: What Really Happened in 1948* (Jerusalem: The Alternative Information Center, December 1991). Ilan Pappé's *The Ethnic Cleansing*, which was published after Morris changed his 1987 conclusions, is of great importance.

21. Benny Morris, "Revisiting the Palestinian Exodus of 1948," in *The War for Palestine: Rewriting the History of 1948*, Rogan and Shlaim, ed. (Cambridge: Cambridge University Press, 2001), 48.

22. Kimmerling, "Merchants of Fear."

23. Morris, *The Palestinian Refugee Problem Revisited*.

24. Ibid., 155, 164.

25. Pappé, *The Ethnic Cleansing*, 12.

26. Ari Shavit, "Survival of the Fittest," *Haaretz*, Friday supplement, January 9, 2004. Republished in *New Left Review* 26 (2004): 37–51.

27. An interview with Tom Segev, December 12, 2004 (Channel 99).

28. Amnon Raz-Krakotzkin, "Post-Zionism and the Bi-National Challenge," *Ofakim Hadashim*, August 24, 2005.

29. Gabriel Piterburg, "Erasures," *New Left Review* 10 (July/August 2001): 31–47, and was translated to Hebrew :*Mechikot, Mitaam* 1 (2005): 29–41. Ilan Pappé, "From an 'Empty land' to the 'Promised Land'" *Mitaam* 1 (January 2005): 79–86.

30. Eisenstadt, *The Israeli Society*; Dan Horowitz and Moshe Lissak, *Troubles in Utopia, The Overburdened Polity of Israel* (Tel Aviv: Am Oved Publishers, 1990); also see Moshe Lissak in reference 394.

31. This is of course not to mention early Palestinian works such as Sabri Jiryis, *The Arabs in Israel* (New York: Monthly Review Press, 1976), or Elia T. Zureik, *The Palestinians in Israel* (London: Routledge, 1979).

32. Kimmerling, *Zionism and Territory*; Shafir, *Land, Labor and the Origins*. Also see Shafir, "Land, Labor and Population in the Zionist Colonization: General and Exclusive Aspects," in *Israeli Society: Critical Perspectives*, edited by Uri Ram (Tel Aviv: Breirot Publishers, 1993): 104–19.

33. Karpel, "All in All."

34. This approach was particularly articulated by Anita Shapira, the leading historian of the

Zionist Labor movement, in her book *Visions in Conflict* (Tel Aviv: Am Oved, 1988), and
by the Department of Sociology at Hebrew University, chaired by Shmuel N. Eisenstadt,
and by Eisenstadt's disciples like Moshe Lissak, Dan Horowitz, and Rivka Bar-Yosef.

35. Kimmerling, "Merchants of Fear."

36. Uri Ram, editor, *Israeli Society: Critical Perspective* (Breirot Publishing: Tel Aviv, 1993),
29; Uri Ram, "The Colonization Perspective in Israeli Sociology," *Journal of Historical Sociology* 6, no. 3 (September 1993): 327–50.

37. Shafir, *Land Labor and the Origins.*

38. See confirmation in Karpel, "All in All."

39. Those who joined the critical sociologists in this dispute were Uri Ram ("The Colonization Perspective," 327–50, and *The Changing Agenda of Israeli Sociology: Theory, Ideology and Identity* [Albany, NY: State University of New York Press, 1995]); and Michael Shalev (*Labor and Political Economy in Israel* [Oxford: Oxford University Press, 1992] and "Time for Theory," in *Theory and Criticism* 8 [Summer 1996]: 225–37). Among additional works by the "old-timers"—that is, critical sociologists who appeared in early 1990s—are those of Baruch Kimmerling and Joel S. Migdal, *Palestinians: The Making of a People* (New York: Free Press, 1993); Baruch Kimmerling, "State Building, State Autonomy and the Identity of Society—the Case of Israel," *Journal of Historical Sociology* 6, no. 4 (1993).

40. Aharon Meged, "The Israeli Suicide Desire," *Haaretz* Supplement, June 10, 1994.

41. For the attack by mainstream social scientists, see Moshe Lissak, interview in *Davar,* March 18, 1994; Yaakov Katz, interview in *Haaretz,* November 18, 1994; Shlomo Aronson, "The New Historians and the Challenge of the Holocaust," *Haaretz,* June 24, 1994; and report on "A Symposium on Post-Zionism," *Haaretz,* October 15, 1995.

   For the positions of critical sociologists published in newspapers, see Kimmerling, "The Merchants of Fear;" Baruch Kimmerling, "Is Being a Part of the Nation a Necessary Condition for Historical Perversion?" *Haaretz,* December 23, 1994; Ilan Pappé, "Post Zionist Sociology," *Haaretz,* January 28, 1994; Ilan Pappé, "The Impact of Zionist Ideology on the Israeli Historiography," *Davar,* May 15, 1994.

42. Uri Ram, "Society and Social Science"; Baruch Kimmerling, "Academic History Caught in the Crossfire: The Case of Israeli-Jewish Historiography," *History and Memory* 7, no. 1 (Spring/Summer 1995): 41–65; Ilan Pappé, "Critique and Agenda: Post Zionist Scholars in Israel," *History and Memory* 7, no. 1 (Spring/Summer 1995): 66–90. Pappé published an early extensive critique of Israeli historiography, "The New History of the 1948 War," *Theory and Criticism* 3 (Winter 1993): 99–114.

   For the attack by mainstream sociology, see Shapira, *Land and Power.* Kimmerling's answer can be found in "Militarism in Israeli Society," *Theory and Criticism* 4 (Autumn 1993) 123–41. Moshe Lissak, "Critical Sociologists and 'Established' Sociologists in the Israeli Academic Community—Ideological Struggles or Professional Academic Discourse," in *An Answer to a Post-Zionist Colleague,* Tuvia Friling, ed., (Tel Aviv: Lemiskal, 2003), 84–109. (Lemiskal is a publishing house established by *Yediot Ahronot* and Sifrait Hemed.) The article was first published in *Zionism—A Contemporary Debate: Research and Ideological Approaches,* Genosar Pinchas and Avi Bareli, eds. (Sede Boker: The Center for Ben-Gurion Heritage, 1996).

   See the entire collection of articles in Friling, *An Answer,* and *Between Vision and Re-*

vision: 100 Years of Zionist Historiography, Weitz Yechiam, ed. (Jerusalem: Zalman Shazar Center, 1996).

43. See introduction in Ram, *Israeli Society,* 7–39; and Baruch Kimmerling, "Sociology, Ideology and Nation-Building: The Palestinians and Their Meaning in Israeli Sociology," *American Sociology Review* 57 (1992): 446–60.

44. Shalev, "Time for Theory," 225–37.

45. See Eisenstadt, *The Social Structure of Israel;* and Eisenstadt, *Israeli Society.* Also see a critical review in Ram, *Israeli Society: Critical Perspectives,* 7–37.

46. Baruch Kimmerling, "Academic History Caught in the Crossfire: The Case of Israeli-Jewish Historiography," *History and Memory* 7, 1 (Spring/Summer 1995).

47. See chapter 5 for a later critique that considers the 1967 occupation not only important for a sociological analysis of Israeli society, but also as part and parcel of the political regime in Israel "proper."

48. Kimmerling, "Merchants of Fear."

49. Ibid.

50. Sand, *Historians, Time and Imagination,* 110.

51. Moshe Lissak, "'Critical' Sociologists and 'Established' Sociologists' in the Israeli Academic Community—Ideological Struggles or Professional Academic Discourse?" in Friling, *An Answer to a Post-Zionist,* 84–109. The article was first published in Pinhas Genosar and Avi Barli, editors, *Zionut bat zmanenu,* The Center for Ben Gurion Heritage and the Center for Study of Zionism, Tel Aviv University, Ben Gurion University Publishing.

52. Ibid., 97.

53. Shalev, "Time for Theory," 228.

54. For his own experience, see the introduction of Shalev, *Labor and Political Economy.*

55. Lissak, "Critical Sociologists," 98.

56. The first wave of settlements, which consisted of farmers who owned their plots of land and called their settlements "colonies"—*moshavot* in Hebrew (like the moshavot of Petah Tikva, Rishon Letzion, and Hadera). However, this was used as a neutral concept and lacked the political connotation attributed to colonization, that is, an organized movement with the aim of taking over the colonized country.

57. Kimmerling, "Merchants of Fear."

58. Lissak, "Critical Sociologists," 99. For "separation" being the cornerstone of Zionist colonization ideology and policies to the present day, see chapter 2.

59. Ibid., 100. Lissak adds that the crystallization of an autonomic economic-social structure alongside the indigenous population was also nourished by the Zionist ideology that aspired to turn "upside down the occupational pyramid" of the Jewish people in the Diaspora—that is, to build a socioeconomic structure in which the Jews will fill all occupational layers and work in all occupations, and first of all as "work-hands" [*Avodat kapaim*]. Only in this way, thought the Labor movement, can the "productivization" of the Jewish people be reached.

60. Ibid., 101. Competition remained concentrated primarily in unprofessional and semi-professional blue-collar jobs, though the rate of Jewish laborers among these forces was declining with the economic and social development of the Yishuv. Furthermore, the impact of the exclusion of Palestinian laborers was not too severe because they were peasants who took jobs in the Jewish sector only as "an additional income for improving their level

of life—since they had an economic base in their villages, although a poor one."

61. See Ghassan Kanafani, *The 1936–1939 Revolt in Palestine* (New York: Committee for a Democratic Palestine, 1972; and London: Tricontinental Society, 1980). See Ted Swedenburg, *Memories of Revolt: 1936–1939, Rebellion in the Palestinian Past* (Fayetteville: University of Arkansas Press, 2003).

62. The "Jewish Settlements' Police" (*Mishteret hayshvim haivriyim*) was a Jewish police force set up by the British in 1936 ostensibly to help defend Jewish lives and property during the 1936–39 Arab revolt in Palestine. Members were recruited almost entirely from the Hagana.

63. Lissak, "Critical Sociologists," 101.

64. Sand, *Historians, Time and Imagination*.

65. Arie Aharoni, *From the Diary of a Candidate for Treason* (Tel Aviv: Sifriat Poalim Publishing, 2000).

66. Ibid., 108. For biological warfare in 1948 and thereafter, see Salman Abu Sitta, "Traces of Poison," *Al Ahram* 627 (February 27–March 5, 2003). A copy can be viewed at http://weekly.ahram.org.eg/2003/627/focus.htm. For more on Israel's use of biological weapons, see Sitta, "Traces of Poison." Also, in 2003 the Israeli daily *Hadashot* published Sara Dar-Leibovitz's comprehensive research on the biological welfare implemented by the army in the 1948 war. She reported that in May 1948, a short time prior to the occupation of Acre, Jewish soldiers inserted Typhus microbes into the water resources, which brought about the breakout of an acute Typhus epidemic in the city. She continues: "The success of the operation in Acre encouraged the decision makers to continue with this line of action. On May 22 two combat soldiers from the Palmach Undercover Unit were sent to a secret intelligence operation in Gaza .... On May 24 the Egyptian intelligence reported on two [Israeli] soldiers who tried to insert Typhus and dysentery microbes into water wells in the Gaza Strip. Chief of Staff Yigal Yadin reported the information to Ben-Gurion who documented it in his diary." Dar-Leibovitz reports that "the two soldiers were executed [by the Egyptians] but no official information about it was publicized nor did Israeli governments thereafter agree to the request of the sister of one of the soldiers to ask the Egyptians to return the corpses." The way Aharoni deals with this event makes him a partner to this policy of silence adopted by the Israeli establishment.

67. Aharoni, *From the Diary*, 106–110.

68. Ibid., 106.

69. Ibid., 108.

Chapter 8: The Postmodernist Current in Post-Zionism

1. See Ram, *The Time of the "Post,"* 121. He emphasizes the influence of Lacan and Derrida on this approach.

2. Ariella Azoulay and Adi Ophir, "A Shortened Dictionary of Citizenship" in *Yamim Raim*, E. Azoulay and A. Ophir, eds. (Tel Aviv: Resting, 2002), 23–43.

3. Ram, *The Time of the "Post,"* 177.

4. On the "imagined" dimensions of Jewish nationalism, see Uri Ram, "Zionist Historiography and the Invention of Modern Jewish Nationhood: The Case of Ben Zion Dinur in

History and Memory" *Israeli Historiography Revisited* 7, no. 1 (Spring–Summer 1995): 91–124 (special issue edited by Gulie Ne'eman Arad); and Yossi Dahan and Henri Wasserman, introduction in *Invent a Nation*, Yossi Dahan and Henri Wasserman, eds. (Raanana: The Open University of Israel, 2006): 11–28.

5. This is the subject of Sand, *When and How*. Sand counters the Zionist claim that today's Jews descend from a single ethno-biological group that was exiled from their homeland after the destruction of the second Temple in 70 CE. Sand's study attempts to prove that most Jews were not exiled. There was a vast presence of Jews throughout the ancient world long before the Roman conquest. The ranks of Jews worldwide in Roman times consisted mostly of converts to Judaism through individuals and collective conversions. In the ninth century the conversion of an entire early medieval European state, Khazaria, situated between the Black Sea and the Caspian Sea, took place. Thus, argues Sand, the bulk of modern Jewry is descended from these converts who joined the Jewish religion during the centuries and who have no ancestral ties to the Biblical land of Israel.

6. Ein-Gil and Machover, "Zionism and Oriental Jews." See also Farajoun, "Class Divisions." Reprints from *Hamsin*, 1976–83.

7. Yossi Yonah and Yehouda Shenhav, "The Multi Cultural Condition" in *Theory and Criticism* 17 (Fall 2000): 163–189; Yehouda Shenhav, "Notes on Identity in a Post National Society," *Theory and Criticism* 19 (Fall 2001): 5–17; Yehouda Shenhav and Hannan Hever, "The Post Colonial Gaze," *Theory and Criticism* 20 (Spring 2002): 9–23. See also Yossi Yonah, *The Virtue of Difference: The Multicultural Project in Israel* (Jerusalem: The Van Leer Jerusalem Institute, Tel Aviv: Hakibbutz Hameuchad Publishing House, 2005).

   Although appearing long before the post-Zionists, the seminal work of Ella Shohat was the first to adopt the approach of cultural identity to depict the nature of Zionism, and the Mizrahim and Palestinians as its victims.

8. A comprehensive and deep analysis of the history of the Mizrahim's oppression and struggle can be found in Sami Shalom Chetrit, *The Mizrahi Struggle in Israel 1948–2003* (Tel Aviv: Am Oved Publishers, 2004).

9. Ein-Gil and Machover, "Zionism and Oriental Jews," 62–76.

10. See S.N. Eisenstadt, *The Absorption of Immigrants* (Jerusalem: The Jewish Agency and Hebrew University, 1964); chapters in *Analysis of Modernization Processes* (Jerusalem: Academon, 1964); *Israeli Society—Background, Developments and Problems* (Jerusalem: Magnes, 1964); *Change and Continuity in Israeli Society* (Jerusalem: The Van Leer Jerusalem Institute, 1974). Also see *The Social Structure of Israel,* S. N. Eisenstadt, C. Adler, R. Bar-Yosef, and R. Kahana, eds. (Jerusalem, Academon 1969).

11. Chetrit, *The Mizrahi Struggle*, 67.

12. See Karl Frankenstein's articles in *Megamot*, 1951–1983. Also see a critical, detailed description of Frankenstein's theories in Chetrit, *The Mizrahi Struggle*.

13. Chetrit, *The Mizrahi Struggle*, 119.

14. Ibid., 124.

15. For the influence of Matzpen on the ideology of the Black Panthers see Chetrit, *The Mizrahi Struggle*, 119–68; Ein Gil and Machover, "Zionism and Oriental Jews." In footnote 19, the authors mention "Matzpen involvement was widely reported and somewhat sensationalised by the Israel press. Thus, for example, a headline in *Haaretz* of 3 March 1971: 'Jerusalem police arrested 13 youths known as "Black Panthers" and members of Matzpen.'

See also *Yediot Aharonot* of 4 March 1971. A leading article by Uri Avnery in *Ha'olam Hazeh* of May 19, 1971, excoriates Matzpen for "trying to manipulate the Panthers and foster the dangerous illusion that the struggle of the Mizrahim is going to overthrow Zionism."

16. Sami Chetrit agreed with sociologist Chana Hertzog, who rightly determined that the social class identity of the Black Panthers was much stronger than their ethnic Mizrahi identity. The Black Panthers did not consider advancing Mizrahi "ethnic" interests as their chief goal. See Chana Hertzog, *Political Ethnicity, Oppression vis-a-vis Reality* (Tel Aviv: Hakibbutz Hameuchad, 1986).

17. Chetrit, *The Mizrahi Struggle*, 154.

18. Quoted in Chetrit, *The Mizrahi Struggle*, 163.

19. On their demonstration against the WZO, see Chetrit, *The Mizrahi Struggle*, 155.

20. Siah—Smol Israeli Hadash (Israeli New Left) was established in 1968 by a group of students at Tel Aviv University, most of them former members of Hashomer Hatzair, and a group of students at the Hebrew University, including former members of the Communist Party of Israel and many new immigrants to the country. The two constituent groups were divided on their relation to Zionism. The Tel Aviv group defined itself as Zionist, and the Jerusalemites considered themselves a-Zionists or even anti-Zionists. The common militant opposition to the deepening occupation and creeping annexation was instrumental in forging an alliance that lasted for five years. The movement dissolved in 1973.

21. See Tikva Honig-Parnass, "Why Are Sash and the Mizrahim Supporters of the Right?" an interview with Sami Shalom Chetrit in Honig-Parnass and Haddad, *Between the Lines*, 195–202. See also Sami Chetrit, "Either the Cake Will Be Shared By All or There Will Be No Cake"; *The Mizrahi Block*, 2001: www.Kedma.co.il/Panterim/.

22. Swirski, *Not Backward But*. See also Dvora Berenstein, "The Black Panthers, Conflict and Protest in Israeli Society," *Megamot* 25 (1979).

23. Ella Shohat, "The Sephardim in Israel: Zionism from the Standpoint of Its Jewish Victims," *Social Text* 19/20 (1988): 1–35. In the article republished (together with three other radical Mizrahim: Sami Shalom Chetrit, Zvi Ben-Dor, and Shiko Behar) in *News from Within*, VIII, no. 1 (January 1997): 29–49 (a special supplement Mizrahim & Zionism), Ella Shohat changed the headline of her article to "*Mizrahim* in Israel: Zionism from the Standpoint of Its Jewish Victims." *Sephardim* (Spanish) was the name of Jews in Palestine before the beginning of the Zionist settlement. The community of Sephardic Jews held a priority status under Ottoman Rule, which they lost to the Ashkenazi minority after the establishment of the British Mandate in Palestine. The notable families among the first originated from non-Arab countries (like Turkey or Greece). Those who emigrated en masse from Arab countries after the establishment of the state were depicted "sefardim." This was part of the official policy focused on wiping out their Arab identity and their potential political consciousness. The Israeli establishment continues to use the term "sefardim" for immigrants from Arab countries and their descendants.

24. Edward W. Said, *Orientalism* (New York: Vintage Books, 1978).

25. Gil Eyal, "Between East and West: The Discourse on the Arab Village in Israel," *Theory and Criticism* 3 (1993): 39–56; and Dan Rabinowitz, "Oriental Nostalgia: The Transformation of the Palestinians into 'Israeli Arabs,'" *Theory and Criticism* 4 (1993): 141–52.

26. On this exclusion by Israeli museums, see Ariella Azoulay, "With Opened Doors: Museums of History and the Israeli Public Space," *Theory and Criticism* 4 (Autumn 1993): 79–96.

27. Chetrit, *The Mizrahi Struggle*, 269.

28. Ibid., 228.

29. It still functions. More information can be found at: www.hila-equal-edu.org.il/.

30. Honig-Parnass, "Why Are Sash and the Mizrahim." For the subversive ideology of the Kedma school in Jaffa, including challenges against the inclusive dimensions of Zionism and its persecution by the Israeli establishment, see Tamar Barkay and Gal Levy, "Kedma School," and Sami S. Chetrit, "Huldai, The Duce and the Local Cop," *News From Within* (June 1999).

31. Ibid. The Van Leer Jerusalem Institute is a leading intellectual center for the interdisciplinary study and discussion of issues related to philosophy, society, culture, and education. It publishes the quarterly journal *Theory and Criticism* which has been home to the post-Zionists of various postmodern streams. See www.vanleer.org.il/default_e.asp.

   Some of the main adherents to the aspects of anti-Zionism and the class-based approach of the "New Radical Mizrahi Discourse," who joined Keshet (like Zvi Ben Dor and Moshe Behar), were then in the midst of their studies toward Phd. degrees. They sharply criticize the identity politics that are dominant among the academics who have led Keshet.

32. The critical presentation of these theories as applied to Israel refers largely to Yonah and Shenhav, "The Multi-Cultural Condition," 163–89; Shenhav, "Notes on Identity," 17; and Shenhav and Hever, "The Post Colonial Gaze," 9–23.

33. Yonah and Shenhav, "The Multi-Cultural Condition," 169. Also see Yonah, "The Virtue of Difference."

34. These years were also witness to the strengthened nationalism of Palestinian citizens and their determined challenge to the Jewish state, as embodied in the establishment of the National Democratic Assembly (NDA) led by Azmi Bishara.

35. Moshe Lissak, *The Big* Alia [Immigration] *of the 50s: The Failure of the Melting Pot* (Jerusalem: Bialik Institution, 1999); Nissin Kalderon, *Pluralists Against Their Will: On the Multiplicity of Cultures in Israel* (Haifa: Haifa University/Zmora Bitan Publishing, 2000).

36. See Amnon Rubinstein, *From Hertzl to Rabin: The Changing Image of Zionism* (Jerusalem: Shoken Publishing House, 1997); Yoav Peled, "The 'Worried Israelis,'" *Theory and Criticism* 3 (Winter 1999): 21–35. Rubinstein answers in the latter as well.

37. Katz Elihu and Hed Sela, *A Culture Policy in Israel* (Jerusalem: The Van Leer Jerusalem Institute and Bracha Foundation, 1999).

38. Zohar Shavit et al., "Culture Certificate—Vision 2000, A Position Paper on Culture Policy of the State of Israel in the 21st Century," The Ministry of Culture and Sport, Jerusalem, 1999.

39. Shavit, "Culture Certificate," 14.

40. Katz and Sela, *A Culture Policy in Israel*, 10.

41. Yonah and Shenhav, "The Multi-Cultural Condition," 178.

42. Ibid., 180.

43. For elaboration on the subversive nature of identity politics, see Shenhav and Hever, "The Post Colonial Gaze," 9–23.

44. Shenhav, "Notes on Identity," 5–17.

45. Eric Hobsbawm, "Identity Politics and the Left," *New Left Review* 17 (May–June 1996): 38–47.

46. Aijaz Ahmad, "Culture, Nationalism and the Role of the Intellectuals: An Interview," in Aijaz Ahmad, *Lineages of the Present* (New Delhi, India: Tulika, 1996), 396–428.

47. Hanan Hever, Yehouda Shenhav, and Pnina Motzafi-Haller, eds., *Mizrahim in Israel: A Critical Observation into Israel's Ethnicity* (Tel Aviv: The Van Leer Jerusalem Institute/Hakibbutz Hameuchad Publishing House, 2002); Yehouda Shenhav, ed., *Space, Land, Home* (Tel Aviv: The Van Leer Jerusalem Institute and Hakibbutz Hameuchad, 2003); and Yehouda Shenhav, ed., *Colonialism and the Post Colonial Condition: Anthology of Translated and Hebrew* [articles] (Tel Aviv: The Van Leer Jerusalem Institute and Hakibbutz Hameuchad, 2004).

48. In addition to Ella Shohat, and for a recent, typical example of this kind of narrative, see Mizrahi theoretican and activist Smadar Lavie, "Colonialism and Imperialism: Zionism," in the *Encyclopedia of Women and Islamic Cultures* vol. 6 (Leiden, Brill, 2007). For a Palestinian Leftist acceptance of this claim, see Palestinian Marxist Adel Samara (who names Israel "Zionist Ashkenazi Regime [ZAR]"), "Why the Socialist Solution in Palestine: and Why the Secular Democratic State Will Serve the Zionist and Arab Comprador Solution," Kana'an e-Bulletin, vol. 8, no. 1592 (2008). See: www.kanaanonline.org/articles/01592.pdf.

49. Ein-Gil and Machover, "Zionism and Oriental Jews."

50. The authors refer the reader to "the masterly materialist account [of racism faced by Mizrahim]" by Raphael Shapiro, "Zionism and Its Oriental Subjects," *Khamsin* no. 5 (1978): 5–26. Reprinted in a collection of articles from *Khamsin*, selected and introduced by Jon Rothschild in *Forbidden Agendas* (London: Al Saqi Books, 1984): 23–48.

51. On criticizing identity politics for not differentiating between the nature of the oppression of Mizrahim and Palestinians in Israel, see Nada Matta, "Postcolonial Theory, Multiculturalism and the Israeli Left: A Critique of Post-Zionism," Holy Land Studies, 2.1 (2003): 85–107.

52. Ahmad, "Culture, Nationalism," 396–428; and Hobsbawm, "Identity Politics."

53. Ahmad, "Culture, Nationalism," 399.

54. Yonah, "In Virtue of Difference," 49.

55. Shenhav and Hever, "The Post-Colonial Gaze," 9–22.

56. Ibid., 13.

57. Ibid., 14.

58. Ibid., 9.

59. Ibid., 9.

60. Ibid., 10.

61. Ibid., 18.

62. See Rabinowitz and Baker, *The Stand-Tall Generation.*

63. Honig-Parnass, "Why Are Sash and the Mizrahim."

64. See Yossi Yonah and Ytzhak Saporta, "Land and Housing Policy in Israel: The Discourse on Citizenship and Its Limits," *Theory and Criticism* 16 (Spring 2000): 129–53. See also Keshet website: www.ha-keshet.org.il/.

65. Jamil Dakwar, "The Palestinians in Israel, Between the Hammer of Privatization of Lands and the Anvil of Nationalization of Lands," on Keshet website: www.ha-keshet.org.il/.

66. Sami Chetrit recognizes that Keshet should have demanded the return of lands to their Palestinian owners in Honig-Parnass, "Why Are Sash and the Mizrahim."

67. Shlomo Swirski, "Whose Lands Are They," *Haaretz*, November 28, 2001.

68. Admitted by Keshet leaders Yossi Yonah and Itzhak Sporta, "Land and Housing Policy," 137.

69. *Jerusalem Post*, July 4, 1998.

70. Ibid.

71. Nabih Bashir, "A Tactical Step?," *Mitzad Sheni*, September 10, 1997.

72. Homi K. Bhabha, ed., *Nation and Narration* (London and New York: Routledge, 1990).

73. Hannan Hever, Yehouda Shenhav, and Pnina Motzafi-Haller, eds., *Mizrahim in Israel: A Critical Observation into Israel's Ethnicity* (Jerusalem: The Van Leer Jerusalem Institute/Hakibbutz Hameuchd Publishing House, 2002), 9–14.

74. Shiko [Moshe] Behar, "The Structured Paradox of Identity Politics," *Haokets*, January 17, 2006. Available at haokets.org. Haokets is a progressive website overseen by Ytzhak Saporta and Yossi Yonah. Behar's piece was a critical response to "multiculturalist" Yossi Yonah (who developed a thesis that Behar named "The Structured Paradox of the Identity Politics"), "The Welfare State and Cultural Heterogenity: The Metamorphosis of a Faltered Romance," in Haokets, January 13, 2006.

75. Shenhav, "The Post Colonial Gaze," 15.

Chapter 9: The Zionist Left and "Peace"

1. Machover, "Conflict and Resolution." For a detailed (and scary) scenario of this sort, see Martin van Creveld, "Sharon's Plan Is to Drive Palestinians Across the Jordan," *Sunday Telegraph*, April 28, 2002. (Martin van Creveld is a leading Israeli military historian.) Also see Ilan Pappé, *The Ethnic Cleansing*. For a summary and analysis of this report, see Shraga Eilam, "'Peace' with Violence or Transfer," in Honig-Parnass and Haddad, *Between the Lines*, 6–11.

2. The principles of the Oslo Accords were already laid down in 1967 in the "Alon Plan." It was composed by the admired Palmach commander Yigal Alon, who served in 1967 as a minister in the Labor government

3. In addition to the first accord, namely, the 1993 *Declaration of Principles on Interim Self-Government, Interim Agreement on the West Bank and the Gaza Strip* (also called *Oslo 2*), signed on September 28, 1995.

4. See Noam Chomsky's criticism on the Oslo Accords in Noam Chomsky and Gilbert Achar, *Perilous Power, The Middle East and U.S. Foreign Policy* (New York: Paradigm Publishers, 2007), 141–214.

5. For a comparison between Apartheid South Africa and the aspired to Palestinian Apartheid, see Virginia Tilley, "Bantustans and the Unilateral Declaration of Statehood," *The Electronic Intifada*, November 19, 2009. See http://electronicintifada.net/v2/article10901.shtml.

   In "Conflict and Resolution," Machover explains that the fragmented enclaves designated for the future "Palestinian state" are not Bantustans, because the main purpose of the Bantustans was to serve as nominally independent dormitories for a reserve labor force on which the South African economy depended. What these proposed enclaves most resemble are American Indian reservations. The various Israeli "peace plans" and accords with willing Palestinian leaders are not unlike the infamous Indian treaties.

6. See note 3. The West Bank was divided into three administrative areas: area A, in which the PA had "full authority" both in security and civic terms, consisted of 17 percent of the

West Bank; area B, 24 percent of the West Bank—over which Israel retained its security control; and area C, 59 percent of the West Bank—over which Israel retained *full* control.

7. See *Haaretz*, September 21, 1993.

8. Bilu is an acronym for "*Beit Israel lecu ve nelcha.*" The first Jewish private farmer colonizers who, in the last decades of the nineteenth century, built the first *Moshavot* (colonies)—for example, Rishon Letzion Hadera and Petach Tikva). Degania was the first kibbutz built by members of Zionist Left immigrants in 1910.

9. An interview with Niva Lanir, *Davar*, September 21, 1993.

10. Adam Hanieh, "Palestine in the Middle East: Opposing Neoliberalism and US Power," ZNet/The Bullet, parts one and two published July 20, 2008, and July 21, 2008, respectively.

11. Hanieh, "Palestine in the Middle East," part one.

12. See introduction for a history of the Zionist Labor movement and the Histadrut's creation of the Israeli capitalist class, and their introduction of neoliberalism into Israel's economy in the mid-1980s. For an elaboration, see Hanieh, "From State-Led Growth," and Hanieh, "Class, Economy, and the Second Intifada," 29–42.

13. The role of bypass roads is to connect settlements and block development of Palestinian communities and Palestinian economy.

14. For details on the 2000 Camp David Summit, see Tanya Reinhart, *Israel/Palestine, How to End the War of 1948* (New York: Seven Stories Press, 2002), 21–51.

15. Baruch Kimmerling, "From Barak to the Road Map," *New Left Review* 23 (September–October 2003).

16. Reinhart, *Israel/Palestine, How to End*, 21–51.

17. Reinhart, *Israel/Palestine, How to End*.

18. Kimmerling, "From Barak."

19. The Camp David document was largely based on the 1995 Beilin-Abu Mazen Plan, from which main elements have remained in most Israeli peace plans since 2000. Reinhart, *Israel/Palestine, How to End*.

20. Azmi Bishara, "Thus an Apartheid Regime Develops," in Honig-Parnass and Haddad, eds. *Between the Lines* (2007 edition), 69–73.

21. For analysis of the breakout of the Intifada and the Palestinian popular forces that carried it on, see Toufic Haddad, "The Thandeem Wild Card," in *Between the Lines* (2007 edition), 61–65.

22. Mati Steinberg of Hebrew University, who was the adviser of four heads of Shabak and of Labor MP Ehud Barak in 2000, is considered one of leading experts in this area. He was interviewed by Akiva Eldar ("Ignoring the Arab Peace Initiative Will Bring About the End of the Zionist Enterprise," *Haaretz*, June 26, 2008) on his upcoming book *Omdim legoralam* (Tel Aviv: Yediot Ahronot Publishing, 2008). Steinberg discloses that he warned Barak his proposal for the forthcoming Camp David negotiations could not be accepted by Arafat. When asked, "What was the effect of Barak's determination that 'there is no partner?'" Steinberg said, "Barak and those who have implemented his policy, Ariel Sharon and his Chief of Staff have created enormous damage. When a PM [Barak] says 'no partner,' it is like a political instruction submitted to the operative levels to act without making a difference between those who want to reach a [peace] settlement and those who don't . . . A straight line leads from such an approach to the destruction of the Palestinian Authority, to the

strengthening of the Iranian intervention and to the unilateral disengagement."

23. On the Zionist Left's betrayal following the 2000 Camp David Summit, see Amnon Raz-Krakotzkin, "Different Aspects of the Bloody Events," in Honig-Parnass and Haddad, eds. *Between the Lines*, 10–15; also see Bishara, "Thus an Apartheid Regime Develops," in *Between the Lines*, 69–73; and Adi Ophir, ed., *The al Aqsa Intifada and the Israeli Left* (Jerusalem: Keter Publishing House, 2001). For abundant quotations from many Israeli intellectuals and authors known for their "liberalism," see Yitzhak Laor, *Tears of Zion*, *New Left Review* 10 (July/August 2001): 47–60.

24. Laor, "Tears of Zion," 47–61.

25. Menachem Brinker, "The Ethics of Pragmatics," *Haaretz*, July 17, 2000.

26. Ram, *The Time of the "Post"*; Sand, *Historians, Time and Imagination*; and Silberstein, *The Post Zionism Debates*.

27. Sand, *Historians, Time and Imagination*, 117.

28. For discussions of these assumed phenomena, see Yoav Peled and Adi Ophir, eds., *From an Enlisted Society to Civic Society* (Jerusalem: The Van Leer Jerusalem Institute and Hakibbutz Hameuchad, 2001).

29. Yonah and Shenhav, "The Multi-Cultural Condition," 170.

30. Gutwein, "Identity vs. Class," 241–259. Gutwein's sharp criticism of Yossi Yonah and Yehouda Shenhav, for their support of the free market, relates especially to their article "The Multi-Cultural Condition," 163–189. It is telling that Gutwein, who expresses a socioeconomic view of Social Democrats, does not relate at all to the Zionist essence of the state of Israel and its implications upon Palestinian citizens. (See chapter 1 on how he ignores the case of Palestinian citizens.) Also see critical analysis of the "free market" supported by post-Zionists in Nada Matta, "Postcolonial Theory, Multiculturalism."

31. Ram, *The Time of the "Post,"* 156.

32. Ibid., 185–186.

33. For the reshuffling of the political map, which indicated the wide consensus among the majority of Israeli society, see Honig-Parnass, "One People, One Leader," 274–280.

34. Route 443 is the main road linking Jerusalem and the West Bank settlements with the bloc of Modi'in communities and the Tel Aviv area in central Israel. Israel paved the road in the 1980s. It used 14 kilometers of an existing route in the West Bank. This 14-kilometer stretch, which is about half the length of the entire road, served for decades as the main Palestinian traffic artery in the southern Ramallah District, dating back to Mandate times. As it passes through the centers of villages lying southwest of Ramallah, it served tens of thousands of Palestinians between the city and the villages.

To pave this part of the road, Israel expanded the existing route by expropriating thousands of dunams of public and private land belonging to Palestinian residents of villages in the area. The landowners filed a petition against the action to the High Court of Justice, which approved the expropriations.

In 2002, following several cases of Palestinian gunfire at Israeli vehicles on the road, in which six Israeli citizens and one resident of East Jerusalem were killed, Israel prohibited Palestinians from using the road, by vehicle or on foot, for whatever purpose, including transport of goods or medical emergencies.

In a report in 2007, following an appeal to the Supreme Court, B'Tselem—The Israeli Information Center for Human Rights in the Occupied Territories—emphasized: "Travel on Route 443 is crucial to the Palestinian villagers living along it. For many of them, this is the way to their farmland, which lies on both sides of the road. It is also the primary access road to Ramallah, the city on which the villagers rely for commerce and for their health and education needs. Many of the villagers also have family and social ties with residents of Ramallah. As a result of the prohibition, more than 100 small shops in villages along its route have closed since 2002, among them floor-tile establishments, flower shops, furniture stores, and restaurants."

35. Akiva Eldar, *Haaretz*, April 4, 2008.

36. For the US-Israeli scheme of unilateral withdrawal from the Gaza Strip and its aftermath, see Toufic Haddad, "Gaza: Birthing a Bantustan," and Tikva Honig-Parnass, eds. "The Misleading Disengagement from Gaza: 'Unilateralism' Replaces 'Peace Process,'" in *Between The Lines* (2007 edition), 280–90 and 265–74, respectively. For the most comprehensive critical review, see Sara Roy, "Praying with Their Eyes Closed: Reflections on the Disengagement from Gaza," *Journal of Palestine Studies* (August 2005); and Sara Roy, "Gaza Future," *London Review of Books* vol. 27, no. 21 (November 3, 2005).

37. Azmi Bishara, "Questions and Answers about Sharon's Disengagement Plan," The National Democratic Assembly, parliamentary office statement, October 27, 2004.

38. See interview with Dov Weisglas, Sharon's closest advisor, conducted by Ari Shavit, *Haaretz,* October 8, 2004, in Honig-Parnass and Haddad, eds. *Between The Lines* (2007 edition), 265–274.

39. Reported by Uri Klein, *Haaretz*, February 15, 2006.

40. Interview with Gideon Alon, *Haaretz*, February 15, 2006.

41. See note 1 in introduction.

42. Amos Oz, "Why Israeli Missiles Strike for Peace," *Evening Standard,* July 20, 2006.

43. Author David Grossman shared Oz's justification of the war in an article published in the UK *Guardian* on the same day that Oz's article was published. See David Grossman, *Guardian,* July 20, 2006.

44. Yitzhak Laor, "A Tale of Love and Darkness," 67–91.

45. Only on August 6, 2006—three weeks after the brutal devastation of Lebanon had begun, and after more than one thousand Lebanese had been killed—did Oz, together with two other Israeli "humanist voices" (authors David Grossman and A. B. Yehoshua) address the Israeli public. They published a large advertisement in the daily newspaper *Haaretz* calling upon the government to agree to a mutual cease-fire. This took place, however, only after the heroic resistance of Hezbollah and the Lebanese people had collectively repelled Israel's attempts to divide them, and were collectively mobilizing for Lebanon's defense. By then it was well known that the Security Council was working toward adopting a cease-fire declaration and that Israeli officials were involved in its articulation. The question which occupied the Israeli establishment's mind at the time was whether Israel should "widen the operation towards the Litani River" in the few days that remained before the UN resolution was put into action. The three writers objected to this expansion, thus joining large parts of the Israeli media. However, the arguments upon which their call was grounded had nothing to do with morally and politically rejecting Israel's "military operation," which they continued to justify. Instead, it was based on the presumption that the "feasible and reasonable goals of the military action have already been achieved" and that there is no justification "for causing more suffering and bloodshed for both sides for

aims that are not feasible." In an effort to deter any similarities that could be drawn between the suffering and bloodshed of "both sides," the writers hastened to add: "The Lebanese nation has no right to demand that its sovereignty be respected if it refuses to enact its full jurisdiction over its territory and citizenry."

46. Beni Tziper, *Haaretz*, Culture and Literature Supplement, September 29, 2006.

47. On January 17, 2011, Ehud Barak, minister of defense and chair of Labor, quit his party to found the "Independence Party." He remained in government while the other Labor ministers quit.

48. Since 2009, while serving as minister of foreign affairs in Netanyahu's Likud government, together with Labor, Lieberman and his colleagues issued bills and ministerial proposals that explicitly aimed to wipe out any remnant of Palestinian citizens' collective memory or national identity and struggle for equality. For example, the so-called "Nakba bill" proposed to cut public funding for institutions that allow the commemoration of the Nakba. See Dana Weiler-Polak, "Israel Has Become a Country Where Human Rights Are Conditional," *Haaretz*, December 6, 2009. See updated information and analysis on the new wave of explicit racist laws in the epilogue.

49. Azmi Bishara, "Ministry of Strategic Threats," *Al Ahram* 818 (November 2006): 1–7.

50. Meron Benvenisti, *Haaretz*, June 30, 2005.

51. Noam Chomsky, "Gaza and its Aftermath," Zspace, February 9, 2009.

52. Chomsky's analysis points to (among other things) the fact that "Israel violated the cease-fire in July 2008, which was observed by Hamas. (Israel concedes that Hamas did not fire a single rocket.) Israel continued its criminal activities in Gaza and the West Bank, including the continued heavy siege imposed on Gaza since January 2006, which brought it to the brink of almost complete strangulation. Later it refused to accept a ceasefire proposed by Hamas shortly before the invasion." See Noam Chomsky, "Undermining Gaza, Foreign Policy in Focus," an interview with Sameer Dossani, January 16, 2009, at www.fpif.org/fpiftxt/5802, and Chomsky, "Obama OKed Israel's Gaza War," *Press TV*, February 21, 2009. Also see Haddad, "The Road to Gaza's Killing Fields," *International Socialist Review* 64 (March–April 2009).

53. Akiva Eldar, "How Much More Killing Till the Tahadiye [cease fire]," *Haaretz*, January 5, 2009.

54. Yitzhak Laor, "*Ma lemeretz ve lesanhedrin,*" *Haaretz*, October 28, 2009.

55. The report, published in September 2009 by the United Nations Fact Finding Mission and headed by Judge Goldstone, was established in April 2009 to investigate the events in "Operation Cast Lead" on Gaza ("The Goldstone Mission"). The report was adopted by the UN Human Rights Council and was further endorsed at the General Assembly.

56. See for example Avi Sagie, "Time to Investigate," *Haaretz*, December 14, 2009. Sagie expresses grave concern over the violation of basic moral values in Gaza—in the center of which is the value of human life. Sagie is a professor at Bar Ilan University and is not considered part of the Zionist Left.

57. Zeev Sternhell, "There Is Nothing [That Needs] Investigation," *Haaretz*, September 25, 2009.

58. For Chomsky's genuine search for a just solution in the framework of the two-state solution, see Chomsky and Achcar, *Perilous Power*, 158–61 and 163–76.

59. For a somewhat different analysis, which emphasizes the Zionist Left's adjustment to

the consensus, rather than vice versa, see Yitzhak Laor, "Why the Left in Israel Vanished," *Haaretz*, November 19, 2009. See: www.haaretz.com/hasen/spages/1129215.html.

60. Ram, *The Time of the "Post,"* 126.

61. Gelsner, "After Post Nationality," 48–55.

62. Brit Shalom was a movement founded in 1925 by Hebrew University intellectuals, among whom were Martin Buber, Yehuda Laib Magnes, and Samuel Hugo Bergman. The movement called for a binational state. Indeed, Martin Buber used ambiguous language and self-righteous arguments for defending free Jewish immigration and settlements in his vision of a binational state. See Martin Buber, "*Beayot Hazman,*" April 1, 1948. "In order to acquire the freedom for the development of the yishuv, there is no need for a Jewish state. In order to achieve it [development] there is need for only granting that extent of Alia [Jewish immigration], which is in our capacity to really absorb from time to time into our economic existence; that *size of settlement,* that we have the real powers to commit; and that measure of independence that is required to establish both. We need time and freedom for our own sake and not for achieving [superiority.] We need *Alia* [Jewish immigration] and settling [the land] and social independence not in order to be stronger than others, but in order that we can mould our life. For all this there is no need for a Jewish state; what is needed is a covenant founded on trust."

63. *Mahsom*, April 17, 2007. See: www.mahsom.com. It is a translation into Hebrew of Bishara's interview on al Jazeera, April 16, 2007, regarding the accusation by the Israeli Shabak of treason, and helping the enemy during a time of war (the 2006 Israeli campaign against Lebanon). Bishara decided not to return to Israel from a visit abroad and resigned from the Knesset, knowing that he would be jailed for many years before a trial began, and years thereafter until a verdict was given.

64. Karpel, "All in All."

65. Among others, the Taba Agreement (2001) and Geneva Initiative (2003).

66. Azmi Bishara, "What We Must Do," *Al Ahram*, April 4, 2008.

67. Karpel, "All in All."

68. Baruch Kimmerling, "The Danger That Lurks in a Constitution," *Haaretz*, March 31, 2005.

69. Kimmerling repeats here the Zionist Left's misleading argument expressed by political scientist Shlomo Avineri (among others; see chapter 5). Unlike Italy, which is not a state of Catholics alone, Israel is the state of only those recognized as Jews by Halacha.

70. Avi Shlaim, "A Reply to Benny Morris," *Guardian*, February 22, 2002. The roundtable talks at Taba, Egypt, took place on January 21–27, 2001. See a detailed report in Tanya Reinhart, *Israel/Palestine*, 209–21.

71. Shlaim, "A Reply."

72. Ben Kaspit, *Maariv*, January 23, 2001. See Tanya Reinhart's conclusion for evidence that the Taba negotiations were a cunning maneuver by Barak to help his reelection campaign. Barak sent three left "dovish" leaders to the talks in Taba (Shlomo Ben Ami, Yossi Beilin, and Yossi Sarid), hoping to acquire an "endorsement" for his candidacy from the Palestinian Authority. He wanted to influence Palestinian citizens not to abstain or boycott the elections and thus prevent a Likud victory (which indeed happened). These three missionaries did indeed convince PA negotiator Abu Ala and his colleagues to sign a declaration stating that the two sides "have never been closer to reaching an agreement," confirmed by Aluf Ben, *Haaretz*, January 28, 2001.

73. Tanya Reinhart, *Israel/Palestine*, 219.

74. Abed Rabbo, known as a Palestinian "Dove," was a cabinet member in several of Arafat's (PNA) governments. He participated in the team that negotiated secretly for the Oslo Accords together with Yossi Beilin. Since 1994, he participated in all negotiations to implement the Oslo Accords, as well as Camp David in 2000, and Taba in 2001.

75. On December 17, 2009, the Geneva Initiative Council held a press conference in which they presented a complete and updated book, "A Regional Peace Plan: The Geneva Initiative Annexes." The session was chaired by Yossi Beilin, who also submitted a copy of the book to Shimon Peres, the Israeli president.

76. Post-Zionist professor Yossi Yonah was among the signatories of the Initiative.

77. Ilan Pappé, "The Geneva Bubble: an Old Version in a New Garment," *Hagada Hasmalit*, January 27, 2004. See www.hagada.org.il/hagada/html/.

78. Post-Zionist professor Yossi Yonah was among the signatories of the Initiative.

79. Yoav Peled, "Zionist Realities," New Left Review 38 (March–April 2006). Peled critically reviews Virginia Tilley's *The One-State Solution* (Ann Arbor: Michigan University Press, 2005).

80. Virginia Tilley, "The Secular Solution, Debating Israel-Palestine," *New Left Review* 38 (March–April 2006). Virginia Tilley's response to Yoav Peled's review of her book *The One-State Solution*.

81. Peled, "Zionist Realities."

82. Tilley, "The Secular Solution."

83. Bishara, "What We Must Do."

Epilogue

1. Aluf Ben, The Man Behind Lieberman, *Haaretz*, October 13, 2011.

2. This is the headline of an article by Hanan Hever in *Haaretz*, October 12, 2010, in which he argues that the new racist laws have only removed the masks behind which the racist nature of the old laws were concealed.

3. Emergency legislations still in use today include:
   The Press Ordinance—1933
   Defense (Emergency) Regulations—1945
   Order for the Extension of the Validity of Emergency Regulations
       (Foreign Travel)—1948
   Prevention of Terrorism Ordinance—1948
   Ship Order (Limitation of Transfer and Mortgaging)—1948
   Fire Arms Law—1949
   State of Emergency Land Appropriation Administration Law—1949
   Prevention of Infiltration (Offenses and Jurisdiction) Law—1954
   The Control of Products and Services Law—1957
   Emergency State Search Authorities Law (Temporary Order)—1969
   Extension of Emergency Regulations Law (Legal Administration and Additional
       Regulations)—1969
   Extension of Emergency Regulations Law—1973

Emergency Powers (Detention) Law—1979

Security Service (Combined Version)—1986

Registration of Equipment and Its Enlistment to the IDF Law—1987

4. According to Adallah, this Apartheid law would apply to about 697 communities, which equals 67.3 percent of the localities in Israel.

5. On March 23, 2011, the Law of Admission Committees passed in the Knesset. It formalizes the establishment of admission committees to review potential residents of Negev and Galilee communities that have fewer than 400 families. These committees would include, in addition to representatives of the communal settlement and the regional council, a representative of the Jewish Agency or the World Zionist Organization.

6. The bill was passed in the Knesset on March 23, 2011. It aroused harsh criticism by Palestinian MKs. MK Hanin Zoabi (Balad) was outraged. "You are creating a monstrous state that will enter the thoughts and emotions of citizens. Is accepting my history considered incitement?" she asked. "The Nakba is a historic truth, not a position or freedom of speech."

7. Another proposal is the amendment to the existing anti-incitement bill. It stipulates that people who deny Israel's Jewish character will be arrested. This extension to the penal code, which has already passed its preliminary reading, would incriminate the majority of Palestinian citizens.

8. Shlomo Avineri, "A Substantive Oath of Allegiance," *Haaretz*, July 25, 2010.

9. For sharp criticism by Ran Greenstein on Avineri's three articles, including the article criticized here, and the debate around them, see the progressive list Alef in its July–October 2010 issues.

10. Shlomo Avineri, "A Palestinian People, Yes, A Jewish People, No?," *Haaretz*, October 5, 2010.

11. Mordechai Kremnitzer, "To Where Has Our Common Sense Disappeared?," *Haaretz*, October 11, 2010.

12. Steven Friedman and Virginia Tilley, "Taken for a Ride by the Israeli Left," *The Electronic Intifada*, January 26, 2007.

13. Uri Avnery, "The State of Bla-Bla-Bla," at www.gush-shalom.org.

14. This indeed is the meaning of the UN decision. However, Uri Avnery ignores the fact that Ben-Gurion and all Zionist political streams have interpreted it as if it called for "a nation state of the entire Jewish People."

15. In *Haaretz*, June 11, 2010, Natasha Mazgovia reported from Washington that Abu Mazen had accepted the central assumption of Zionism—the Jewish right to the land. Two days before, he announced, "he will never deny the right of the Jewish people to the land of Israel." This was said in a meeting with around thirty members of the Jewish community in the United States, ex-members of the US government, and researchers who asked about "Palestinian incitement and their readiness to begin direct negotiations with Israel." In the same week, PLO Secretary Yasser Abed Rabbo said in an interview that his organization would be willing to recognize Israel as a Jewish state if Israel agreed to give the Palestinians a state based on 1967 borders. "We would be willing to recognize Israel as whatever the Israelis want, even as a Chinese state," said Abed Rabbo.

16. Jonathan Cook, Arab Citizens are Not a Negotiating Chip," Antiwar, October 3, 2010, at http://original.antiwar.com/cook/2010/10/03/israels-arab-citizens-are-not-a-negotiating-chip.

17. Uri Avnery, "Fayyad's Big Gamble," Gush Shalom, November 4, 2010. See www.gush-shalom.org.

18. Aisling Byrne, "Businessmen Posing as Revolutionaries: General Dayton and the 'New Palestinian Breed,'" Conflicts Forum at Beirut, published November 2009 in www.conflictsforum.org. Aisling Byrne updated information and analysis to the 2009 essay in a paper presented at a conference called "The Development of Neo-Colonial Structures Under the Guise of 'State-Building,'" The Center for Development Studies, Bir Zeit University and Ghent University, September 2010.

19. See also updated information in Tobias Buck, "Jerusalem, Allegations of West Bank Torture Increase," *Financial Times*, November 21, 2010.

20. Nahum Barnea, "Anatomy of a Victory," *Yediot Ahronot*, October 9, 2009.

21. *In The Trap of the Green Line [bemalkodet hakav hayarok]: A Jewish Political Essay* (Tel Aviv: Am Oved Publishers, 2010).

22. Tom Segev, "The State of All Its Mizrahim," *Haaretz* Weekend Supplement, February 19, 2010.

23. Shenhav, *Trap of Green Line*, 55.

24. Ibid., 56.

25. Ibid.

26. For continued emphasis on the "cultural" and "identical" approach to Mizrahim, see interview with Sami Shalom Chetrit by Samia Dodin in *Sephardic Heritage Update* issue 132, 1 (December 2004); and Smadar Lavie, "Colonialism and Imperialism: 'Zionism,'" in *Encyclopedia of Women and Islamic Cultures*, vol. 6 (Koninklijke, Netherlands: Brill, 2007).

27. See Ein-Gil and Machover, "Zionism and Oriental Jews," 2008.

28. Shenhav, *Trap of Green Line*, 112.

29. Ibid., 156.

30. Omar Barghouti emphasizes as exceptional the recently formed group Boycott! Supporting the Palestinian BDS, Call from Within. See www.boycottisrael.info. It is particularly praiseworthy, as it unconditionally accepts BDS as defined and guided by the Palestinian BDS National Committee, and is therefore regarded by the BNC as a reliable and principled partner in the movement.

31. The BDS Call, signed by over 170 Palestinian civil society organizations in July 2005 (http://bdsmovement.net/?q=node/52) and, in the academic and cultural fields, from the Palestinian Call for Academic and Cultural Boycott of Israel, issued a year earlier in July 2004 (www.pacbi.org/etemplate.php?id=869) Palestinian Campaign for the Academic and Cultural Boycott of Israel (PACBI) is part of the BDS National Committee in Palestine.

32. Omar Barghouti, "Boyott Ariel and the Rest—They Are All Complicit," PACBI, February 10, 2010. See http://pacbi.org/etemplate.php?id=1175.

33. Machover, "Israelis and Palestinians"; and Moshé Machover, "Resolution of the Israeli-Palestinian Conflict, A Socialist Viewpoint," February 29. See http://matzpen.org/index.asp?p=resolution-machover. Published under the title "Breaking the Chains of Zionist Oppression," in *Weekly Worker*, 757 (February 19, 2009). See www.cpgb.org.uk/article.php?article_id=1001091.

Index

"Passim" (literally "scattered") indicates intermittent discussion of a topic over a cluster of pages.

About Haymarket Books

Haymarket Books is a nonprofit, progressive book distributor and publisher, a project of the Center for Economic Research and Social Change. We believe that activists need to take ideas, history, and politics into the many struggles for social justice today. Learning the lessons of past victories, as well as defeats, can arm a new generation of fighters for a better world. As Karl Marx said, "The philosophers have merely interpreted the world; the point, however, is to change it."

We take inspiration and courage from our namesakes, the Haymarket Martyrs, who gave their lives fighting for a better world. Their 1886 struggle for the eight-hour day reminds workers around the world that ordinary people can organize and struggle for their own liberation.

For more information and to shop our complete catalog of titles, visit us online at www.haymarketbooks.org.

Also from Haymarket Books

Between the Lines: Readings on Israel, the Palestinians, and the U.S. "War on Terror" • Edited by Tikva Honig-Parnass and Toufic Haddad

Gaza in Crisis: Reflections on Israel's War on the Palestinians
Noam Chomsky and Ilan Pappé

Boycott, Divestment, Sanctions: The Global Movement for Palestinian Civil Rights • Omar Barghouti

Israelis and Palestinians: Conflict and Resolution • Moshé Machover

Midnight on the Mavi Marmara • Edited by Moustafa Bayoumi

The Palestine Communist Party 1919–1948: Arab and Jew in the Struggle for Internationalism • Musa Budeiri

The Pen and the Sword: Conversations with Edward Said
David Barsamian

Diary of Bergen-Belsen, 1944–1945 • Hanna Lévy-Hass, foreword and afterword by Amira Hass

About the Author

Tikva Honig-Parnass was raised in the Jewish community of pre-state Palestine, fought in the 1948 war, and served as the secretary of the then-radical left Zionist party of Mapam (the Unified Workers Party) in the Knesset (1951–1954). In 1960 she definitively broke with Zionism and joined the ranks of the Israeli Socialist Organization, known as "Matzpen." Since then she has played an active role in the movement against the '67 occupation as well as in the struggle for Palestinian national rights.